Lecture Notes in
Introduction to
Corporate Finance

World Scientific Lecture Notes in Finance

ISSN: 24249955

Series Editor: Professor Itzhak Venezia

Published:

Vol. 1   Lecture Notes in Introduction to Corporate Finance
by Ivan E. Brick (Rutgers Business School at Newark and New Brunswick, USA)

Forthcoming Titles:

Lecture Notes in Fixed Income Fundamentals
by Eliezer Z. Prisman (York University, Canada)

Lecture Notes in Behavioral Finance
by Itzhak Venezia (The Hebrew University of Jerusalem, Israel)

Lecture Notes in Market Microstructure and Trading
by Peter Joakim Westerholm (The University of Sydney, Australia)

Lecture Notes in Risk Management
by Zvi Wiener and Yevgeny Mugerman (The Hebrew University of Jerusalem, Israel)

World Scientific Lecture Notes in Finance – **Vol. 1**

Lecture Notes in Introduction to Corporate Finance

Ivan E Brick

Rutgers Business School at Newark and New Brunswick, USA

EW JERSEY · LONDON · SINGAPORE · BEIJING · SHANGHAI · HONG KONG · TAIPEI · CHENNAI · TOKYO

Published by

World Scientific Publishing Co. Pte. Ltd.
5 Toh Tuck Link, Singapore 596224
USA office: 27 Warren Street, Suite 401-402, Hackensack, NJ 07601
UK office: 57 Shelton Street, Covent Garden, London WC2H 9HE

Library of Congress Cataloging-in-Publication Data
Names: Brick, Ivan E., author.
Title: Lecture notes in introduction to corporate finance / Ivan E Brick
    (Rutgers Business School at Newark and New Brunswick, USA).
Description: 1 Edition. | New Jersey : World Scientific, [2017. | Series: World scientific lecture
    notes in finance ; Volume 1 | Includes bibliographical references and index.
Identifiers: LCCN 2017001764| ISBN 9789813149885 (hardcover) | ISBN 9789813149892 (pbk.)
Subjects: LCSH: Corporations--Finance.
Classification: LCC HG4026 .B6676 2017 | DDC 658.15--dc23
LC record available at https://lccn.loc.gov/2017001764

British Library Cataloguing-in-Publication Data
A catalogue record for this book is available from the British Library.

Desk Editor: Shreya Gopi

Typeset by Stallion Press
Email: enquiries@stallionpress.com

Printed in Singapore

CONTENTS

ABOUT THE AUTHOR

Professor Ivan Brick joined Rutgers Business School at Newark and New Brunswick in 1978. He has been the Chair of the Finance and Economics department since 1996. Professor Brick has published numerous papers in academic journals such as the *Journal of Finance, Journal of Financial Quantitative Analysis, International Economic Review, Review of Economics and Statistics, Journal of Industrial Economics, Journal of Corporate Finance*, and *Financial Management*. His research interests include corporate finance, optimal security design and corporate governance. Currently, he is an associate editor for the *Review of Quantitative Finance and Accounting*. Previously, he has served as an Associate Editor of *Financial Management* and *Multinational Finance Journal*. Professor Brick has received several teaching awards at the Rutgers Business School. He received the "Outstanding Educator Award" by the 1995 Executive MBA Class. Professor Brick was awarded the "Farrokh Langdana Excellence in Teaching Award" by the 2011 MBA Class. In 2012, the Newark Undergraduate Program awarded him the Dean's Advisory Council Award for the "Most Knowledgeable Finance Professor", "The Most Caring Finance Professor", as well as "The Most Motivational Finance Professor". For his outstanding service, Professor Brick was awarded the RBS Dean's Service Award in 2013 and 2016.

CHAPTER 1

INTRODUCTION

What is Finance?

Consider a Euro coin. On the right side of the coin are the investors who wish to invest. They invest in financial securities such as stock and debt securities. They also invest in commodities, real estate and derivative securities such as options. Many investors invest their money in banks in the form of deposits. The left side of the coin represents the issuers. The government that supplies Treasury securities and municipal debt are the issuers. Issuers also include corporate entities that issue both stock and debt securities to the public. The proceeds of these sales are used to finance the business operations of the issuers.

The thickness of the coin represents the medium where the two meet. We can think of the thickness of this 'coin' as the Financial Institutions. The job of the Financial Institutions is to match the investors demand for investment with the supply offered by the issuing entities. Financial institutions include banks that take savers' deposits and lend them to a homeowner who wants to buy a house or to a business that uses the money to expand operations. They include investment banks, which "sell" new securities issued by corporations to the public.

Now that you know something about the players of finance, we can now answer the question "What is finance?" Finance studies the interaction of investors and issuers of securities and how it impacts upon the return received by investors and the price obtained by issuers. It examines how investors make decisions regarding the choice of investments. Finance seeks to explain the factors that determine how firms finance their operations and whether to expand or contract. Finance also explains how firms use the markets to learn something about themselves. Finance describes how the organization of financial markets impacts upon the prices of securities. Finally, finance explains the operations of financial institutions as they perform the important function of bundling of investors' funds and transforming their investments into financing vehicles that are essential for the well-being of firms and governments.

In this course, we provide an introduction to finance. There are chapters that describe some of the financial securities that are available for investors. We will explain how risk and return are related and their impact upon choices made by firms and investors alike. We will provide you with basic tools to make rational decisions. We believe that mastering the subject matter will enable you to do your job better and help you plan your own personal investments. We will examine how firms allocate their resources and how they finance their operations. Finance is somewhat technical and it requires understanding of the use of spreadsheets. We will provide you with a tutorial for that purpose. In addition, you will need to learn accounting fundamentals because the language of firms is accounting and you cannot evaluate firms without understanding income statements and balance sheets. We believe that you will learn much about finance and hopefully, you will enjoy the experience of working through this textbook.

What do Investors Want?

One of the first questions you face as an employee is how you want to allocate the contribution to your 401(k) retirement plan. (Your employer will also ask about health care plans but that is another course. More importantly, you should figure out who will be your mentor and how to manage your career! But that is also for another day.) Your 401(k) retirement plan may offer several alternatives. One plan invests in the stock of your company. Another invests in the

US domestic stock market. A third plan invests in overseas equities. A fourth plan only offers choices of treasury securities. A fifth plan invests in corporate bonds. How do you decide which plan is best for you? Before deciding, let us give a brief description of some basic investment vehicles.

Savings Accounts: Most people have their own checking account. Many banks offer a minimal interest rate for keeping money in the checking account. Banks also offer Certificates of Deposits (CDs), with greater yields provided that you are willing to tie up your money for 1 year or more. For the most part, these investments are secure because of government insurance offered by the Federal Deposit Insurance Corporation (FDIC).

Treasury Securities: These securities are offered by the US government and are considered essentially free of any chance of default. Why? Because the government has the unique privilege of being able to run the printing press to pay its bills. They are very liquid and have current maturities from 1 month to 30 years. Treasury Securities with more than 1-year maturity pay interest twice a year and you receive the final principal payment on the last day of maturity. The current yield of 10-year Treasury as of June 6, 2016 is 1.723%. To find the current yield of a 10-year Treasury go to http://finance.yahoo.com/. Why are some bank CD rates higher than the treasury securities? For example, Discover is offering a 7-year CD for 2.10% as of June 6, 2016. One reason is that the CDs are not liquid (cannot be sold by the holder) and banks have to offer a higher yield to attract depositors.

Municipal Bonds: These securities are issued by municipalities like states, counties and cities. The current yield of AAA (triple A) rated 10-year municipal bond as of June 6, 2016 is 1.65%. First, what do we mean by triple A rated? And why are municipal bonds offered at a lower rate than treasury securities?

To answer these questions, one must realize that municipalities can default on their debt. New York City almost defaulted on its debt back in the 1970s. Orange County, California, the wealthiest county in the US as measured by per capita annual income, defaulted in the late 1980s. Remember, the US government can always print money to ensure payment of the loan, but municipalities cannot. If taxes and fees collected by the municipality are insufficient to pay off the loan, the municipality is not required to raise taxes and it has the right to default on the loan. There are rating agencies such as Moody's and Standard & Poor's (S&P) that rate the safety of such bonds. Triple A rated bonds are considered to be the safest.

This answers the first question, but what of the second question? Income from municipal bonds are tax exempt from federal taxes and frequently exempt from state and local income taxes. As a result, the required yield of highly rated municipal bonds can be lower than treasury securities because the holder of municipal bonds does not have to pay taxes on the interest income.

Corporate Debt: Most corporate debt securities have original maturities of greater than 5 years, pay interest semi-annually, and repay the principal amount at the final maturity date. Corporations enjoy limited liability, which means if the firm cannot make the payments it owes the debt holders, the owners of the firm do not have to make up the difference. Instead, the corporation can default on its loan obligations. Moody's, S&P and others agencies provide credit ratings for all of these bonds. The current yield of triple A rated 10-year corporate bond as of June 6, 2016 is 2.28%. To find current yields of triple A rated bonds go to http://finance.yahoo.com/bonds/composite_bond_rates. The average yield of high yield, or "junk bonds", (bonds that the rating agencies do not regard to be safe bets) as of June 6, 2016 is 7.40%. The source for this yield is the Federal Reserve Bank of St. Louis at https://research.stlouisfed.org/fred2/series/BAMLH0A0HYM2EY.

Common Stock: Holders of common stock are the theoretical owners of the firm. The shareholders appoint the board of directors who oversees management on behalf of shareholders. The return of common stock is made up of two components: dividends and capital gains. Dividends come out of the firm's earnings. Capital gains represent the percentage change in the stock price from the time of purchase. The average return of stock as measured by the S&P 500 Index has been over 12% per annum since its inception more than

50 years ago. Note that there have been years that the stock returns have been much lower. For example, return for the stock market in 2002 as measured by the percentage price change of the S&P 500 Index was approximately −22.1%.

Retirement Investment Vehicles: One of the earliest private retirement investment vehicles is the Traditional Individual Retirement Arrangements (IRAs). The contributions to the IRA can be tax deferred (and you do not pay taxes on the earnings until you begin withdrawing from the account). Distributions from the IRA may not begin before you are 59.5 years old. No matter what, you must begin withdrawing by the time you are 70.5 years old. The distributions are considered taxable income. The maximum contribution you can make into the Traditional IRA account as of 2013 is $5500 for people younger than 50 and $6500 for people aged 50 and over. Contributions can be used to reduce your taxable income but there are income limitations: In some cases, you can lose the total tax deductibility of the contribution if your income exceeds $69,000. For more information, go to http://en.wikipedia.org/wiki/Traditional_IRA. Note the above is accurate as of January 2013. The law does not restrict the type of investments you make for your IRA. Another type of IRA is known as the Roth IRA. The contributions made to this type of IRA are not tax deductible. Like the traditional IRA, the earnings of these investments are not taxable. Unlike the Traditional IRA, distributions after you reach the age of 59.5 are not taxed at the ordinary income tax rate, and nor do you have to take any distribution once you reach the age of 70.5.

Many companies offer qualified pension retirement plans. Most of the plans in the corporate world are now defined contribution plans. In these plans, you contribute a percentage of your income. Often these contributions are matched by the employer. The contributions to these plans are tax deductible and you do not pay taxes on the plan's earnings until you begin your withdrawal. The maximum amount one can contribute to these corporate plans is $17,500 as of 2013.

Mutual Funds and ETFs: Investment in the stock market is risky, as evidenced by the 2002 return for the S&P index of stocks.

Moreover, many investors would like to leave the investment picking to the professionals. It is also prudent to diversify investments, but the amount of money needed to economically diversify can be substantial. Mutual funds are another investment vehicle that allow diversification. Mutual funds claim to offer both trading expertise and the ability to diversify cheaply. In particular, these funds are actively managed whereby professionals of the fund are trying to buy and sell mispriced stock (or bonds). Most funds specialized by following a specific investment style. There are mutual funds that invest only in equity (Equity Funds), bonds (Fixed Income Funds) or short-term liquid investments (Money Market Funds). Mutual funds also have different risk profiles within a specific category of investment. For example, there are mutual funds that invest in income (dividend) paying stocks, in growth stocks or in international stocks. Some mutual funds track stock indices such as the Dow Jones or the S&P 500 and are therefore passively managed. Mutual funds offer a dizzying set of fees to compensate the mutual fund managers for their time and effort. Fees include a Front-Load Sales Charge (an upfront fee based upon the amount invested with the fund), an expense ratio (the percentage of the value of the investment that is charged by the fund to cover its costs) and/or Back-Load Sales Charge (a fee that is paid upon exiting the mutual fund). Obviously, a fund beating the overall market can charge higher rates than those that do not. On average, mutual funds do not beat the market, especially after taking into account the fees. Nevertheless, mutual funds serve a good social purpose in that most of us do not have the expertise or resources to create a well-diversified portfolio.

Fortunately, there are equity investment vehicles that allow you to cost effectively diversify. One of the cheapest (in terms of transaction costs needed to make a diversified investment) is the Exchange Traded Funds. This is an investment fund that tracks a stock index. One of the more famous of these funds is Standard & Poor's depositary receipt (SPDR), an investment fund that tracks the S&P index. Vanguard offers VIPERs and Barclays Global Investors offers iShares. These ETF funds cover a wide range of indices and economics sectors. For the most part, these investment funds are passively managed in the sense that the manager is not trying to pick undervalued stocks or sell overvalued stocks. Rather the firm selling these funds is essentially offering services to buy equities that track a particular index or sector. In making your choice, one should learn about how well the funds actually track the particular index and learn about the fund's expense ratio.

Alternative Investments: There are several alternative investments individuals can consider. The biggest alternative investment is real estate. For many people the investment in residential quarters not only serves as a place to live, but a sizable wealth component of the individual. Investors who are interested in becoming a real estate mogul without committing to millions of dollars can invest in Real Estate Investment Trust (REIT). According to Wikipedia (http:// en.wikipedia.org/wiki/Real_estate_investment_trust), "In the United States, a REIT is a company that owns, and in most cases operates, income-producing real estate. Some REITs finance real estate. To be a REIT, a company must distribute at least 90 percent of its taxable income to shareholders annually in the form of dividends." Investors can also invest in commodities such as gold, silver or platinum. Finally, investors can speculate on asset prices by buying or selling derivative securities such as call or put options.

A call option is a derivative security which gives the holder the right to buy the underlying security at a specified price (known as the Exercise Price). A put gives the holder the right to sell the underlying security at a specified price. One may view these derivatives as a useful vehicle for speculative investing. If one believes that stock price will rise (decline), one can buy the call (put) option. But one may also use these derivative securities for hedging. For example, you bought IBM at $162 per share. The price is now $182. You are not ready to sell the stock but you want to hedge against IBM falling below $175. You can buy a put option on IBM with an exercise price of $175. Two months hence you wish to sell your IBM stock. Consider two scenarios: Either IBM is worth $150 per share or $200 per share. If IBM is worth $150 per share, you can exercise your put option and make sure that you actually receive $175. But should IBM's price increase to $200 a share, you simply do not exercise your put option and sell IBM for $200. Note the put option in this case is used as an insurance mechanism.

Your Investment Decision: Assume that you decided to invest a $10,000 signing bonus. How would you invest? Certainly, you will be considering the tradeoff between risk and return. For example, you could put all of your money in the treasury market. Your return will be very certain, but it is not very high. You can earn a lot more by investing your money in the junk bond market or in common stock. But you will also be taking a greater chance of not getting any return should the firm default. You also have to consider the liquidity of your investment. In other words, how easy will it be for you to sell your security at a fair price if you quickly need your money? Similarly, the choice of investment will depend upon your tax bracket, since municipal bonds can offer higher after-tax returns on your investment if your tax bracket is sufficiently high. Finally, you would have to consider the longevity of your investment. Do I want to invest in a 2-year Treasury or 20-year Treasury?

There is no right or wrong answer as to how to invest. You might choose high risk investments because you like the higher expected returns and you are willing to lose your shirt. On the other hand, some of you are very risk averse and will not invest in anything other than a short-term Treasury Security. The main point is that investors should choose their investment based upon expected after-tax return, risk and liquidity of the investment. In this course, we will provide you with both tools and more information so that you can make better personal investment decisions.

What are the Concerns of Corporate Management?

Corporate officers have various responsibilities to ensure the well-being and viability of their company. The first responsibility of the management is to *manage the flow of funds of the company*. Flow of funds implies two activities. One is managing the sources of funds and the other is managing the uses of these funds. In particular, management must be able to secure financing for the operations of the company. And they have many choices. For example, they can raise the necessary amount by borrowing money from banks, issuing new debt to the public, using more of the available current earnings (and as a result, giving out less dividends to current shareholders) or issuing new common stock. The process determining the optimal financing arrangement is known as the *financing decision.*

The table on the next page provides an illustrative set of financing options for corporate officers to finance operations. As illustrated, firms can use short-term, intermediate term or long-term financing. Short-term financing arrangements (i.e., financial arrangements that require payments within 3 years) include not paying cash for goods and services received (known as trade credit), getting lines of credit from banks (akin to owning a credit card whereby the firm has maximum limit to how much it can borrow), issuing commercial paper, short-term public issued debt only available to credit worthy borrowers, selling accounts receivables to a third party (this is known as factoring) or borrowing short-term loans collateralized by short-term assets such as accounts receivables and inventory.

The firm can raise money on a more long-term basis. For example, firms can borrow money by issuing Bonds (debt which has first lien on a set of assets), Debentures (holders of this type of debt are considered to be general creditors and get paid only if bondholders are fully paid), by entering a lease arrangement, issuing equity (preferred or common stock[1]), retention of earnings or sale/liquidations of assets.

Once the company receives these funds, the corporate officers are responsible to allocate the monies among many competing uses and demands. For example, management must determine which investments are profitable enough. Firms have to decide how much money to invest in long-term assets such as plant, property, and equipment. This class of assets is the tangible assets of the firm. The firm also has

---

[1] A preferred stock usually has a set coupon that determines the annual dividend payment. However, if the firm does not pay the dividends, preferred stockholders cannot force the firm into bankruptcy. On the other hand, common stockholders cannot receive any dividends until the preferred stockholders' claims are paid in full.

ILLUSTRATIVE
SOURCES OF FUNDS

SHORT-TERM   ISSUES

TRADE CREDIT & TRADE RELATED ⎤

BANKS & FINANCIAL INSTITUTIONS │

COMMERCIAL PAPER   │

INTERMEDIATE - TERM

BANKS & FINANCIAL INSTITUTIONS

INTERMEDIATE - TERM NOTES   SENIOR V. JUNIOR
                                             SECURED V. UNSECURED
                                             CURRENCY DENOMINATION
LEASING / SALE LEASEBACK   VARIABLE V. FIXED RATE
                                             PUBLIC V. PRIVATE

LONG - TERM

BONDS & DEBENTURES

LEASES / SALE - LEASEBACK

SPECIAL INSTRUMENTS / CONTINGENT
CLAIMS CONTRACTS

STOCK
    PREFERRED
    COMMON   ⎦
CASH RETAINED FROM OPERATIONS
SALE / LIQUIDATION OF ASSETS

to manage its intangible assets. For example, management provides training programs for their employees to ensure that the employees have the appropriate skill set. Corporate officers also invest in processes to ensure the reputation and quality of product and service. Management also determines how much to invest in short-term assets. For example, firms carry inventory so that they are able to satisfy demand for their products. The process for determining the optimal allocation of funds across all investment opportunities is known as the *capital budgeting decision*.

The second responsibility of management is to **manage the firm's exposure to risk**. There are at least five primary types of risks. *Business Risk* is the impact to the firm's bottom line as a result of the strategic responses of the firm's competitors, suppliers and customers to actions of the firm. For example, all public firms must file financial documents with the Security Exchange Commission. These documents can be read by investors and potential competitors. Potential competitors can learn about the profitability of the company and if the firm is doing very well, this information may induce others to enter the market, creating a dampening effect upon future profits. Managers would have to create economic barriers to prevent increased competition or prevent customers from switching allegiances. For the latter case, just think of the difficulty for customers to switch their wireless phone contracts to another carrier before the contract expires. Most if not all wireless companies will charge a termination fee if you switch before the contract expires. Not only that, but every time you update your cell phone, your contract is automatically extended for at least 1 year.

Financing Risk is the risk that the firm may not be able to satisfy all of its financial obligations. Management must use an appropriate amount of borrowing to finance its operations so that the probability of financial ruin is not so high.

Political Risk involves the impact of government regulation and changes in business law on the bottom line. For example, President Obama and the Democratic Congress passed a law requiring that either business must provide health insurance for all of its employees or that they pay a fee that will finance health care insurance coverage for the uninsured. Clearly, this law has had a major impact upon bottom line of many firms.

Interest Rate Risk is the risk associated with the firm facing a more hostile interest rate environment when it re-enters the loan market. For example, there are some firms that finance their operations through the commercial paper market. Commercial paper is a loan with a maturity of less than 270 days. Generally, firms roll over their commercial paper obligation by issuing new debt to finance the maturing debt. However, if interest rates rise, the new commercial paper will carry a higher interest costs, thereby affecting the bottom line. (There is one advantage of short-term borrowing; it is usually cheaper than long-term loans.)

Currency Risk is the risk associated with changing value of currency. If, for example, you are an importer of fine wines from Europe, and the Euro appreciates in value *vis à vis* the dollar, you will find that your imported wine products have become more expensive. The area of finance that is useful to management to manage exposure to risk is the area of corporate risk management.

Firms try to alleviate both interest rate and currency risk by employing a matching strategy or using the derivative market to hedge against risk. For example, let us say that an American based-firm has a sizable investment in Canada. Let us say that now 1 Canadian dollar equals 1 American dollar. Should the Canadian dollar become stronger (i.e., the Canadian dollar buys more than 1 American dollar), then the value of the Canadian earnings will increase as far as the American company is concerned. On the other hand, if the Canadian dollar value *vis a vis* the American dollar decreases, the value of the Canadian earnings will decrease. The American firm can reduce its risk by financing the Canadian operations by borrowing in Canada based upon Canadian currency. Thus, if the Canadian dollar becomes stronger, then value of earnings will increase but simultaneously the Canadian liability will also increase in value. On the other hand if the Canadian dollar weakens, both the Canadian assets and liabilities decrease in value. Putting this in the context of stockholders equity, by matching, the firm is reducing the expected volatility of stockholders equity.

Alternatively, the firm can use the futures market to reduce currency risk. Assume that the Canadian division is expected to generate $10 million Canadian dollars in the coming fiscal year. The firm may enter a future contract that requires the firm to sell 10 million Canadian dollars for $9,803,921.57 in a year from now. Implicitly, the contract is fixing the Canadian dollar equal to $0.98 (approximately). Let us say, 1 year hence, the Canadian dollar is worth $0.89. Thus, if the firm is expecting earnings worth 10 million Canadian dollars, then the earnings from the Canadian division will be worth only $8,900,000. But the firm can reverse the futures contract by buying the futures contract for $0.89 per Canadian dollar. The difference between the selling price and the buying price is the futures profits of $0.09 per Canadian dollar, which makes up the loss engendered in value of the Canadian earnings.

The third responsibility of the corporate officers is defining the *objective of the firm*. A well-defined objective of the firm is one that provides a clear direction for management to make both the capital budgeting and financing decisions. Many companies provide a mission statement or corporate credo to explicitly communicate their vision to its employees. In other words, a clear objective will allow the management to determine the optimal source of finance and to rank competing capital budgeting projects. Financial Theory dictates that the objective of the firm is to maximize the value of shareholder wealth. We will go into this in more detail in the next section, but for now recall that the shareholders own the firm and therefore should call the shots. Finally, a properly defined objective of the firm will help the firm to set up corporate risk management strategies that enhance the value of equity.

What is the Objective of the Firm?

If you are reading this material, you certainly have a notion as to what should be the objective of the firm. Before we champion maximizing the value of the common stock, let us discuss some other objectives that seem to be appropriate.

Maximizing the firm's profit: This is the classic objective discussed in economics classes and generally, it is not wrong, but it is not adequate either. All firms make investments. The nature of investments is to reduce current cash flows and profits in the hope of obtaining even greater cash flows and profits in the future. What this means is that we need a tool that will allow us to account for the time profile of profits so that we can rank alternative corporate investment strategies.

Minimizing firm risk: This is not an appropriate objective. After all, firms can minimize risk by simply investing all of the money into Treasuries. If you were a shareholder of the firm, is this what you want corporate management to do? Of course not, since you can make this type of investment on your own.

Maximize market share: This is a classic objective of marketing managers. This can be achieved by reducing the prices of the firm's products and services. But again, to what end? If you are the biggest guy on the block but you are earning no profits, will the board of directors pat you on the back and say: "You are doing a great job!" Maximizing market share can be part of a strategy to boost profits. For example, by maximizing market share the firm might be able to achieve economies of scale savings that reduces costs and reduces the effectiveness of competition from rival firms, but the idea behind the strategy is the creation of profits. Sometimes it might be better for a firm to pick a niche for itself than to compete directly with the larger players. This is exactly the strategy of regional banks and airlines. And they are among the most profitable firms in their respective industries!

Maximize growth: This is not an appropriate objective because it can lead the firm to financial ruin. If a firm grows too fast such that its operations outstrips management's capabilities, then strategic mistakes can be made which dampens profits and increases the chance of bankruptcy. Firms obsessed with growth might begin acquiring other companies to maximize growth. Such firms are likely to overpay for these assets, causing irreparable harm to the bottom line.

Maximizing society welfare: It is very hard to knock down such an objective since who can argue that firms should not be cognizant of their actions upon the community in which they reside and on the environment. Nor would we want to argue that business should be concerned solely about maximizing the stock price with no regard for ethical issues. Generally speaking though, maximizing society welfare is ambiguous and it does not take into account the role of competition and consumer demand in affecting a firm's policymaking.

For example, we are all concerned about outsourcing. One can argue that outsourcing takes jobs away from Americans. Consider two competing firms with similar products, say television sets. AllAmerica Inc. refuses to outsource any part of its manufacturing. Multinat Inc. outsources at least 45% of the manufacturing to Indonesia. As a result, unit costs of Multinat Inc. are significantly lower than AllAmerica Inc. Consequently, AllAmerica televisions sell for $379 and Multinat television sets sell for $299. Assuming the same quality, there is a reasonable chance that most of the consumer market will be drawn to Multinat products. If AllAmerica continues its patriotic ways, it might find itself with insufficient demand to remain in business.

Please do not get us wrong. We should not be oblivious to societal concerns and there is no room for unethical behavior, but reconciling societal concerns and profits is beyond the scope of this course.

Why Maximize the Value of the Stock?

The quick and dirty answer to the above question is that technically the stockholders are the real bosses of the firm, but let us explain how stock price maximization maximizes the welfare of all stockholders.

"Congratulations! You are a stockholder of Smart Set Financial Advisors!" CEO Rofeh Ben announces at the annual shareholder meeting that the firm had a wonderful year. He tells the audience that this was supposed to be the last year and therefore, the proposed liquidating dividend per share should be $1000. Wonderful you say to yourself. I paid $500 for this stock 3 years ago and I doubled my money. Then you hear the dreaded "But! We have a deal for you. If each of you gives back the $1000 dividend, the firm will invest the money in one last project. This project is the last project of the company and it is federally guaranteed. In other words, the US Treasury guarantees that if the firm makes an investment of $10,000,000, it will get next year $10,800,000. In other words, your $1000 investment will provide you with $1080 next year. However, if one of you does not surrender your dividend, the deal is off!"

There is hushed silence. Suddenly, a person next to you jumps up and states: "Mr. Ben, I own 1000 shares of this company. Why should

I surrender my dividend? I can certainly do better in the stock market than 8%! And besides, I was planning to use some of this money to build an extension to my house."

Rofeh Ben anticipated the question and provides the following answer. "Sir, I am glad that you are fortunate enough to own a house. That means you have access to the home-owner equity market which allows you to borrow at 6%. You can go to the bank and put up your shares as collateral. The bank would understand that within 1 year you will be receiving with certainty $1,080,000. What will be the maximum amount of money the bank will be willing to lend you!" He immediately goes to his laptop and the computer projector projects on the screen the following:

$$\text{Loan} \ (1.06) = \$1,080,000.$$

Rofeh Ben continues: "In this equation, we are solving how much you can borrow. Note I am assuming that you can borrow at 6%. That is the same rate that the bank will be willing to lend the firm if we were to pledge the assets of this investment as collateral. If you borrowed $1,000,000 from the bank, you will be required to pay back $1,000,000 in principal and $60,000 in interest, or $1,000,000(1.06). The above equation tells you that you can actually borrow more than $1,000,000. Actually, you will be able to borrow $1,018,868. If you throw your lot with us, you will have almost $19,000 more to play with! In fact, if you were to sell your one share of shares to an outsider, that outsider will be willing to pay up to $1,018,868, assuming that we all agree to do the project. Your stock price is effectively higher, is that not good?"

"Of course, if your and the firm's borrowing rate are greater than the 8% return, then you will be right not to surrender your dividend and we would be crazy to even make such a suggestion. Let us say the borrowing rate is 12%. Then the maximum you would be able to borrow from the bank would only be $964,286. And, any rational investor would not pay more than that amount for your shares."

The individual sits down, nodding his head with approval. He understands that by the firm maximizing the stock price, he is better off. The audience agrees and votes unanimously to surrender the dividend for one more last hurrah with Smart Set Financial Advisors.

Efficient Markets

In this course, we are assuming that markets are efficient. It implies that there is no systematic mispricing of securities. Efficient markets imply that security prices incorporate information instantaneously. There are three types of efficient markets. The Weak Form of Market Efficiency implies that there are no statistical return trends that can be profitably exploited. If Weak Form is a 100% accurate, it would call to question the usefulness of Technical Analysis that use pricing trends to indicate if a stock price will increase or decrease in the near future. The semi-strong form of market efficiency states that all publicly available information is impounded in market prices. The strong form of market efficiency argues that all information is impounded in market prices. These latter two definitions of market efficiency imply that it would be tremendously difficult if not impossible to find asset mispricing (either overvalued or undervalued). This would call into question the validity of fundamental asset analysis that uses both public and private (but not insider, illegal) information to ascertain the value of the asset. All assets are priced correctly and therefore an investment strategy based upon identifying mispriced securities will reduce the overall return of trading strategy.

EMPIRICALLY, MOST FINANCIAL MARKETS ARE FAIRLY EFFICIENT, AT LEAST IN THE WEAK FORM AND SEMI-STRONG FORM SENSE.

There are several implications for corporate finance managers if we are to assume that markets are efficient. First, the corporate manager can rely on market prices to deduce the required rate of return the market is expecting from the firm. Second, the manager should not use accounting gimmicks that do not increase cash flow of the firm in order to report higher earnings. Third, managers should not seek merger partners that do not increase the cash flow pie.

Remaining Misgivings Concerning Value Maximization

Although you have agreed to surrender that $1000 dividend because you know that you can sell your one share of stock for $1018.86. But you wonder how valid are Rofeh Ben's arguments in other situations? You meet your old professor from business school, Professor Eli Ivanofski, and you tell him about the experience earlier in the day and about your misgivings.

"What would happen if the project is not so certain?" you ask.

"This should not be a problem. You would require a higher interest rate because the bank would charge you a higher interest rate. For example, had the project promised an 8% return as suggested by the CEO and the bank would have charged 12% because of the risk, then everyone would agree the project is not sound!" the professor replies. "Furthermore, if the project is risky and the rate of borrowing for that risk class is 6%, then everyone would agree the project is worthwhile because the stock price would be higher."

"That is fine. But what if as a shareholder, I do not like to take on that risk? Or what if I disagree with the projections of the management?" You shot back!

The professor smiles and replies: "These are better questions than you used to ask me as a student! In any case, if individual stockholders disagree over the outcomes of the projects or disagree on the optimal level of risk the firm should bear, management should still select projects that they believe earn a return greater than it costs to fund. The market determines that interest rate. The disaffected stockholders can sell their shares at a profit and invest their money in other securities that they regard more to their liking."

"Okay! But you make it sound that the market is all-knowing!" you exclaim.

The professor absentmindedly picks off lint from the lapel of his jacket and says: "The market represents the consensus of individuals and the academic literature finds that they generally do a good job. In actuality there are two ways for corporations and investors to use the market. One way is to rely on the efficiency of the market and use the prices and interest rates to govern actions and decisions. This is what the CEO is doing. The other way is to attempt to find when the market is wrong. This is hard work and that is what mutual funds, hedge funds and private equity firms try to do. But it is almost lunch time. How about going to the university cafeteria and having lunch together. My treat!"

A higher stock price and a free lunch! You are having a good day! Then you notice that the professor is taking out his latest research paper. You remember the old economic maxim, "There is no such thing as a free lunch."

CHAPTER 2

TIME VALUE OF MONEY

The Time Value of Money

The value of money a year from now is less than the value of that money today. Why is that? The reason is that you can invest money today and hopefully receive a larger amount in the future. Since money has a time value associated with it, financial analysts must consider the present value (PV) of future cash flows when they are making financial decisions.

Learning how to take present value of future cash flows is one of the most important lessons in finance. Why? As we will discuss later, the price of any asset is the present value of its cash flows. Moreover, present value provides the framework that allows managers to rank competing capital projects and to help determine the cheapest source of financing.

Finding the Present Value of Future Cash Flows

Imagine that our bank is willing to offer us 10% interest on a $100 deposit. At the end of the year the future value (FV) of our investment should be our initial investment of $100 plus the promised interest of 10% on our investment or $110. Another way of saying this is that the promised future value of $110 one year from now has a present value of $100 today. In fact, an investor should be indifferent from receiving $100 today or $110 one year from now because the investor is able to invest $100 today at an interest rate of 10% and receive $110 at the end of the year.

Let us analyze our problem more closely so that we can generalize the relationship between present value and future value. We made the observation that if we invested $100 at 10% it will be worth $110 at the end of year 1. That is, we will receive our original investment of $100 and interest of 10% of that $100. Mathematically this is written as:

$$\$100(1.1) = \$110.$$

By dividing both sides of that equation by 1.1 we find the present value of the $110 or PV = $110/(1.1) = $100. The more general mathematical formula for PV is given by:

$$PV = CF_T/(1 + R)^T, \qquad (2.1)$$

where CF_T is the cash flow at time T and R is the interest rate. In the example above, R is the annual interest of 10%. In our example, $T = 1$ because the $110 will be received 1 year from now.

Assume that your distant uncle promises you $121 on your 30th birthday. You just turned 28. If you can get 10% interest from the bank, then the present value can be obtained by using Equation (2.1). In this example, $T = 2$ because the promised payment is 2 years from now. And the future value or $CF_2 = 121$. Mathematically, PV $= \$121/(1.1)^2 = \$100$.

We can give two economic interpretations of present value. The *first* interpretation states that the present value of a cash flow is the minimum amount of funds an individual must invest in the capital markets to "earn" the future cash flow.

Here is an example that will illustrate the first economic meaning of the time value of money. Let us assume the interest rate is 10% per year. What is the present value of receiving $110 at the end of the first period and $121 at the end of the second period? Using our present value formula, we have:

$$PV = \$110/1.1 + \$121/(1.1)^2 = \$200.$$

Ok, so the present value is $200, what about the economic interpretation that we promised? Well, if we invest $200 in the capital markets (let us say a bank) earning 10% a year, we would be able to withdraw $110 in the first year and $121 in the second year. How do we know this?

If we invest $200 in the bank earning 10% per annum, we will earn $20 in interest in the first year. Our account balance is then $220. Now assume we withdraw $110 from our account after we have been credited for the interest. We will be left with $110 which we will leave in the bank for another year. Again, with a 10% interest rate, we can earn another $11 by the end of the second year. We will now have $121 ending balance which we can now withdraw for our own personal consumption. Terrific!

The *second* interpretation states that the present value is the maximum amount one can borrow against the future cash flow. Our example can also be used to illustrate the second economic meaning of the time value of money: the maximum amount one can borrow against the cash flow.

Imagine if we had two promissory notes from Uncle Sam (that means that they are risk free) one promising to pay us $110 in year 1 and the other paying us $121 in year 2. If the bank lending rate is 10%, then the most that any bank will lend us against our future cash flow is $200. Just think of the bank as the investor in the following table.

Bank lends us today	$200
Interest earned at end of year 1	$20
We make our first loan payment at the end of year 1	$110
Our balance at the end of year 1	$110
Interest earned at end of year 2	$11
We make our second loan payment at the end of year 2	$121
Balance at the end of year 2	$0

Imagine if you wanted to peddle the two promissory notes from Uncle Sam. If there was an auction for these notes and many people came to the auction (which in a sense this is exactly what traders are doing at stock and bond exchanges), would you not expect that the competition among buyers will push up the price of the two promissory notes to $200? Hopefully, you are beginning to see that present value of the promissory notes is also its price.

Using Excel to Calculate Present Value

We can also use Excel to calculate the present value. In the following set of examples, we will illustrate present value concepts and the various present value functions of Excel. Let us begin by actually using Excel to calculate the present value of receiving $110 in period 1 and $121 in period 2 assuming an interest rate of 10%. The following table represents an Excel worksheet. In cells B1 and C1, you will find the cash flows for times 1 and 2, respectively. Note that in cell B2, we put in the Excel function, *npv(rate,pmt1, pmt2, ..)* That must be entered to get the correct answer of $200.

	A	B	C
1	CASH FLOW	110	121
2	PRESENT VALUE	=NPV(0.1,B1:C1)	

Rate is the interest rate and is entered in the format of percentage (10%, in our example) or in the format of a number (0.1, in our example). The payments could either be entered as a cell location separated by commas (in our example as B1, C1,) or as a range (in our example B1:C1). Excel always assumes that the cash flow of the first cell in the npv function (B1 in our example) is the cash flow at time 1. We will do a similar problem with the financial calculator on page 14.

Let us do another example. Assume you are expecting to receive cash flow as depicted in the following table.

TIME	0	1	2	3	4	5
CASH FLOW	$100	0	0	$1,000	0	$5,000

Below, we present how you might enter these numbers in the Excel worksheet to get the present value. The letters in bold represent the columns in the excel sheet. The numbers in bold represent the rows in the excel sheet. Please note in this example our interest rate is 12% or 0.12.

	A	B	C	D	E	F	G
1	TIME	0	1	2	3	4	5
2	CASH FLOW	100	0	0	1,000	0	5,000
3		=NPV(0.12,C2:G2)+B2					

Note that you must not omit any cash flow that is zero so that Excel 'knows' the timing of the cash flow. That is why the excel function specifies cells C2:G2 so that the excel calculator "knows" that at times 1 and 2 the cash flow is zero. Also, note that you will have to enter the cash flow of time 0 separately. Hence, cell C3 adds '+B2' following the NPV function. The answer you should get is $3,648.91. Now you try. The financial calculator can also be used to do this problem, but you must consult your manual as to its usage. For now, we do not provide an explanation in these notes since each calculator has a unique procedure for this calculation. But later in the notes, we provide how to use the HP — 12c for these types of calculations.

Excel also has several other useful functions that can be used to do time value problems. We will work through several examples.

Lump Sum Example

Assume that you will receive $1,000 in year 10 assuming an interest rate of 10% per year. According to Equation (2.1) the present value is given by PV = $1,000/(1.1)^{10}. We could also use the NPV function as used above to find the present value of receiving the lump sum of $1,000 in year 10. But this would take some hard work. As an illustration, consider the following Excel sheet table depicted below. The first row represents the columns and rows are identified by integers, 1, 2 and 3. Note that we would have to create a spreadsheet that allows for an entry of zero value for years 1–9 (as depicted in cells C2 to K2) and then an entry of 1,000 in year 10 (cell L2). In cell C3, we place the NPV function as shown and it will yield an answer equal to $385.54.

A	B	C	D	E	F	G	H	I	J	K	L
1	TIME	1	2	3	4	5	6	7	8	9	10
2	CF	0	0	0	0	0	0	0	0	0	1,000
3		=NPV(0.1, C2:L2)										

Instead, we can use another useful Excel present value function. This function is PV(rate, nper, pmt, fv, type) where rate is the interest rate, expressed as a percentage (e.g., 10%) or as a decimal (e.g., 0.10), nper is the number of periods, pmt is the payment per period, fv is the future value of the lump sum payment, and type = 0 if the payments are received at the end of the period and type = 1 if the payments are received a the beginning of the period.

Thus, for our previous example where we asked what is the present value of receiving $1,000 at the end of period 10 assuming an interest rate of 10%, then we set rate = 0.1, nper = 10, pmt = 0, fv = 1,000, type = 0. Note you must set pmt = 0 so that Excel "knows" that is there are no payments until time 10, at which point you will receive $1,000 at the end of year 10. More formally, you can type the following in any cell = PV(.1,10,0,1000,0). Do not forget to type the equal sign in front of PV otherwise Excel will treat the expression as text and not a mathematical function.

Assuming you are following along using an Excel sheet, you will find that if you type such a formula you will obtain (−$385.54). Excel is telling you that if you wanted to buy a security that promises to pay you $1,000 at the end of year 10, you will have to pay $385.54 assuming that the interest rate is 10% per annum. Why must you pay this amount? Because if you were to invest $385.54 in a bank that promises to pay 10% per annum on all deposits, you will have $1,000 at the end of 10 years.

You might ask, "What sort of security pays only a lump sum payment at the end of certain number of years?" One such security is a zero-coupon bond that pays no interest until the final maturity date. But at the final maturity date, the bond pays a lump sum. Back in the early 1980s, many corporations issued zero-coupon bonds to finance their activities. For reasons beyond the scope of this presentation, most firms now avoid issuing such bonds. However, you can still purchase zero-coupon bonds today. For example, STRIPs, an acronym for Separately Traded Registered Income Proceeds, are zero-coupon Treasury securities.

So by now you are saying to yourself, that the above discussion is interesting but would it not be more appropriate to discuss these investments in some other chapter? The real reason for the discussion is not only to show you how STRIPs might be priced, but also make sure you understand that in the real world, no one is going to ask what is the present value of a lump sum amount. But they may ask, how do you price a zero-coupon bond!

Using a Financial Calculator to Calculate Present Value

There are financial calculators that one can use to evaluate present value. Each of these calculators has the following five symbols.

$$N \quad i \quad PV \quad PMT \quad FV$$

The N represents the number of periods in the future when the payment is received. The symbol i interest rate. PV is the present value. PMT is the periodic payment and FV can be viewed as the future lump sum payment. We will define each term more concretely in the following set of examples. It will help, of course, that you read the manual associated with your financial calculator.

Lump Sum Example

Assume that you are promised a future lump sum payment of FV at time N. What is the present value? According to Equation (2.1), the present value is given by

$$PV = FV/(1+i)^N.$$

Let us do two examples:

(a) Assume that you receive $500 in year 10, the interest rate $i =$ 10%. In this case, FV = $500 and N =10%. According to Equation (2.1) PV = $500/(1.1)^{10}$. You can use the financial calculator by plugging the numbers as shown in the next table.

N	i	PV	PMT	FV
10	10	?		500
		−192.77		

The second row of the above table represents the numbers you put in the calculator. Note that you enter 10 (as in 10%) and not 0.1 (as you did for the excel sheet) for i. Also, make sure that your calculator sets as a default for PMT as one payment per year. The "?" in the table indicates that you use that button (in this case, the PV button) to calculate the answer. Please also note that your calculator will yield an answer of −192.77. *WHY THE MINUS?* The calculator is essentially saying that if you wish to receive $500 in the future, you will have to pay $192.77. (The +/− sign in the PV, PMT, and FV functions can be taken to indicate the *direction* of the Cash Flow, where "+" represents Cash coming in, and "−" represents Cash going out.)

Recall our discussion on page 27. In the real world no one asks, "WHAT IS THE PRESENT VALUE OF A PARTICULAR CASH FLOW?" The real world uses terms as "what is the price" or "what is it worth". For example, assume that the interest rate (Wall Street usually calls the interest rate as the yield) is 10%. A security, a zero-coupon bond called a STRIP, offers to pay $500 at the end of year 10. No interim payment will be made before year 10. What should be the price for such a security? We already know that answer, it is worth $192.77.

(b) Consider now another example. Assume that you receive $250 in year 1 and another $400 in year 2. Again, assume that the interest rate is 10%. What are these cash flows worth today? The present value equation is given by

$$PV = \$250/(1.1) + 400/(1 + 0.10)^2 = \$557.85.$$

To do this problem, using a financial calculator, you must calculate the present value of each cash flow separately. (*HINT: ACTUALLY, THERE IS AN EASIER METHOD TO DO THIS BUT YOU MUST CONSULT YOUR MANUAL. WE ARE SIMPLY TRYING TO CONCENTRATE ON LEARNING THE CONCEPTS.*) In other words:

N	i	PV	PMT	FV
1	10	?	0	250
		−227.27		

The first cash flow of $250 at time 1 is worth $227.27.

N	i	PV	PMT	FV
2	10	?	0	400
		−330.58		

The second cash flow is worth $330.58. The sum of the two cash flows equals $557.85.

The Present Value of An Annuity

An annuity is a cash flow received at the end of each year for a specified number of years. Your car or mortgage payment is probably structured as an annuity. To find the present value of receiving $100 per year for the next 15 years, we use the following formula:

$$PV = \sum_{t=1}^{n} \frac{100}{(1+R)^t},$$

where n is the number of periods in an annuity and R is the interest rate. $\sum_{t=1}^{n}$ is the Greek letter sigma, which represents addition from period 1 to n in mathematics. The letter t is a time index. Hence, the above equation is telling us to do the following mathematical operations:

$$100/(1+R) + 100/(1+R)^2 + 100/(1+R)^3$$
$$+ 100/(1+R)^4 + \cdots + 100/(1+R)^n.$$

Fortunately, we can use the PV(rate, nper, pmt, fv, type) function of Excel to evaluate annuities. Let us illustrate this with a few concrete examples:

Example 1: Your mother (who introduces you to her friends as "My son/daughter, the investment banker!") is asking you for investment advice. She would like to receive $5,000 per year for the next 20 years as part of her retirement income. Of course, she wants to bear very little risk. An insurance company rated very highly advertises an annuity rate of 6% per year. How much must you invest of your mother's money to obtain her annuity? Note, that we do not ask "what is the present value of a $5,000 annuity for 20 years at 6%?" But of course, that is exactly the question being asked. Why? The reason is that the insurance company is going to charge a premium for the promise of paying out $5,000 per year for 20 years. They will take the premium and invest in the market earning at least 6% so that they can afford the promise. In other words, we are asking: What is the minimum amount of funds your mother must invest in the capital markets to "earn" the $5,000 per annum for 20 years! This is exactly the first economic interpretation of what is present value (see page 23). Using Excel, we can obtain the correct answer by setting the PV function as PV(0.06,20,5000,0,0). If you try this on your Excel sheet (and you should), you will obtain an answer of ($57,349.61).

You can also solve this using the financial calculator. This time we will use the PMT button instead of the FV button. The PMT button represents the amount of the annuity per year. Refer to the table below:

N	i	PV	PMT	FV
20	6	?	5,000	0
		−57,349.61		

What will happen to the amount needed for the investment if interest rises to 10%? Now our PV function is PV(0.10,20,5000,0,0) which will yield ($42,567.82). Note that present value declines as interest rates go up. It also means that the amount of money required to obtain the future cash flows will decline as interest rates go up. By the way we get an identical answer if we use the financial calculator as follows:

N	i	PV	PMT	FV
20	10	?	5,000	0
		−42,567.82		

If interest rates decline to 3%, the PV function will yield ($74,387.37). As interest rates decline, present value increases. As interest rates decline, the amount of money required to obtain future value cash flows increases. Again, using the financial calculator, we get the identical answer.

N	i	PV	PMT	FV
20	3	?	5,000	0
		−74,387.37		

Example 2: You recently stashed your $50,000 year-end bonus in the bank. You are interested in a studio condominium in Brooklyn Heights, a stylish neighborhood across the river from Manhattan. The asking price for your pad is $375,000. Based upon your compensation, you estimate you can afford to pay a monthly mortgage (including escrow) payment of $3,500 per month. Assume that the current mortgage rate is 8% per year for a 15 year mortgage. You must put down in cash 10% of the purchase price. Can you afford the condo?

Before answering the above question, we must explain why this is a present value problem. According to the second economic interpretation we gave on page 23, present value is the maximum amount you can borrow against future cash flows. Hence, we are essentially asking how much can you borrow if you are promising to pay in the future (starting one month from now) $3,500 per month for the next 15 years. Our point is very simple. If you are looking at a finance situation involving money over time, you are dealing with present value.

Note that paying $3,500 per month for 15 years is an annuity. But now the periods are defined in months as opposed to years. This should not slow us down. We just need to reinterpret the parameters of the PV function. In particular, we must divide the annual interest rate of 8% by 12 to obtain the monthly rate. Thus, the rate is now 2/3% or 0.00667. To obtain the value of nper for the excel sheet, we multiply 15 years by 12, which equals 180 months, the monthly duration of the mortgage. Hence, our function now looks like PV(0.08/12,180,3500,0,0) which will yield ($366,242.07). This means you can afford to borrow up to $366,242.07. If you put down $37,500, then you will need to borrow $337,500 from the bank, well within the maximum you can afford to borrow. Welcome to Brooklyn!

How do we use the financial calculator to get this answer? Note that the interest rate we use is not 0.08/12 but rather 8/12 as in percent. See the following table:

N	i	PV	PMT	FV
180	8/12	? −366,242.07	3,500	0

Example 3: Another important application of present value is that it can be used to evaluate a debt security. A typical debt security pays an annual coupon payment based upon a stated coupon rate. In addition it pays a lump sum payment at the end of its maturity. That lump sum payment is known as the face or par value of the bond. The annual interest rate is given by multiplying the coupon rate and the face value. Typically the face value or par value of debt is $1,000. If the coupon rate is 9% and the maturity of the bond is 15 years, then you are expecting to receive 0.09*$1,000 or $90 per year for the next 15 years and in addition you will receive $1,000 in year 15. The price of such a bond depends upon the prevailing interest rate in the market. For example, this debt may have been issued by the company 5 years ago when interest rates were 9%. But now interest rates are 12%! (In Wall Street parlance, the yields are now 12%!) Now if you were buying this debt security, you would not pay the same amount as another debt with maturity of 15 years and a coupon rate of 12%. The 9% coupon is only paying $90 while the new debt security that was just issued is paying $120. How much less will you pay?

To answer this question, note that this debt security is a combination of a $90 15-year annuity and a lump sum of $1,000 at the end of year 15. Our PV function will be useful here as well. In particular, we can set the parameters as follows: PV(0.12, 15,90,1,000,0). This will yield a price of ($795.67). We can also use the financial calculator:

N	i	PV	PMT	FV
15	12	? −795.67	90	1,000

Note that if the interest rate is only 9%, then PV(0.09, 15,90,1000,0) will generate a price of $1,000. That is, whenever the interest rate or bond yield is equal to the coupon rate, the price of the debt security will equal the security's par or face value, $1,000. If the yield is higher than the coupon rate, then the price will be below par. If the yield or interest rate is lower than the coupon rate, then the price of the security will be greater than par.

And let us not forget to use the financial calculator. For this last example, the table is as follows:

N	i	PV	PMT	FV
15	9	? −1,000	90	1,000

Example 4: In all of the above annuity examples, we assume that you either paid or received the first annuity payment exactly one year from now. But not all annuities are paid out so quickly. You have probably read about the crushing pension and healthcare liabilities of General Motors, Ford, and Chrysler faced in 2008. The question is how do we determine these liabilities and how do we know whether or not the liability is unfunded? Let us illustrate these concepts in the following example. We are going to use overly simplistic assumptions that will make our analysis more tractable but does not take away from the fact of the importance of present value for these calculations.

Assume that the average employee of Overextended Inc. will retire in 25 years and there are 10,000 employees. Furthermore the company promises to pay an annual retirement benefit of $20,000 per year beginning at the date of retirement. Ms. Actuary tells management that they should assume that the average duration of this liability is 15 years. Assume further that the company has set aside $200 million to cover the promised payout for the retirement and it has no plans to make any further payments. As the CFO, you must figure out whether or not the firm has put away enough money.

To solve this problem, we must determine how much money the firm must have in each employee's retirement account at the exact time the employee retires. Assume that the company can earn 7% on its investments. We can solve this problem in two ways. One way is to recognize that starting at time 25, the firm is paying 15 payments of $20,000 but paying it at the beginning of the period. Hence, using the Excel PV function, we must set type = 1. Consequently, you should enter in your Excel sheet (do not forget the equal sign) =PV(0.07,15,20000,0,1). When you do this, Excel will provide an answer of ($194,909.36). If you set type = 0, as we have done normally, you are assuming that the first retirement payment is made on the first anniversary of the retirement.[1]

You can also come up with this answer using the financial calculator. The default of the financial calculator is that the cash flows are taking place at the end of the period. Each financial calculator allows you to change the format to the beginning of the period. For example in the HP-12C, you can touch the g button and then seven so that the financial calculator interprets your cash flow entries as the beginning of the period. (Again, please consult your manual!)

---

[1] Of course, you could have come up with the identical answer had you typed on your worksheet =PV(0.07,14,20000,0,0) − 20,000. Why the minus sign? Remember that the PV function always assumes that you will be paying at time of the first payment the amount given by the PV function. This latter approach recognizes that at time 25 each employee receives $20,000 immediately and then 14 additional payments all occurring on the anniversary of the retirement.

The appropriate table now becomes:

N	i	PV	PMT	FV
15	7	?	20,000	0
		−194,909.36		

Now remember you need to have $194,909.36 at time 25. How much must the firm have in the retirement account today, time 0? We can treat the $194,909.36 as a lump sum to be received at time 25. Accordingly, let us use the PV function, =PV(0.07,25,0,194909.36, 0) which yields ($35,911.89). (Before proceeding any further, note we do not use commas for 194,909.35 in the PV function since the Excel function uses commas to separate the required parameters.) If there are 10,000 employees, then the firm needs $359,118,892.71 right now, but your firm has only put away $200 million for the retirement benefits. Hence, the unfunded liability will equal $159,118,892.71.

Again, we can use the financial calculator to get the identical results as above. Before proceeding, if you are using the financial calculator, write down the $194,909.36 on a separate piece of paper because you will need to clear the register (see your manual) to proceed further. Once you clear the register, you will lose the $194,909.36 figure from the calculator's memory. Also note, as in the excel sheet, we place $194,909.36 in FV. In other words:

N	i	PV	PMT	FV
25	7	?	0	194,909.36
		−35,911.89		

Repeating ourselves — if there are 10,000 employees, then the firm needs $359,118,892.71 right now, but your firm has only put away $200 million for the retirement benefits. Hence, the unfunded liability will equal $159,118,892.71.

Example 5: Let us continue with the above example. As the CFO of the firm, you recognize that the company is in serious financial shape because of its unfunded liability. In fact, you must report the unfunded liability in a footnote in the financial documents that you file with the SEC. Once this information is submitted to the SEC, it becomes publicly available and you expect that the stock price of Overextended Inc. will drop. You also realize that the company cannot afford to borrow the money to fully fund the retirement liability. It is a shame since the company is expecting a 25% increase in profits this year, the highest growth the company has enjoyed since its inception. What to do?

One way out is for the firm to continue making annual payments to the retirement accounts. Of course, you do not need to make a total payment of $159,118,892.71 over the 25 years period. The magic of compounded interest (and appropriate money management) will help reduce your annual payment. What we want to find out is the annual payment for 25 years that has a present value equal to the unfunded liability $159,118,892.71. Fortunately, Excel has a payment function, =pmt(rate, nper, pv, fv, type), that we can use to answer the question. In particular, we type the function as =pmt(0.07,25,159118892.71,0,0) in the worksheet and you will find that the answer is ($13,654,074.48). Note that Excel gives you a negative number. This is because you entered the unfunded liability as a positive number for pv. Thus, Excel is saying that if you are willing to pay $13,654,074.48 per year for 25 years, you can borrow $159,118,892.71 today. Now that you have determined the annual contribution the firm must make, and assuming that you set up the process so that the payment is made, Overextended Inc. will no longer have an unfunded pension liability.[2]

---

[2] Actually, there will still be a reported unfunded liability as far as the accountants are concerned. Financial theory would say there is none since you have set up an account to fund the liability over time. Who is correct, the accountants or we finance types? You can answer this question yourself by answering the following question: If the company has money problems anytime in the future, what incentives does a manager have for keeping up with the payment schedule as you have calculated? Clearly there will be a strong incentive for the manager not to

Can we get the same answer using the financial calculator? Of course!

N	i	PV	PMT	FV
25	7	159,118,892.71	?	0
			−13,654,074.48	

Note the number of steps we had to take to find the required annual contribution $13,654,074.48. First, we had to find out the amount of money needed in the retirement account at time 25 (Answer: 10,000*$194,909.36 or $1,949,093,600). Then we had to find the present value of this liability (Answer: $359,118,892.71). Once we knew the liability, we subtracted out the $200 million to find the unfunded portion of the liability. And then, for the final step, we figured out the annual contribution such that the present value of the annual payments is equal to the unfunded portion of the liability.

Is there a way to cut out the second step? Absolutely! Just type in your Excel sheet =pmt(0.07,25,−200000000, 1949093600,0) and you will get the same answer as above or ($13,654,074.48). In other words, the arguments used in your pmt function is equivalent to stating the following: What must your payment be, so that the future value (fv) of the amount of money currently set aside ($200 million) earning 7% per annum will be worth in 25 years, the amount of money available ($1,949,093,600) to pay off the retirees. A word of caution is in order. You must be very careful about the minus signs for pv and fv. Note that above, we set pv to be equal to −200000000. Why? Because Overextended Inc. must pay that amount to the retirement account

---

make the annual contribution and hope for a better tomorrow. Sadly, we must admit the accountants are right on this one. Pension accounting is much more complicated than is presented in this footnote but a further discussion is beyond the scope of these notes.

(as well as making annual contributions) in order to be able to take out $1,949,093,600 at the end of 25 years.[3]

Similarly, we can skip the second step using our financial calculator. More formally:

N	i	PV	PMT	FV
25	7	−200,000,000	? −13,654,074.48	1,949,093,600

Example 6: Congratulations! Because of your quick thinking, Overextended Inc. no longer has an unfunded retirement liability. The problem is that the firm will not have sufficient cash flow to fund this year's retirement contribution because of extensive investment commitments the firm has made. You estimate that you will need to borrow $14 million. Mr. Gizbar, your banker, is willing to provide the loan as a 5-year mortgage that would require the firm to make equal semi-annual payments. The coupon rate is 8%. How much would the firm have to pay every 6 months?

Essentially, the present value of the payments must equal the current value of the loan. We can again use our pmt function, noting that pv is set to $14 million, rate is set to 4% or 0.04 (because if the annual rate is 8% then the semi-annual rate is half that number) and nper is set to 10 (because there are 10 6-month periods in a 5-year period). If you type on your Excel worksheet =pmt(0.04,10,14000000,0,0), you will get as an answer ($1,726,073.22), implying a semi-annual payment of $1,726,073.22.

---

[3]You could have also typed in =pmt(0.07,25,200000000, -1949093600,0). This time you would have gotten a positive $13,654,074.48. The interpretation here is that the firm is first creating a savings asset of $200 million and it continues to save $13,654,074.48 per annum so that by the end of the 25th year, the firm can pull out $1,949,093,600. Note that pv and fv are opposite signs since the direction of the money are going in opposite ways. The initial investment and annual contribution is being paid into a 7% bearing asset. At the end of the 25th year, you are taking the money out.

We can get a similar answer using the financial calculator. Please see the following table:

N	i	PV	PMT	FV
10	4	−14,000,000	?	0
			−1,726,073.22	

Note, when you borrow $14 million at an annual rate of 8%, the amount of interest you pay at the end of 6 months is $560,000. If you are paying $1,726,073.22, then the difference between the semi-annual payment and the interest payment of $560,000 is the principal payment. (OK, now for my pet peeve! Note, the spelling is not "PRINCIPLE"!!!) Hence at the end of 6 months, you will pay down $1,726,073.22 − $560,000 = $1,166,073.22. This in turn implies that at the end of 6 months, the balance of your loan is $12,833,926.78. This is important to know not only if you want to pay off the loan at the end of 6 months. It is also important because now the interest payment at the end of the first year will be lower than what the firm paid six months earlier. In fact, the interest payment at the end of the year is now 0.04($12,833,926.78) = $513,357.07. The principal payment will be the difference between the total semi-annual payment and the interest payment, or $1,726,073.22 − $513,357.07 = $1,212,716.15. For a mortgage, while the periodic interest payment declines, the principal payment increases commensurately so that the total periodic mortgage payment remains the same. Table 2.1 describes the amortization schedule of this loan.

Note, that in order for us to know how much the loan is outstanding at the end of period 6 (after 3 years have passed), we have to amortize the loan for 6 periods. In other words, we have to figure out how much principal we pay over the entire 3 years. The schedule of principal payment is known as the amortization schedule of the loan.

Is there an easier way to get that answer? Do you have to ask! We just need to realize that the principal balance of the loan outstanding is the present value of the remaining payments. Note that

Table 2.1: Loan Amortization Schedule of Example 6

Period	Loan Outstanding	Interest Payment	Principal Payment
0	$14,000,000.00		
1	$12,833,926.78	$560,000.00	$1,166,073.22
2	$11,621,210.63	$513,357.07	$1,212,716.15
3	$10,359,985.83	$464,848.43	$1,261,224.80
4	$9,048,312.05	$414,399.43	$1,311,673.79
5	$7,684,171.31	$361,932.48	$1,364,140.74
6	$6,265,464.94	$307,366.85	$1,418,706.37
7	$4,790,010.32	$250,618.60	$1,475,454.62
8	$3,255,537.51	$191,600.41	$1,534,472.81
9	$1,659,685.79	$130,221.50	$1,595,851.72
10	$0.00	$66,387.43	$1,659,685.79

at period 6, there are four payments left to go to completely pay off the loan. Hence, if you type =PV(0.04,4, 1726073.22,0,0) in your Excel worksheet you will obtain ($6,265,464.94), the same answer as we have in Table 2.1 for period 6. Using the financial calculator, we get an identical answer. More formally:

N	i	PV	PMT	FV
4	4	? $-6,265,464.94$	1,726,073.22	0

Example 7: Mr. Gizbar calls you back and says that he can alternatively lend you the $14,000,000 at 8% with semi-annual payments but this time with a balloon payment of $4 million at the end of the loan's life. Note that with this arrangement the firm will be paying a good portion of the loan on the final maturity date. Whereas in the previous example, the firm is paying the original $14 million total principal payment spread over 10 payments, in this example, you are only paying $10 million principal over the 10 payments, leaving the last day to pay off the remaining $4 million balance.

First let us determine the semi-annual payment by typing in the Excel worksheet =pmt(0.04,10,14000000,−4000000,0) which yields

($1,392,909.44). Note that the balloon payment of $4 million is the negative entry of fv of the pmt function. Please notice that the semi-annual payment has been reduced by $333,163.78. Also, please note that we enter the balloon payment as −4,000,000 in the FV function. That is you are receiving $14 million today but you must pay $4 million at the end of year 5 (and as it turns out an additional payment of $1,392,909.44 every 6 months). Similarly, we can get the periodic payment using the financial calculator.

N	i	PV	PMT	FV
10	4	14,000,000	?	−4,000,000
			−1,392,909.44	

The amortization schedule for this loan is given by Table 2.2. If we compare the entries of Table 2.2 with that of Table 2.1, you will see that the periodic interest payments are higher with the exception at period 1 for the loan with the $4 million balloon payment. Similarly, the principal payments of the $4 million balloon payment loan are lower except in period 10 where it becomes significantly greater.

Table 2.2: Loan Amortization Schedule of Example 7

Period	Loan Outstanding	Interest Payment	Principal Payment
0	$14,000,000.00		
1	$13,167,090.56	$560,000.00	$832,909.44
2	$12,300,864.74	$526,683.62	$866,225.82
3	$11,399,989.88	$492,034.59	$900,874.85
4	$10,463,080.03	$455,999.60	$936,909.85
5	$9,488,693.79	$418,523.20	$974,386.24
6	$8,475,332.10	$379,547.75	$1,013,361.69
7	$7,421,435.94	$339,013.28	$1,053,896.16
8	$6,325,383.94	$296,857.44	$1,096,052.01
9	$5,185,489.85	$253,015.36	$1,139,894.09
10	$0.00	$207,419.59	$5,185,489.85

What is happening in period 10? First, you are still paying the periodic payment of $1,392,909.44, of which $207,419.59 is interest and $1,185,489.85 is applied to principal. But you are also paying an additional $4 million principal or balloon payment.

Which loan do you think is best for the firm? Note that the cost of the loan as characterized by the coupon payment is the same for both loans! The aggregate total payment of the loan in Example 6 is 10 times the semi-annual payment or $17,260,732.21. The aggregate total payment of the balloon payment loan of Example 7 is 10 times the loan's semi-annual payment (of $1,392,909.44) plus the $4 million balloon payment or $17,292,909.44. That is not much of a difference between the two loans given that you are able to reduce your semi-annual payment by $333,163.78 with the $4 million dollar balloon payment loan for period 1–9. Hence, the answer will depend upon the cash flow profile of the company. If the cash flow is very tight at the beginning of the loan and you expect the cash flow to significantly improve over the next few years, the firm might prefer the balloon payment option. If the cash flow of the firm will not improve significantly, or having the ability to borrow in 5 years to finance future growth is very important, the firm should prefer the mortgage loan of Example 6.

Internal Rate of Return-Yield to Maturity

In present value calculations, we know the interest rate and the cash flows while the unknown is the price or present value. However, some times we know the cash flow and the price, also known as the present value. We want to know the interest rate that equates the present value of the cash flow to the current price. This interest rate is known as either the yield to maturity, return on investment or the internal rate of return. (By now you are asking yourself, "why there are so many different names for the interest rate?" It is a good question and it is unfortunately way beyond the scope of this course or author and so let us move on!)

For example, the asking price of a building is $2 million. The estimated profit is −$150,000 at time 1, $25,000 at time 2, $350,000 per year for periods 3–6 and you expect to sell the building for $4 million at the end of the sixth year. If the return on the investment is greater than your cost of borrowing, then you know you are making money. If not, you are losing money and the price is too high. Mathematically, you are solving the following equation:

$$\$2,000,000 = -\$150,000/(1+R) + \$25,000/(1+R)^2$$
$$+ \$350,000/(1+R)^3 + \$350,000/(1+R)^4$$
$$+ \$350,000/(1+R)^5 + \$4,350,000/(1+R)^6.$$

The above equation is a polynomial equation and cannot be solved algebraically. In fact, calculus was created just to solve equations such as the one above. Fortunately, we can solve the equation by brute force, which is a method of trying different interest rates until we find the one that satisfies the above equation. Even more fortunate, with computers and the Excel time value function irr, we can solve this equation very easily. The following table, replicating an Excel worksheet, lays out the cash flow.

	A	B	C
1	Time	Cash Flow	ROI
2	0	−$2,000,000	=irr(B2:B8)
3	1	−$150,000	
4	2	$25,000	
5	3	$350,000	
6	4	$350,000	
7	5	$350,000	
8	6	$4,350,000	

In the above table, column B lays out the cash flow of the real estate investment. The negative sign in cell B2 represents the price we pay (and therefore we are laying out) for the real estate investment. In cell C2, we introduce a new Excel time value function, irr(values, guess). You enter the cells B2:B8 to highlight the cash flows of the investment. You can ask the Excel function to begin its iterative process with a certain interest rate. But for most problems, you can just leave it out. If we type =irr(B2:B8) as is illustrated in cell C2, we will get 18.50% or 0.1850. If you are not getting this answer, make sure you properly format the cell. By the way, commercial mortgage rates are currently 8.5%. Thus, go buy the building and become a land baron. Watch out Donald Trump! (The latter is not a political statement!)

Can this be done using the financial calculator? Of course, but have you looked at your manual yet? Hmmm . . . OK, I will show you how to do this problem using the HP-12C. Those of you using other calculators, please read your manual but essentially you are using the cash flow register function of your calculator. Note that the HP-12C has different notations in Row 3 below the n, i, PV, PMT, and FV buttons and other notations above those buttons in Row 1. In particular:

AMORT	INT	NPV	RND	IRR
N	i	PV	PMT	FV
12X	12÷	CF_0	CF_j	N_j

Note also that on the bottom of the calculator there is an **f** and **g** buttons. The **f** and **g** buttons help us move from Row 3 to Row 1 settings. We will first concentrate on the relevant buttons in Row 3. CF_0 represents the cash flow at time 0. CF_j represents the cash flows after time 0. N_j will allow us to enter the number of times that a cash flow repeats itself. The following table tells you the steps to take to get the IRR. Note that you first punch in **f** and clx to clear the register. Then you enter the first cash flow of −$2 million, hit the **g** button and then the CF_0 button. Step 3 instructs you to enter −$150,000 and then hit the **g** and the CF_j buttons. The next step is to enter $25,000 and then hit **g** and the CF_j buttons. Step #5 tells you to enter 350,000 and then hit the **g** and **CF$_j$** buttons. Since you are expecting to receive $350,000 in years 3–5, implying receiving that amount three times, you can either repeat Step 5 two more times or you can instead as indicated in the table below, enter 3 and hit the **g** and the **N$_j$** buttons. The final cash entry of $4,350,000 is now entered and you hit again the **g** and the **CF$_j$** buttons. Now you want the IRR. Note that in the previous table, the **IRR** button is in Row 1. Therefore, you hit the **f** key and then the **IRR** button to obtain our answer.

Step 1	f	clx
Step 2	−2,000,000	**g CF$_0$**
Step 3	−150,000	**g CF$_j$**
Step 4	25,000	**g CF$_j$**
Step 5	350,000	**g CF$_j$**
Step 6	3	**g N$_j$**
Step 7	4,350,000	**g CF$_j$**
Step 8	f	**IRR**

Just like in the present value of money, there are special Excel functions that we can use to find the present value of an annuity or lump sum, there is the Excel function rate(nper, pmt, pv, fv, type, guess) that can be used to find the return on investment or yield of an annuity or lump sum. Below we present three such problems.

Example 1: The *XYZ* bond is priced at $828 per $1,000 par. The coupon rate is 5% and the maturity of the bond is 3 years. This implies that the annual coupon payment is $50 per year for 3 years and that at the end of the third year, the holder of the bond also receives $1,000. Find the yield of the bond. In essence, we are determining the interest rate that equates the present value of the promised cash flows of the bond to the current price of $828. The excel rate function is =rate(nper, pmt, pv, fv, type, guess). We can type in the Excel worksheet =rate(3,50,−828,1000,0) [we can ignore a value for guess] and we will get 0.1218 or 12.18%. Equivalently, we can use the financial calculator using the i button.

N	i	PV	PMT	FV
3	?	−828	50	1,000
	12.18			

The 12.18% answer is known as the yield of the bond. Note that we set the pv parameter as −828. The reason for this is that to get the $50 coupon payment for three years and the $1,000 principal payment at the end of year 3, you have to pay (or layout) $828.

An investor uses the yield of the bond to make a comparison among different debt securities so that she can determine which debt security to buy. In addition, corporate officers may want to know the yield of the debt securities currently outstanding because such knowledge provides an estimate of how much it would cost the firm to borrow under current market conditions.

Before we proceed further we should explain the difference between coupon rate and yield. The coupon rate determines the cash flow of the financial security. The yield determines the price of the security. The difference can be seen in how we use the pv and pmt excel functions. With the pv function, PV(rate, nper, pmt, fv, type), we set rate using the yield of comparable financial securities to find the price of that security. In our mortgage problems, we are interested in finding the periodic payment. Hence, when we use the rate parameter in the pmt function, =pmt(rate, nper, pv, fv, type), we use the coupon rate.

Example 2: The price of a zero-coupon bond with a par value of $1,000 and maturing in 10 years is $500. What is the yield to maturity of the bond? Again, we can use the rate function in excel as rate(10,0,−500,1000,0). Using this function we will obtain an answer of 0.0718 or 7.18%. Similarly, using the financial calculator:

N	i	PV	PMT	FV
10	?	−500	0	1,000
	7.18			

Example 3: In the United States, all corporate debt securities pay interest semi-annually. In contrast, most corporate debt securities issued in Europe pay interest only one time per year. Thus, to find the yield of US debt securities, we must adjust our calculations to take into account the semi-annual payment. Assume a 20-year bond whose current price is $900 and a coupon rate of 8%. Interest payments are paid semi-annually and the $1,000 principal payment is paid at the end of the 20th year. In this case, N is set to 40 representing the 40 semi-annual payments during the 20-year duration of the bond. In addition, pmt is set to ($)40 because an 8% coupon implies an annual payment of $80 but a semi-annual payment of ($)40. Thus, if we type as in our Excel worksheet =rate(40,40,−900,1000,0), we will get an answer of 4.5471% or 0.045471. To find the annual yield of the bond, we multiply the answer by 2, yielding 9.09%. Now, using the financial calculator we can get the same periodic rate of 4.5471%:

N	i	PV	PMT	FV
40	?	−900	40	1,000
	4.5471			

In the above paragraph, I suggested that you multiply the periodic rate of 4.5471% by 2 since there are two periods in a year. This is known as the *Bond Equivalent Yield*. In fact, when you are quoted a yield by Wall Street vendors, this is the yield they use. However, this yield ignores the compounding of interest rates. To understand the importance of compounding, consider the following. Eurobonds, that is, bonds issued by the capital market exchanges in Europe, pay interest only once a year. In contrast, corporate bonds traded in the US pay interest twice a year. Consider the following choices offered to you as an investor. Both bonds mature in 10 years. However, one bond, a Eurobond, is offering a bond with a coupon rate at 9%, paying $90 (yes, Eurobonds can be denominated in US dollars) once a year. Another bond of the same risk is offered in the US also with a 9% coupon. Both bonds are priced at $1,000. Clearly, you prefer the American bond because of the time value of money. The American bond will give you half the annual interest in 6 months compared to the Eurobond that will pay $90 in 12 months. If you were to find the bond equivalent yield of the US bond, you will find it is equal to 9%. It would appear that you should be indifferent between the two. Hence the bond equivalent yield is not telling you the whole story. There is another metric that we can use known as the *Effective annual yield* (*EAY*). The EAY takes into account the frequency of payments in a year. The greater the frequency, the more opportunities there are to reinvest that money, and therefore the greater will be the effective annual yield. The formula for EAY is given by:

$$\text{EAY} = [1 + \text{Periodic Rate in decimal terms}]^2 - 1. \qquad (2.2)$$

That is, $(1 + 0.045471)^2 - 1 = 0.093$ or 9.3%. Clearly, the American Bond is better.

Valuing Perpetuities

We have already stated that present value can be used to evaluate assets. We have also used present value to evaluate debt securities, but debt securities have a finite life. There are other assets with indefinite lives. For example, the United Kingdom issues gilts, treasury securities with an infinite maturity. In the United States, investors can buy preferred stock or common stock with no set maturity date. Financial theory states that the prices of these financial securities must equal the present value of the expected payments, but how does one find the present value of a financial security with an indefinite or infinite lifespan!? Fortunately, one can use a mathematical trick that helps us do that. In particular, if the dividends are expected to grow at a constant rate forever, then the price of that security is given by

$$PV = \text{Div}/(R - G), \qquad (2.3)$$

where Div is the expected dividend payment at time 1, R is the appropriate interest or discount rate for that security and G is the expected growth rate. We will talk about the appropriate discount rate for equity in another chapter but for now, let us be satisfied in understanding how to apply the above formula. Let us call the above model, the Dividend Growth Model.

Example 1: Assume that the appropriate discount rate for a preferred stock is 18%. The par value of the preferred stock is $100 and the stated coupon rate is 3%. This implies that the expected annual dividend is $3 in perpetuity (3% of a $100). What should be the current price of preferred stock? In this example, G = 0 and therefore the formula is $3/.18 or $16.67. Let us see the logic of this answer. Imagine if you invested $16.67 in Overly Generous Bank, Ltd. This bank offers depositors an 18% interest rate. How much money can you take out of the bank at the end of every year without reducing the available principal of $16.67? The answer, of course, is 0.18($16.67) or $3 per year. Hence, it makes sense that a preferred stock promising to pay $3 per annum in perpetuity would have a value of $16.67.

Example 2: Now consider a common stock, which is expected to pay $3 next year. The dividend is expected to grow at a constant rate of 10% per annum. Note that the dividends beginning at time 2 will be strictly greater than the dividends that are promised in Example 1 and therefore, clearly the common stock price must be greater than $16.67. Applying the formula $PV = \text{Div}/(R - G)$ or $3/(0.18–0.1), we will get an answer of $37.50.

Let us further analyze this answer. Assume that you bought the stock today for $37.50. What is the expected stock price you should receive if you were to sell the stock after holding it for exactly 1 year and receiving the first dividend of $3? Assume that the required interest rate does not change and the market still expects a dividend growth rate of 10%. Imagine being transported by H.G. Wells' time machine 1 year hence. Looking over the landscape, market participants are expected that this common stock is expected to pay $3.30 in the following year, corresponding to a 10% increase in dividends. Using the Dividend Growth Model, PV = Div/(R − G), the expected price should be given by $3.30/(0.18–0.1) = $41.25. Let us analyze your return. As you know, return that an investor earns from investing in common stock is divided into two parts. One part is the return obtained in the form of capital gains. In this case, you would be selling the stock for $3.75 more than you bought it. Given your initial investment of $37.50, you will be earning a capital gains return of $3.75/$37.50 of 10%. Note that the capital gains portion of your return corresponds exactly with the expected growth rate of dividends. Hence, according to financial theory, it is the expected growth of dividends that spur capital gains. Finally, part of your return comes from dividends. Note that your dividend yield is $3/$37.50 = 8%. Hence, your total return is the sum of the capital gains return of 10% and dividend yield of 8%, equaling 18%, the number that we used as our discount rate in the dividend growth example.

Example 3: You are considering purchasing an apartment building in downtown Manhattan. You expect to earn $3 million in profits next year and you expect profits to increase by 10% per annum. You require a rate of return of 18%. What is the maximum price you should pay for this building? Okay, this is not really another example. It is simply restating the previous example, but that is the exactly the point. The Dividend growth model is not only applicable to analyze price of equity, it can be used for any growth situation. Based upon what we did in Example 2, clearly the answer is $37.5 million.

We can also use the dividend growth model to calculate the expected return on investment or the required rate of return for situations whereby the cash flows or dividends are expected to grow at a constant rate. This is strictly analogous to the internal rate of return discussion above.

Example 4: After solving the problem of the unfunded pension liability, you receive a higher than usual bonus from the board of directors. Now, they have a harder task for you. Mr. Curmudgeon, who has been a member of the board of directors for the past 18 years, asks you, as the CFO of Overextended, Inc., as to what stockholders want! You observe that the current stock price of Overextended, Inc. is $32. Next year's dividend is expected to be $2.50 per share, and historically, the dividend growth rate has been 5% per annum. You see no reason why this should not continue for the foreseeable future. Note that in this case, you know the stock price (present value) and the cash flow. Consequently, you can use the Dividend Growth model to back out the rate of interest the market is using to price the security. Mathematically, we can directly solve for R, the required rate of return:

$$R = \text{Div}/\text{Price} + G. \qquad (2.4)$$

Plugging the known information into the formula, we have R = $2.50/$32 + 0.05 = 0.1281 or 12.81%. You can now tell Mr. Curmudgeon, that the firm needs to earn at least 12.81% as a return on equity. Otherwise, the stock price would drop. You assure Mr. Curmudgeon that under current investment plans, we should be able to satisfy current stockholders.

Example 5: You are expecting the shopping mall that you wish to buy to generate $5 million in profit next year. You expect, because of recent real estate development in the area that such profit will increase by 12% per annum until and including year 5. Henceforth, the growth rate should only be 2% per annum in perpetuity. Assuming you require a 15% annual return, what should be the maximum price that you should pay for the shopping mall?

Clearly you cannot simply use the dividend growth model since the cash flows start to grow in perpetuity sometime in the future. Before answering the question, let us develop the formula for a deferred growth annuity. Let CF_N be the cash flow at time N and assume that the cash flow will henceforth grow at a rate of G. If you used HG Wells' time machine and travelled to period $N - 1$, then period N is one period from period $N - 1$. We can use the dividend growth model to find the value of the cash flows at period $N - 1$. That is PV $= \mathrm{CF}_N/(\mathrm{R} - \mathrm{G})$. But that is the value of the cash flow at time $N - 1$ and we are interested in the value at time 0. Well that is not so hard; we treat the PV of time $N - 1$ as a lump sum cash flow at time $N - 1$ and we simply divide the PV by $(1 + R)^{N-1}$. In other words, the formula is:

$$\text{PV of a Deferred Growth Annuity } = \mathrm{CF}_N/[(R - G) * (1 + R)^{N-1}]. \tag{2.5}$$

Now we can find the value of the shopping mall using excel. We present below the table that depicts an excel sheet. The columns and the rows are in bold. Column A delineates the time periods. Column B delineates the cash flow for each time period. Column C provides the present value of the cash flow. In C6, the number represents the PV of the cash flow from time 1–5. This is obtained by using

	A	B	C
1	time	Cash Flow	PV
2	1	$5,000,000.00	
3	2	$5,600,000.00	
4	3	$6,272,000.00	
5	4	$7,024,640.00	
6	5	$7,867,596.80	$20,634,119.24
7	6	$8,024,948.74	$30,690,906.26
8		sum	$51,325,025.50

the excel function =NPV(0.15, B2:B6). The number in C7 is the present value of the deferred growth annuity found by using Equation (2.5) or $30,690,906.26/((0.15−0.02)*(1.15)^5)$. In Row 8, we sum cells C6 and C7 to obtain the value of the mall, which is $51,325,025.50. That is the maximum price you should pay for the mall.

Future Value

In this chapter, we have learned much about the present value of money. But sometimes, you would like to know how much money you will have at some future date. That is, you want to know the future value of money. Mathematically, the formula is:

$$CF(1 + R)^T = FV.$$

Example 1: You have put $500 in the bank as a deposit. The bank gives you 7.18% return. You want to know that if you leave that money in the bank for 10 years, how much money will you have? According to the above formula, you will have $500 $(1.0718)^{10}$ = $1,000.25. You could figure this out using the excel function = FV(rate, nper, pmt, pv, type). As with the other time value functions of excel, we need to be cognizant of signs. Hence, if you use =FV(0.0718,10,0,500,0) you will obtain −$1,000.25. On the other hand, if you use =FV(0.0718,10,0,−500,0) you will obtain $1,000.25.

We can also get the same answer using the financial calculator and we use the FV button to calculate the future value. In other words:

N	i	PV	PMT	FV
10	7.18	−500	0	?
				1,000.25

Example 2: Next year you will put $500 in a bank as a deposit. Assuming an interest rate of 7.18%, how much money will you have at the end of year 11? The answer again will be $1,000.25. Note that nper in the Excel function FV represents the number of compounding periods. The n button of the financial calculator also represents the number of compounding periods. In Example 1, there are 10 compounding periods between time 0, today, when you deposited $500 in the bank and time 10 when you withdraw $1,000.25. In this example, you will deposit the money at the end of this year. You will

leave the money in the bank until year 11. Again, there are only 10 compounding periods.

Example 3: Assume you plan to invest in your retirement account at a rate of $1,200 per year. Assume you can earn 7% per annum. How much money will you have at the end of 25 years? Since you are withdrawing the money at the end of 25 years, that is sometime in the future, you again have a future value problem. In this case, we can use =FV(0.07,25,1200,0,0) which will yield ($75,898.85). Had you used =FV(.07,25,−1200,0,0), you would obtain $75,898.85. Hence, you see that the sign obtained for the answer is opposite of the input in the FV function. This becomes more important in the next example. In either case, you are expecting to have $75,898.85 at the end of the 25th year. By now you must realize that the financial calculator can also do the same.

N	i	PV	PMT	FV
25	7	0	−1,200	?
				75,898.85

Example 4: Assume you plan to invest in your retirement account at a rate of $1,200 per year. Assume you can earn 7% per annum. In addition, your current retirement account has $75,000. How much money will you have at the end of 25 years? In this case, we can use =FV(0.07,25,1200,75000,0) which will yield ($482,956.29). Had you used =FV(0.07,25,−1200,−75000,0), you would obtain $482,956.29. Note that sign for 1,200 and 75,000 must be the same sign otherwise you will have a wrong answer. Finally, the next table shows you how to use the financial calculator.

N	i	PV	PMT	FV
25	7	−75,000	−1,200	?
				482,956.29

Below, we give you 20 practice questions to see if you understand the concepts presented so far. Good luck! The correct answer is in bold font.

1. What is the PV of $1,000,000 to be received in 10 years at an interest rate of 8.5%?

    a. $1,085,000.85
    b. $85,000
    c. $442,285.42
    d. $2,129.52

2. You receive $200 in year 10, with an interest rate of 8%. What is the Present Value?

    a. $92.64
    b. $93.57
    c. $100
    d. $200

3. Assume you receive a $50 payment at the end of each of the next 3 years at an interest rate of 6.5%. What is the Present Value of these payments?

    a. $46.95
    b. $124.18
    c. $150
    d. $132.42

4. If you are offered $300 a year for the next 15 years at an interest rate of 7%, then what is the Present Value?

    a. $4,500
    b. $1,631.01
    c. $2,732.37
    d. none of the above

5. If you receive $100 in the second year and $250 in the fourth year at an interest rate of 5.5%, what is the total PV of these lump sums?

    a. $250
    b. $350

   c. **$291.65**

   d. $100.76

6. What is the PV of an investment that yields $500 to be received in 5 years and $1,000 to be received in 10 years at an interest rate of 4%?

   a. **$1,086.53**

   b. $1,500

   c. $694.79

   d. $1,159.71

7. You receive $1,000 in year 5, $1,200 in year 10, $1,350 in year 15, and $1,500 in year 20. With an interest rate of 10%, what is the PV of these monies?

   a. **$1,629.72**

   b. $1,262.50

   c. $5,050

   d. $750.65

8. You receive $100 for 3 years at an interest rate of 7%, what is the Present Value?

   a. $100

   b. $275.51

   c. **$262.43**

   d. $300

9. You are currently 30 years old. You will receive $10,000 annually for the next 20 years. If the interest rate is 8%, what would the PV of these cash flows be?

   a. $200,000

   b. $10,000

   c. **$98,181.47**

   d. $9,937.73

10. You are currently 60 years old. You want to receive $10,000 annually beginning at the age of 60 for 20 years. If the interest rate is 8%, how much money must you have in your bank account today?

   a. **$106,035.99**

    b. $200,000

    c. $49,755.01

    d. $42,909.64

11. You receive $200 a year in years 6–10 at an interest rate of 10%. What would the PV of this cash stream be at time 0?

    a. $758.16

    b. $1,000

    c. $470.76

    d. $620.92

12. You want to buy a car. The list price is $10,000. You are able to put down $6,000. The dealer tells you, that he is willing to lend you money at an annual interest rate of 6% but you must be able to pay off the loan in 3.5 years. You can afford $100 monthly payments. How much can the dealer lend you?

    a. $3,526.40

    b. $4,452

    c. $3,881.35

    d. $3,779.83

13. Assume that the bank lends you $175,000. The annual interest rate is 6%. You are expected to make quarterly installments over a 15-year period. What is the amount you expect to pay each quarter?

    a. $2,625

    b. $4,443.85

    c. $5,541.67

    d. None of the above

14. What is the yield to maturity of a bond paying interest annually with a $1,000 par value, a 7% annual coupon rate, 25 years to maturity, and currently selling for $804?

    a. 9

    b. 7

    c. 14

    d. None of the above

15. What is the bond equivalent yield on a bond paying interest semi-annually with $1,000 face value, a 7.5% annual coupon for 20 years assuming a bond price of $863?

   a. 4.35%
   b. 7.5%
   c. 8.99%
   d. 20%

16. Assume that your annual mortgage payment is $24,000. The original mortgage is $180,000 and the mortgage is paid off in 15 years. Determine the annual interest rate of the mortgage.

   a. 10.25%
   b. 10.43%
   c. 10.59%
   d. 11.01%

17. Assume that your semi-annual mortgage payment is $12,000. The original mortgage is $180,000 and the mortgage is paid off in 15 years. Determine the annual (bond-equivalent yield) interest rate of the mortgage.

   a. 10.25%
   b. 10.43%
   c. 10.59%
   d. 11.01%

18. Assume that your monthly mortgage payment is $2,000. The original mortgage is $180,000 and the mortgage is paid off in 15 years. Determine the annual (bond-equivalent yield) interest rate of the mortgage.

   a. 10.25%
   b. 10.43%
   c. 10.59%
   d. 11.01%

19. Assume that you are now 35 years old. You would like to retire at age 65 and have a retirement fund of $5,000,000 at the time of your retirement. You have already $100,000 at age 35 in the retirement account. You expect to earn 6% per year. The amount

of money you must set aside each month to reach your retirement goal is:

a. **$4,377.98**
b. $5,577.08
c. $6,134.42
d. None of the above

20. Assume that you want a monthly retirement income of $4,500 beginning on your 65th birthday. You expect to live for 25 years and you want to leave $600,000 in the retirement account for your heirs which you will give to your heirs when you are a month shy of your birthday. Assuming you can earn 8% per year, the amount of money you must have in your retirement account by the end of the month prior to your 65th birthday is:

a. $589,167.49
b. **$664,782.26**
c. $1,300,215.17
d. None of the above

More Advanced Problems

1. You have finally found an auto insurance company which will insure your car for $750. The company offers you an option to pay the insurance in quarterly payments of $195. Payment is due at the end of each quarter. Would you select the installment option or take $750 from your 8% interest-bearing savings accounts?

2. Assume that the interest rate on a $3,770,000 loan is 14%. Assuming you pay off the loan in 10 equal (end-of-the-year) annual (mortgage) installments, and assuming your tax rate is 50%, what is your after-tax payment in year 7?

3. As the firm's pension manager, you select the securities which maximize the pension fund's return. You are required to invest in only investment grade bonds. You are considering two such bonds, each of which has been given an AAA rating. One bond, issued by the Safebett Company, is selling at par with a 12% coupon.

Another bond, issued by Betach, Inc., with a coupon rate of 5% is selling at $828 ($1,000 face value). Both bonds have a 3-year maturity. What are the yields of the two bonds?

4. Assume that the price of common stock is $16.32. The present yearly dividend is $1.50 which has just been paid. Consequently, the current price does not reflect the dividend just paid, but rather the value of the future dividends. You are expecting the dividend to grow 12% per annum for the first 2 years, and 4% thereafter. What is the approximate yield of this stock?

5. XYZ is considering buying the Toutedesuite Building for $10 mm. Bank A will give XYZ a 10-year loan, payable in equal yearly (mortgage) installments, with an annual interest rate of 18%. Bank B will also give a 10-year loan, payable in equal yearly (mortgage) installments, with a stated coupon rate of 15%. In addition Bank B will charge an upfront commitment 3.5% fee (of the loan). Which financial package is better?

6. Elimelech, who is 30, wants to save money to meet two objectives. First, he would like to be able to retire 20 years from now and have a retirement income of $30,000 per year for at least 30 years. The first retirement check will be received when Elimelech is 51 and his last check will be when he is 80. Second, he would like to purchase a speed boat 5 years from now, at an estimated cost of $20,000. He can afford to save only $12,000 per year for the first 10 years beginning when he is 31. Elimelech expects to earn 8% per year on average from investments over the next 50 years. What must his minimum annual savings be from years 11–20 to meet his objectives?

7. King Noodles' bonds have a 7.5% coupon rate and a $1,000 par value. Interest is paid semi-annually. The bond has a maturity of 8 years. If the (bond equivalent) yield on similar bonds is 6.6%, what is the value of King Noodles' bonds?

8. ABC borrows $1 million at 14% interest from the bank. The firm must prepay the interest at the beginning of the year. The principal is repaid at the end of the year. What is the approximate yield of debt?

Solution to More Advanced Problems

1. Find the present value of the quarterly payments.

N	i	PV	pmt	FV
4	2	?	195	0
		-742.51		

Hence, select the installment option.

2. First Step: Find the annual equal installments.

N	i	PV	pmt	FV
10	14	3,770,000	?	0
			$-722,760$	

Second Step: Find the book value of the loan at the end of the 6th year, which is the present value of the remaining payments:

N	i	PV	pmt	FV
4	14	?	722,760	0
		$-2,105,914$		

Third Step: Determine the interest and principal payment in year 7.

$$\text{Interest}_T = (\text{Interest Rate})(\text{Book Value}_{T-1})$$
$$= (0.14)(\$2,105,914) = \$294,828,$$
$$\text{Principal} = \$722,760 - 294,828 = \$427,932.$$

Fourth Step: Determine the total after tax-payment.

$$\text{After-tax} = \text{Interest}(1 - \text{Tax Rate}) + \text{Principal}$$
$$= (\$294,828)(1 - 0.5) + \$427,932$$
$$= \$575,346.$$

3. To obtain the solutions for this problem, you equate the price of the bond to the present value of the cash flows. Using the financial calculator:

Safebett

N	i	PV	pmt	FV
3	?	−1,000	120	1,000
	12			

Betach

N	i	PV	pmt	FV
3	?	−828	50	1,000
	12.18			

4. Equate the present value of the cash flows to the price of the stock:

$$\$16.32 = \frac{1.50(1.12)}{1+R} + \frac{1.50(1.12)^2}{(1+R)^2} + \frac{1.50(1.12)^2(1.04)}{(1+R)^2(R-0.04)}.$$

The first two terms represent the present value of the cash flow at times 1 and 2. The last term is the present value is the value of a deferred growth annuity. You must use excel to find the answer to this question since you have to use trial and error to find the answer, that is $R = 15\%$.

5. I am assuming that XYZ needs exactly $10 million to buy the Toutedesuite Building. Thus the firm will borrow the commitment fee. Since Bank B charges a 3.5% tax on the book-value of the

loan, then XYZ's borrowing requirement is given by the following relationship:

$$(1 - \text{Tax}) \text{ Loan} = \$10,000,000$$
$$\text{or}$$
$$\text{Loan} = \$10,000,000/.965 = \$10,362,694.30.$$

The annual mortgage payment of Bank B's loan is found by equating the present value of the mortgage payments to $10,362,694.30. Similarly, the annual mortgage payment of Bank A's loan is found by equating the present value of the mortgage payments to $10,000,000.

Bank B

N	i	PV	pmt	FV
10	15	10,362,694.30	?	0
			−2064788.21	

Bank A

N	i	PV	pmt	FV
10	18	10,000,000	?	0
			−2,225,146.41	

Since the annual payment of loan B is lower than that of Loan A, XYZ is better off borrowing from Bank B.

6. Set the present value of the liabilities equal to the present value of the assets. Before proceeding, I will introduce new notation. The present value of receiving $1 per year for n periods at rate i is given by the following formula.

$$PV = \sum_{t=1}^{n} \frac{1}{(1+i)^t}.$$

$\sum$ is the Greek letter sigma. In mathematics it represents addition from period 1 to n. The letter t is a time index. Hence, the above equation is telling us to do the following mathematical operations:

$$1/(1+i) + 1/(1+i)^2 + 1/(1+i)^3 + 1/(1+i)^4 + \cdots + 1/(1+i)^n.$$

Of course, this becomes a cumbersome notation. Instead, we can use $A_{n,i}$ to represent the present value of an annuity of \$1 per period for n periods at rate i. The equation below represents the "first steps" for solving the above problem. The left-hand side of the equation is the present value of the payout that Mr. Smith wants. The right-hand side of the equation is the present value of the savings plan.

$$30,000A_{30,8\%}/(1.08)^{20} + 20,000/(1.08)^5$$
$$= 12,000A_{10,8\%} + X\ A_{10,8\%}/(1.08)^{10}$$

Now consider the payout first. The second term is the present value he needs for the boat. He needs to have \$20,000 in year 5 and therefore the present value is simply $20,000/(1.08)^5$. Using the financial calculator, this is equal to

N	i	PV	pmt	FV
5	8	?	0	20,000
		−13,611.66		

Now the annual retirement payment of \$30,000 per year has a present value *at time 20 of* $30,000A_{30,8\%}$. We are assuming for simplicity that the payments are received at the end of each year. Note that this is the present value at time 20 but we need to know the present value of this retirement plan at time 0. Therefore, we need to divide that present value by $(1.08)^{20}$. To find the present value of this second payout, we follow the same procedure we did

for Example 4 on pages 34–36. In other words we solve this in two
steps:

Step 1:

N	i	PV	pmt	FV
30	8	? −337,733.50	30,000	0

Step 2:

N	i	PV	pmt	FV
20	8	? −72,460.12	0	337,733.50

Now let us proceed to the savings plan. To solve the first term of
the right-hand side equation, we do:

N	i	PV	pmt	FV
10	8	? −80,520.98	12,000	0

Now, how do we evaluate the last expression of X $A_{10,8\%}/(1.08)^{10}$.
How do we put an X in our financial calculator? Ignore the X
and concentrate on the other terms. Note that $A_{10,8\%}$ is simply
an annuity of $1 for 10 periods at 8%. We can solve everything

but X in the following two steps:
Step 1:

N	i	PV	pmt	FV
10	8	? −6.710	1	0

Step 2:

N	i	PV	pmt	FV
10	8	? −3.108	0	6.710

Now we have all the pieces together, we can solve the following equation:

$$30,000A_{30,8\%}/(1.08)^{20} + 20,000/(1.08)^5$$
$$= 12,000\ A_{10,8\%} + X\ A_{10,8\%}/(1.08)^{10}$$
$$72,460.12 + 13,611.66 = 80,520.98 + 3.108X,$$
$$X = \$1,785.97.$$

8. Find the present value of the cash flows, noting that the periodic rate is the bond equivalent yield divided by 2.

N	i	PV	pmt	FV
16	3.3	? 1,055.25	37.5	1,000

9. The cash flow at time 0 is $1 million $-\$140,000 = \$860,000$. The cash flow at $t = 1$ is $1,000,000. Hence,

$$860,000 = 1,000,000/(1 + R),$$
$$R = 16.28\%.$$

CHAPTER 3

RISK AND RETURN

Introduction

What are investors looking for? That is easy — investors want to get the biggest bang for the buck! What does this mean though? In Finance, we assume that investors want high returns. The problem is that in the real world high returns come with a price and are usually associated with high risks. So before we can answer the question as to what investors are looking for, we need to understand what we mean by return and what we mean by risk.

Assume that you bought 100 shares of IBM stock on January 3, 2007 at the opening price of \$97.18 and you sold the IBM at the closing price of \$104.69 on January 2, 2008. Table 3.1 the historical prices of IBM during 2007. What return did you make? Return is made up of two components. The first component is capital gains defined as the difference of the price at the time you sell the stock and the price of the stock at the time of purchase divided by the stock price at the time of purchase. Mathematically, P_t is defined as the price of the stock at time t. Then the capital gains portion of return is $(P_t - P_{t-1})/P_{t-1}$. For our example, the IBM capital gains portion is $(\$104.69 - \$97.18)/\$97.18 = .0773$ or 7.73%.

The second component of the return is the dividends the holder of the stock receives. IBM paid out \$.30 in February, 2007, and \$.40 dividend in May, August and November, 2007. The total dividend paid is \$1.50. The dividend return is defined as the $\text{Dividend}/\text{Price}_{t-1}$,

Table 3.1

Date	Open	High	Low	Close
1/3/2007	97.18	100.9	94.55	99.15
2/1/2007	98.97	100.44	92.47	92.94
3/1/2007	90.25	95.81	88.77	94.26
4/2/2007	94.51	103	93.91	102.21
5/1/2007	102.06	108.05	101.35	106.6
6/1/2007	106.62	107.24	101.56	105.25
7/2/2007	105.39	118.82	104.58	110.65
8/1/2007	110.39	117.35	103.7	116.69
9/4/2007	116.34	118.89	114.3	117.8
10/1/2007	117.61	121.46	110.96	116.12
11/1/2007	115.5	116.09	99.27	105.18
12/3/2007	105.55	112.19	104	108.1
1/2/2008	108.99	108.99	104.17	104.69

which for our example is $1.50/$97.18 or 1.54%. Your total return for the year is the sum of these two components, which equals 9.27%.

We can incorporate the two components of returns in one easy formula. In particular return for a given period is defined as:

(Selling Price + Dividend Received − Buying Price)/Buying Price.

$$(3.1)$$

In our example, we assume that you sold IBM stock at $104.69 and bought it at $97.18. In addition, during the year, you received a total dividend of $1.50. Hence according to Equation (3.1), the annual return is:

($104.69 + $1.50 − $97.18)/$97.18 = 9.27%.

Let us leave aside whether or not this was a good investment. Note that the return you received depends upon when you bought and sold the stock. For example, we assumed that you bought the stock at the opening bell of the New York Stock Exchange on January 3, 2007, at 9:30 am and sold it at 4:00 pm, the closing bell of the NYSE on January 2, 2008. But what if you bought the stock at the high price of January 3, 2007, which was $100.90? Furthermore, assume that you sold IBM stock at the low price of January 2, 2008, which was $104.17. Your total return would have only been 4.73%.

(Please verify these calculations!) This implies that should you come up with an idea as to how to beat the market, and you want to test the model using historical prices, then you must take into account the timing of the trade execution since the return results can be very sensitive to the timing of the trade execution.

Expected Return

Now that you know how to measure return, you are almost ready to become the next Warren Buffet. (Perhaps not, there is lot more to learn that is way beyond this course, like how to do financial statement analysis and forecasting of earnings. That is why we offer so many other courses at the Rutgers Business School, where I am a faculty member, but you need to know the basics before you take those electives.) Obviously, you want to pick the best investment vehicle with the high expected returns. One way of determining the best performing stocks is examining how well those stocks have done in the past. However, please note, this is only one approach since the past is not necessarily the best guide for the future. In addition, our estimates should be based upon one more observation. Many financial practitioners calculate the monthly returns of a particular stock for the previous 60 months to increase the number of observations and then find the average monthly returns by summing the 60 monthly observations and dividing the sum by 60. Mathematically, the average monthly return is given by:

$$AR = \sum_{t=1}^{n} Ret_t/n, \qquad (3.2)$$

where Ret_t is the monthly return at time t. Recall that Ret_t is given by Equation (3.1) or in short notation, it is given by $(P_{sell} - P_{buy} + div_t)/P_{buy}$ where div_t is the dividend that is paid out in month t. Finally n is the number of observations.

Let us go back to our original IBM example, but this time, assume that you buy and sell IBM at the closing price at the beginning of each month. The table below presents the closing price, the cash dividends and monthly returns of IBM for each month. Note, that the table tells you the closing price of the first trading day of the month. Consequently, the closing price of IBM on January 3, 2007 is $99.15 while the closing price on February 1, 2007 is $92.94. The dividend of $.30 is paid sometime in the month of February (but after February 1).

Using Equation (3.1), we can find the monthly return for each month. The return for January is based upon the assumption that you buy the stock at the beginning of January at a price of $99.15 and sold it for $92.94. Hence, the return for January is simply ($92.94 − $99.15)/ $99.15 or −6.2632%. On the other hand, the return for February assumes that you bought the stock on February 1 at $92.94, sold it for $94.26 on March 1 and sometime in February (say, February 10), you received a dividend of $0.30. Thus, monthly return for February is ($94.26+$0.30−$92.94)/$92.94 = 1.7431%.

We can compute the average monthly return by summing all of the individual monthly returns (which you should verify) in the far right column of Table 3.2 (which by the way, the sum is equal to 8.3357%), and dividing that sum by 12, the number of monthly observations. You should be able to verify that the monthly average is equal to 0.6963%. Multiplying the monthly average by 12 (since

Table 3.2

Date	Close	Dividend	Return(%)
1/3/2007	99.15	0	N/A
2/1/2007	92.94	0.3	−6.2632
3/1/2007	94.26	0	1.7431
4/2/2007	102.21	0	8.4341
5/1/2007	106.6	0.4	4.2951
6/1/2007	105.25	0	−0.8912
7/2/2007	110.65	0	5.1306
8/1/2007	116.69	0.4	5.4587
9/4/2007	117.8	0	1.2940
10/1/2007	116.12	0	−1.4261
11/1/2007	105.18	0.4	−9.4213
12/3/2007	108.1	0	3.1565
1/2/2008	104.69	0	−3.1545

there are 12 months in the year), we get an average expected yearly
return of 8.3357%.

Risk

Is 8.3357% a good return? Well that depends how certain you will
get that return every year. For example, IBM as of August 20, 2008,
closed at $122.51. Ignoring dividends the stock has gone up $17.82
since the close of January 2, 2008. But, most of us realize that stock
prices can go down as well, resulting in a negative return. In other
words, we need some measure that will quantify the level of risk you
undertake by holding IBM stock. The measure that most practitioners use is the standard deviation of the returns. (Now, now, I know
you learned this statistic in your other classes. But do not sweat it,
I will offer you a review.)

To find the standard deviation, one must first find the variance
since the square root of the variance is the standard deviation. The
formula to find the (sample) variance is given by:

$$\text{VAR} = \sum_{t=1}^{n} (\text{Ret}_t - \text{AR})^2 / (n - 1) \tag{3.3}$$

The table below summarizes the calculation of the variance.

The first 4 columns of Table 3.3 are identical to that of Table 3.2
with the exception that returns are now expressed in decimal terms
as opposed to percentage. (Sorry, I find it less confusing for me to
do it this way!) Recall that the average monthly return for IBM was
0.006963 or 0.6963%. The last column represents $(\text{Ret}_t - \text{AR})^2$ for
each month. So for the month of February, the entry of 0.004844
is obtained by taking $(-0.062632 - 0.006963)^2$ to obtain 0.004844.
Summing all of numbers of the last column, we get 0.029533. Divide
this by 11 (n − 1) and our monthly variance is 0.002685.[1] Taking
the square root of this last number, we get the monthly standard
deviation of 0.051815 or approximately 5.182%.

---

[1]For those of you following units, as is done in the sciences, the variance of
0.002685 is 26.85 percentage *squared*. Now you know why I prefer using decimal
terms when doing these calculations.

Table 3.3

Date	Close	Dividend	Return	$(Ret_t - AR)^2$
1/3/2007	99.15	0	N/A	N/A
2/1/2007	92.94	0.3	−0.062632	0.004844
3/1/2007	94.26	0	0.017431	0.00011
4/2/2007	102.21	0	0.084341	0.005987
5/1/2007	106.6	0.4	0.042951	0.001295
6/1/2007	105.25	0	−0.008912	0.000252
7/2/2007	110.65	0	0.051306	0.001966
8/1/2007	116.69	0.4	0.054587	0.002268
9/4/2007	117.8	0	0.012940	3.57E-05
10/1/2007	116.12	0	−0.014261	0.00045
11/1/2007	105.18	0.4	−0.094213	0.010237
12/3/2007	108.1	0	0.031565	0.000605
1/2/2008	104.69	0	−0.031545	0.001483

You might ask, what does that mean? Good question. Let us assume that IBM returns are normally distributed. Then we know that 95% of return observations should fall between the mean return +1.96(standard deviation) and mean return −1.96(standard deviation). That is, for IBM, we expect that 95% of all observations should be greater than 0.6963%.−1.96(5.182%) or −9.46% but less than 0.6963%+1.96(5.182%) or 10.5%. Now, the 1-year Treasury Bill rate as of August 21, 2008 is approximately 2% per year or 0.16667% per month. I would think you can make a rational choice between investing in treasury securities where you know with certainty what you would earn every month compared to the IBM stock where in a given month, you can lose (with 2.5% probability) almost 10%. By the way, there is no right choice, *per se*. If you are very risk averse, you will select the treasury option. The less risk averse, the more likely you will choose the IBM stock.

The Mean-Standard Deviation Framework

Finance academicians and its practitioners accept the notion that investors rank their investment choices by taking into account their personal trade-off between risk and return. Assume that you as an investor calculated the expected return and its standard deviation

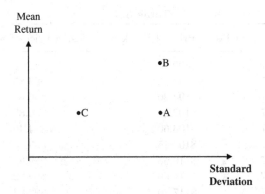

Figure 3.1

for three different common stocks. Assume that you have plotted the expected return and standard deviation for stocks A, B and C, as denoted in Figure 3.1. The y-axis denotes the mean return and the x-axis denotes the standard deviation of the return. According to Figure 1, security A has the same expected return as security C, but C has lower risk as measured by the standard deviation. Security B has a much higher expected return than security A. But security B has the same risk level as security A. Under these conditions, no rational investor would invest in security A. High risk averse investor might choose security C while low risk averse investors will pick security B.

This assumes, that investors pick only one stock. However, we know that investors hold a portfolio or combination of stocks. To get an idea as to whether a combination of securities increases our opportunity set consider the historical prices of securities A and B as depicted in Table 3.4.

Assume that stocks A and B offer no dividends. Now you should take the trouble in calculating the monthly returns for each stock, but since I cannot wait until you do this calculation, I do this for you in Table 3.5. But it would be good practice for you to verify the results. Your assignment now is to verify that the average monthly return for stock A is 0.5779% while the average return of stock B is 4.4221%. Similarly, verify that the standard deviation of both stocks is 5.169%. Assuming that my numbers are correct, a rational investor would select stock B and not stock A.

Table 3.4

Date	Closing Price of Stock A	Closing Price of Stock B
1/3/2007	$99.15	$75.36
2/1/2007	$92.94	$83.85
3/1/2007	$94.26	$86.85
4/2/2007	$102.21	$83.87
5/1/2007	$106.60	$84.46
6/1/2007	$105.25	$89.75
7/2/2007	$110.65	$89.63
8/1/2007	$116.69	$89.22
9/4/2007	$117.80	$92.83
10/1/2007	$116.12	$98.80
11/1/2007	$105.18	$113.05
12/3/2007	$108.10	$115.56
1/2/2008	$104.69	$124.99

But then again, who wants to be rational? Let us take a chance. What if you would invest 50% of your money in stock A and 50% in stock B? For example, you started off with $1,000 and put $500 in stock A and $500 in stock B. The investment in stock A would have declined by 6.2632% or would be worth at the end of January (or beginning of February) $468.68. In contrast, the $500 investment in Stock B would be worth 11.2632% more. In other words, at the end of January the original $500 investment is now worth $500*(1.112632) or $556.32. Your total investment at the end of January is now $1,025 and your portfolio experienced a 2.5% return. Now let us rebalance the portfolio so you put $512.50 in stock A and $512.50 in Stock B. Proceed as above to calculate how much each investment is worth by the end of February. Interestingly, you will find that it is worth $1,050.625, implying another 2.5% return. Well, you may not believe this unless you tried this for the other months, but you will find that every month, your return will be exactly 2.5% return. If that is so, the risk of the portfolio, where you constantly have half of your money in Stock A and half of your investment in Stock B, will be zero (i.e., the standard deviation of the portfolio is *zero*). I bet that some of you would like this portfolio, a portfolio that does require you to make some investment in the "inferior" Stock A. What this means to you is that you will now have to learn about the mathematics of investment portfolios, but since this is an introductory course, we will only concentrate on understanding how the mathematics works with only two securities. I leave the more complicated cases for the finance electives, but really, with excel, it is not too hard!

Introduction to Portfolio Finance

In this subsection, you will be introduced to the basic mathematics of portfolio theory. Let us begin with something very easy, the expected return of the portfolio, $E(R_p)$. It is simply the weighted average of the expected return of each stock in the portfolio. Let w represent the proportion of your wealth invested in Stock A of the previous subsection and $(1-w)$ represent the proportion of your wealth invested in Stock B. Recall that the average monthly return for stock A is 0.5779% while the average return of Stock B is 4.4221%. Assuming you put 50% of your wealth in stock A and 50% in Stock B. Then you find the expected monthly return of your portfolio as:

$$0.5E(R_A) + 0.5E(R_B) = 0.5(0.5779\%) + 0.5(4.4221\%)$$
$$= 2.5\%$$

We can generalize the formula as follows:

$$E(R_p) = wE(R_1) + (1 - w)E(R_2). \tag{3.4}$$

Example 1: Determine the expected monthly return of the portfolio consisting of Stock A with an average monthly return of .5779% and Stock B with an average monthly of 4.4221%, where the portion of money invested in Stock A, w, is 20%, 40%, 60% and 80%, respectively.

To solve this, we simply apply Equation (3.4):

$E(R_p) = wE(R_1) + (1 - w)E(R_2).$
For $w = 20\%, E(R_p) = 0.2(0.5779\%) + 0.8(4.4221\%)$

$$= 3.65326\%.$$

$$\text{For } w = 40\%, \text{E}(R_p) = 0.4(0.5779\%) + 0.6(4.4221\%)$$

$$= 2.88442\%.$$

$$\text{For } w = 60\%, \text{E}(R_p) = 0.6(0.5779\%) + 0.4(4.4221\%)$$

$$= 2.11558\%.$$

$$\text{For } w = 80\%, \text{E}(R_p) = 0.8(0.5779\%) + 0.2(4.4221\%)$$

$$= 1.34674\%.$$

Example 2: Assume that you have \$100,000 to invest. Assume further you would invest \$25,000 in Stock A of Example 1 and \$75,000 in Stock B. What is your expected return of this portfolio?

To answer this question, we must recognize that by investing \$25,000 in Stock A, your $w = \$25,000/\$100,000 = 0.25$. Hence,

$$\text{For } w = 25\%, \text{E}(R_p) = 0.25(0.5779\%) + 0.75(4.4221\%)$$

$$= 3.46105\%.$$

Example 3: By now, you are recognizing that Stock A is dragging your average return down. You are an aggressive investor and you decide that you might be better off if you can invest much more than \$100,000 in Stock B. But where do you get the additional money? In Wall Street, individuals can borrow stock from another person, sell it, and use the proceeds to invest in other investments. This is known as shorting the stock. At the end of the period, you have to buy back the stock to give it back to the original owner. If the stock price of the shorted stock goes up, you lose money and if the price of the shorted stock goes down you make money. Of course, if you short Stock A and even if it goes up its average amount of 0.5779% per month, it should be no different than borrowing money and promising to pay 0.5779% per month of interest. Assume that you want to invest \$125,000 in Stock B. To get the extra \$25,000 to supplement your original \$100,000 you had for investment, you will go to your broker and ask her to short the equivalent of \$25,000 of Stock A. Based upon these actions, what is your expected return?

Again, once we calculate w, we can easily calculate the expected return of this portfolio. In this case, that amount of money invested

Table 3.5

Date	Return of A(%)	Return of B (%)
1/3/2007		
2/1/2007	−6.2632	11.2632
3/1/2007	1.4203	3.5797
4/2/2007	8.4341	−3.4341
5/1/2007	4.2951	0.7049
6/1/2007	−1.2664	6.2664
7/2/2007	5.1306	−0.1306
8/1/2007	5.4587	−0.4587
9/4/2007	0.9512	4.0488
10/1/2007	−1.4261	6.4261
11/1/2007	−9.4213	14.4213
12/3/2007	2.7762	2.2238
1/2/2008	−3.1545	8.1545

in A is −\$25,000/\$100,000 so that $w = -0.25$ and $1 - w = 1.25$. Note that you are investing \$125,000 in Stock B, so you are investing 125% of your wealth in Stock B. The expected monthly return of this portfolio is now:

$$E(R_p) = -0.25(0.5779\%) + 1.25(4.4221\%) = 5.3815\%.$$

Before you get too excited and start shorting your least favorite stocks, shorting is not exactly like a loan. Shorting will increase the risk of your portfolio. Remember you are shorting Stock A, which can have a good month. Go back to Table 3.5 and see what happened in April of 2007. In that month Stock A had a return of 8.4341% and Stock B declined by 3.4341%. Had you implemented your shorting strategy in that month, your return would have been:

$$E(R_p) = -0.25(8.4341\%) + 1.25(-3.4341\%) = -6.401\%.$$

This is our segue to learn about portfolio risk. Unlike expected return, the return variance of the portfolio is not a weighted average of the standard deviation of the components of the portfolio. You were asked on page 75 to verify that the standard deviation of both Stocks A and B is 5.169%. I am certain that you have done so by now. In any case, you were shown that had you invested 50% of your wealth in Stock A and 50% of your wealth in Stock B, the risk of

Table 3.6

Date	Closing Price of Stock A	Return of A (%)	Closing Price of Stock B	Return of B (%)
1/3/2007	$99.15		$75.36	
2/1/2007	$92.94	−6.2632	$83.85	11.2632
3/1/2007	$94.26	1.4203	$86.85	3.5797
4/2/2007	$102.21	8.4341	$83.87	−3.4341
5/1/2007	$106.60	4.2951	$84.46	0.7049
6/1/2007	$105.25	−1.2664	$89.75	6.2664
7/2/2007	$110.65	5.1306	$89.63	−0.1306
8/1/2007	$116.69	5.4587	$89.22	−0.4587
9/4/2007	$117.80	0.9512	$92.83	4.0488
10/1/2007	$116.12	−1.4261	$98.80	6.4261
11/1/2007	$105.18	−9.4213	$113.05	14.4213
12/3/2007	$108.10	2.7762	$115.56	2.2238
1/2/2008	$104.69	−3.1545	$124.99	8.1545

the portfolio was exactly zero. Yet, if you were to take the weighted average of the standard deviation of that portfolio, your answer would have been 5.169%. Obviously, something is missing.

What is missing is that the weighted average approach does not take into account the co-movement of the two stocks. Below, we reproduce the historical price and return table for Stocks A and B. Note that in any month, Stock A does better than its average return of 0.5779%, Stock B does worse than its mean of 4.4221%. Similarly, in any month Stock A does worse than its average return of 0.5779%, Stock B does better than its mean of 4.4221%. In this situation, we say that Stock A and Stock B commove in opposite directions. There are two statistics that one can use to measure this co-movement. The first is known as the Covariance. The formula is a bit messy, but it is easy to implement, as you shall see. The covariance of the return of stock i with the return of stock j is given by:

$$\mathrm{Cov}(R_i, R_j) = \sum_{t=1}^{n}(R_{it} - \mathrm{AR}_i)(R_{jt} - \mathrm{AR}_j)/(n - 1) \qquad (3.5)$$

where R_{it} and R_{jt} are the returns of stock i and stock j, respectively for month t and AR_i and AR_j are the average monthly returns of stock i and stock j, respectively. Let us proceed with calculating

Table 3.7

Date	R_{At}	$R_{At} - AR_A$	R_{Bt}	$R_{Bt} - AR_B$	Product
1/3/2007					
2/1/2007	−0.0626	−0.0684	0.1126	0.0684	−0.0047
3/1/2007	0.0142	0.0084	0.0358	−0.0084	−0.0001
4/2/2007	0.0843	0.0786	−0.0343	−0.0786	−0.0062
5/1/2007	0.0430	0.0372	0.0070	−0.0372	−0.0014
6/1/2007	−0.0127	−0.0184	0.0627	0.0184	−0.0003
7/2/2007	0.0513	0.0455	−0.0013	−0.0455	−0.0021
8/1/2007	0.0546	0.0488	−0.0046	−0.0488	−0.0024
9/4/2007	0.0095	0.0037	0.0405	−0.0037	0.0000
10/1/2007	−0.0143	−0.0200	0.0643	0.0200	−0.0004
11/1/2007	−0.0942	−0.1000	0.1442	0.1000	−0.0100
12/3/2007	0.0278	0.0220	0.0222	−0.0220	−0.0005
1/2/2008	−0.0315	−0.0373	0.0815	0.0373	−0.0014

$Cov(R_A, R_B)$. Consider Table 3.7. The monthly return at time t for stock A, R_{At}, and Stock B, R_{Bt}, are denoted as decimals. The third column gives you the deviation of monthly return for Stock A at time t from its average return, AR_A. Similarly, the fifth column gives you the deviation of monthly return for Stock B at time t from its average return, AR_B. Note that the entries found in the 5th column are −1 times the entries in the third column noting that the two stock move in opposite directions from each other. The sixth column is simply the product of the entries of the third and fifth columns. If you sum the entries of the last column and dividing by n-1 which in our case is 11, we obtain −0.00267 or 26.7 percentage squared (26.7%^{2}). (See footnote 1 of this chapter.) We are now ready to write the general formula for the variance of a two-stock portfolio:

$$Var(R_p) = w^2 Var(R_A) + (1 - w)^2 Var(R_B)$$
$$+ 2w(1 - w)Cov(R_A, R_B). \quad (3.6)$$

Recall that the standard deviation of both Stocks A and B are 5.169%. Converting that number to a decimal format, the standard deviation is 0.05169 and the variance is therefore the square of 0.05169, or 0.00267. We can now plug into Equation (3.6) to find the variance of the portfolio when we invest 50% of the money in A

Table 3.8

	A	B	C	D	E
	Date	Closing Price of Stock A	Return of A (%)	Closing Price of Stock B	Return of B (%)
1					
2	1/3/2007	$99.15		$75.36	
3	2/1/2007	$92.94	−6.26	$83.85	11.26
4	3/1/2007	$94.26	1.42	$86.85	3.58
5	4/2/2007	$102.21	8.43	$83.87	−3.43
6	5/1/2007	$106.60	4.30	$84.46	0.70
7	6/1/2007	$105.25	−1.27	$89.75	6.27
8	7/2/2007	$110.65	5.13	$89.63	−0.13
9	8/1/2007	$116.69	5.46	$89.22	−0.46
10	9/4/2007	$117.80	0.95	$92.83	4.05
11	10/1/2007	$116.12	−1.43	$98.80	6.43
12	11/1/2007	$105.18	−9.42	$113.05	14.42
13	12/3/2007	$108.10	2.78	$115.56	2.22
14	1/2/2008	$104.69	−3.15	$124.99	8.15
15					
16	Average		0.5779		4.4221
17	Std. Dev.		5.169		5.169
				Covariance	−0.2672

and 50% in B. In other words,

$$\text{Var}(R_p) = w^2\text{Var}(R_A) + (1-w)^2\text{Var}(R_B) + 2w(1-w)\text{Cov}(R_A, R_B)$$
$$= 0.25(0.00267) + 0.25(0.00267)$$
$$+ 2(0.5)(0.5)(-0.00267) = \mathbf{0}.$$

Before we go to the next example, is there a way to use Excel functions to get the identical results as above? The answer is of course yes. Consider Table 3.8.

The Excel columns and rows are denoted in bold font. Note that A1:E14 is a replication of Table 3.6. Note that cells C16 and E16 are the average monthly returns of Stock A and B, respectively. To obtain the average go to Cell C16 of your spread sheet (after you have copied Table 3.7 onto your Excel sheet) and type in =average(C3:C14).[2] You will get 0.58%. To get the answer we obtained, you will have to format

---

[2]Cell C3 should be interpreted as −6.26%.

the cell to yield four significant digits. By the way, 0.5779% is equal to 0.005779 in decimal terms. You can simply convert percentages to decimals by dividing the percentage by 100. Similarly, we can obtain the standard deviation by typing in cell C17, =Stdev.S (C3:C14). Now go to E18. You can obtain that number (after formatting the cell for four decimal places) by typing =Covariance.S(C3:C14,E3:E14). Although the excel function will provide an answer of −0.2672%, you can convert the answer into decimal terms by dividing the number by 100 to get −0.002672. Now comes the tricky part. The correct covariance is either −0.002672 or 26.72%^{2}. The latter is obtained by multiplying the decimal by 10,000. Understanding the units is important. Now, you can show that by investing half of the money in Stock A and half in Stock B, the variance equals to zero if we use the percentage units as shown below:

$$\mathrm{Var}(R_p) = w^2\mathrm{Var}(R_A) + (1-w)^2\mathrm{Var}(R_B)$$
$$+ 2w(1-w)\mathrm{Cov}(R_A, R_B)$$
$$= 0.25(5.169)^2 + 0.25(5.169)^2$$
$$+ 2(0.5)(0.5)(-26.72\%^2) = \mathbf{0}.$$

Example 4: Determine the variance and the standard deviation of monthly return of the portfolio consisting of Stock A and Stock B, both with a standard deviation of 5.169%, where the portion of money invested in Stock A, w, is 20%, 40%, 60% and 80%, respectively.

To solve this, we simply apply Equation (3.6):

$$\mathrm{Var}(R_p) = w^2\mathrm{Var}(R_A) + (1-w)^2\mathrm{Var}(R_B)$$
$$+ 2w(1-w)\mathrm{Cov}(R_A, R_B)$$

For $w = 0.2, \mathrm{Var}(R_p) = 0.04(0.00267) + 0.64(0.00267)$
$$+ 2(0.2)(0.8)(-0.00267) = 0.000962.$$
For $w = 0.4, \mathrm{Var}(R_p) = 0.16(0.00267) + 0.36(0.00267)$
$$+ 2(0.4)(0.6)(-0.00267) = 0.000107.$$
For $w = 0.6, \mathrm{Var}(R_p) = 0.36(0.00267) + 0.16(0.00267)$
$$+ 2(0.6)(0.4)(-0.00267) = 0.000107.$$

For $w = 0.8$, $\text{Var}(R_p) = 0.64(0.00267) + 0.04(0.00267)$
$$+ 2(0.8)(0.2)(-0.00267) = 0.000962.$$

To find the standard deviations, simply take the square root of the variances. For $w = 0.2$ or $w = 0.8$, the standard deviation is 0.031014 or 3.1014% and for $w = 0.4$ or $w = 0.6$, the standard deviation is 0.010338 or 1.0338%.

Example 5: Assume that you want to invest \$125,000 in Stock B. To get the extra \$25,000 to supplement your original \$100,000 you had for investment, you will go to your broker and ask her to short the equivalent of \$25,000 of Stock A. Based upon these actions, what are the monthly variance and standard deviation of this portfolio?

To solve this, we simply apply Equation (3.6), noting that $w = -0.25$ and $(1 - w) = 1.25$:

$$\text{Var}(R_p) = w^2\text{Var}(R_A) + (1 - w)^2\text{Var}(R_B)$$
$$+ 2w(1 - w)\text{Cov}(R_A, R_B)$$

For $w = -0.25$, $\text{Var}(R_p) = 0.0625*0.00267 + 1.5625*0.00267 + 2(-0.25)*1.25(-0.00267) = 0.006012$ and the standard deviation is 0.077535 or 7.77535%. Note that the risk of this portfolio, which involves leveraging your return or equivalently shorting a stock, significantly increases the overall risk of the portfolio compared to any of the portfolios depicted in Example 4.

There is a second measure of co-movement known as the correlation coefficient. The correlation coefficient scales the Covariance for size of the variable. While theoretically covariance can be anywhere between $-\infty$ and $+\infty$, the correlation coefficient will range between -1 and $+1$. The correlation coefficient, ρ, of the returns of stocks i and j is given by:

$$\rho_{ij} = \text{Cov}(R_i, R_j)/\sigma_i\sigma_j \qquad (3.7)$$

where σ_i is the standard deviation of Stock i. The correlation coefficient of the returns of Stocks A and B can be found using Equation (3.7). Recall that the covariance of Stock A is -0.002672 and a standard deviation for both Stock A and B of 0.05169. Hence,

$-0.002672/(0.05169)^2$ is equal to -1. Now you do the calculation but this time use the percentage format, whereby the standard deviation is 5.169% and the covariance is 26.72%^{2}.

We can rewrite the formula for Var(Rp) of Equation (3.6) using the correlation coefficient. In particular:

$$\text{Var}(R_p) = w^2\text{Var}(R_i) + (1-w)^2\text{Var}(R_j)$$
$$+ 2w(1-w)\rho_{ij}\sigma_i\sigma_j \qquad (3.8)$$

This formula allows us to examine two very special cases when $\rho_{ij} = 1$ and when it is equal to -1. It turns out that when $\rho_{ij} = 1$, the standard deviation of the portfolio is simply the weighted average of the standard deviations of the components of the portfolio. That is when $\rho_{ij} = 1$

$$\textbf{Standard Deviation}(\textbf{R}_\textbf{p}) = \sigma_\textbf{p} = w\sigma_\textbf{i} + (1-w)\sigma_\textbf{j}. \qquad (3.9)$$

Example 6: Stock k has an expected return of 12% and a standard deviation of 10%. Stock j has an expected return of 18% and a standard deviation of 20%. Determine the expected return and variance of a portfolio consisting of Stocks k and j, assuming that you put 30% of your wealth in Stock k. Assume that $\rho_{kj} = 1$.

We know that the expected return of the portfolio is the weighted average of the expected return of the components. In this case, $E(R_p) = 0.3{*}12\% + 0.7{*}18\% = 16.2\%$. We also know that because $\rho_{kj} = 1$, that the standard deviation of the portfolio is also a weighted average of the standard deviation of the stock components of the portfolio. Hence, $\sigma_p = w\sigma_i + (1-w)\sigma_j = 0.3(10\%) + 0.7(20\%) = 17\%$. The variance is simply the square of 17% or 289%^{2}.

The case for when $\rho_{ij} = -1$ is even more interesting. In this case,

$$\sigma_\textbf{p} = |w\sigma_i - (1-w)\sigma_j|. \qquad (3.10)$$

We are taking the difference between the weighted standard deviation components. But since the standard deviation must be positive, we take the absolute value of this difference, in the event that the difference proves to be negative.

Example 7: Redo Example 6 but now assume that $\rho_{kj} = -1$.

Note that the expected return of this portfolio is not affected by the correlation coefficient and therefore it still remains as 16.2%. The standard deviation is now given by:

$$\sigma_p = |w\sigma_k - (1-w)\sigma_j| = |0.3^*10\% - 0.7^*20\%| = |-11\%| = 11\%.$$

The variance is the square of 11% or $121\%^2$.

Example 8: Let us go back to our portfolio of A and B, whose correlation coefficient was equal -1. Recall that the standard deviation for both of these stocks is 5.169%. What are the portfolio weights that will result in a zero risk portfolio? Now we already know that answer since when the concept of portfolio risk was first introduced, you saw that if you invest 50% of your money in Stock A, we obtained a riskless portfolio. Let us derive using Equation (3.10).

To solve this problem, we must set $\sigma_p = |w^*\sigma_A - (1-w)^*\sigma_B| = 0$.

Mathematically, this implies that $w^*\sigma_A = (1-w)^*\sigma_B$. Since $\sigma_A = \sigma_B$, then $w = 1 - w$ to obtain equality. In which case $w = 0.5$. While we are at it, let us derive the general formula for the case when the standard deviations are not equal. In this case:

$$w\sigma_A = (1-w)\sigma_B = \sigma_B - w\sigma_B.$$

Rearranging terms, we have

$$= w(\sigma_A + \sigma_B) = \sigma_B.$$

Solving for w, we have

$$w = \sigma_B/(\sigma_A + \sigma_B).$$

Note when the correlation coefficient $= -1$, we obtain a riskless portfolio when $w = 0.5$ if and only if the standard deviation of both securities are identical. Otherwise, w will not equal 50%.

Example 9: Actually, this example is not about computing portfolio risk but to "dramatically" demonstrate the benefits of diversification. Let us begin with the following table that provides summary statistics for 27 of the current day members of the Dow Jones Index. Three are missing since these stocks did not have return data from January 2008 to December 2013 from the Center for Research in

Security Prices (CRSP) tapes. (The CRSP tapes provide historical return and price data for all stocks beginning from December 1925.) Note that there are five columns. The first column lists the name of the company. The second company gives you the ticker symbol as of December 2013. The next column provides the average monthly return for each company. The following column summarizes the standard deviation for each company. The last two columns are statistics that have not been covered yet and this table will be reproduced in our next chapter.

Name of the Company	Ticker Symbol	Average Return (%)	Standard Deviation (%)	Beta	R^2
AMERICAN EXPRESS CO	AXP	1.70	13.75	1.5197	0.4799
BOEING CO	BA	1.21	8.56	0.9862	0.5220
CATERPILLAR INC	CAT	1.22	11.61	1.3937	0.5662
CISCO SYSTEMS INC	CSCO	0.20	8.70	0.9459	0.4641
CHEVRON CORP NEW	CVX	0.86	6.01	0.5086	0.2817
DU PONT E I DE NEMOURS & CO	DD	1.26	8.73	1.1747	0.7112
GENERAL ELECTRIC CO	GE	0.46	10.10	1.2179	0.5715
GOLDMAN SACHS GROUP INC	GS	0.37	10.35	1.2142	0.5406
HOME DEPOT INC	HD	2.04	6.87	0.5914	0.2914
INTERNATIONAL BUSINESS MACHS COR	IBM	1.07	5.42	0.5628	0.4238
INTEL CORP	INTC	0.54	7.67	0.7959	0.4235
JOHNSON & JOHNSON	JNJ	0.82	4.44	0.3990	0.3171
JPMORGAN CHASE & CO	JPM	1.14	10.40	1.0396	0.3929
COCA COLA CO	KO	0.78	4.90	0.3200	0.1675
MCDONALDS CORP	MCD	1.04	4.13	0.2446	0.1379
3M CO	MMM	1.12	6.15	0.6838	0.4862
MERCK & CO INC	MRK	0.40	7.07	0.4629	0.1683
MICROSOFT CORP	MSFT	0.53	7.19	0.7002	0.3725

(*Continued*)

(*Continued*)

Name of the Company	Ticker Symbol	Average Return (%)	Standard Deviation (%)	Beta	R^2
NIKE INC	NKE	1.65	7.42	0.6534	0.3052
PFIZER INC	PFE	0.97	5.85	0.4703	0.2538
PROCTER & GAMBLE CO	PG	0.51	4.76	0.3078	0.1645
TRAVELERS COMPANIES INC	TRV	1.11	5.79	0.4578	0.2457
UNITEDHEALTH GROUP INC	UNH	0.89	9.24	0.7884	0.2860
UNITED TECHNOLOGIES CORP	UTX	0.96	6.39	0.8507	0.6964
VERIZON COMMUNICATIONS INC	VZ	0.85	5.47	0.2582	0.0875
WAL MART STORES INC	WMT	1.00	4.71	0.1470	0.0383
EXXON MOBIL CORP	XOM	0.43	4.92	0.2983	0.1443
Averages		0.93	7.28	0.7034	0.3533
Portfolio Statistic		0.93	4.93	0.7034	0.7989

The last two rows are the main focus of this discussion. The row entitled averages is the average of all of the numbers directly above it. Hence, the average under the column of the standard deviation which equals 7.28% is the average of all of the standard deviations of the firm listed in that table. However, if one formed an equal-weighted portfolio of these 27 firms and computed the standard deviation of the returns of that portfolio, the actual standard deviation is 4.93%. Hence, diversification reduced the overall volatility from 7.28% to 4.93%, representing a 32% reduction in the volatility.

When we discuss the Capital Asset Pricing Model, we will go back to this table and learn more about Beta and R^2.

Now it is time to do practice problems. **The correct answer is in bold font.**

Risk and Return Problems

Problems 1–3 rely on the following chart. The chart provides the closing price of Johnson & Johnson at the end of the first trading day in a given month. For example, the closing price on July 1, 2008 was $68.47. The chart also gives you the dividend per share. Note that the row listing March-08, there is an entry of $0.42 dividends. This means that sometime in the month of March of 2008, Johnson & Johnson paid 42 cents of dividends per share.

Date	Price	Dividends
August-08	$68.10	$0.00
July-08	$68.47	$0.00
June-08	$64.34	$0.46
May-08	$66.74	$0.00
April-08	$67.09	$0.00
March-08	$64.87	$0.42
February-08	$61.96	$0.00
January-08	$63.14	$0.00
December-07	$66.70	$0.42
November-07	$67.74	$0.00
October-07	$65.17	$0.00
September-07	$65.70	$0.42
August-07	$61.79	$0.00
July-07	$60.50	$0.00
June-07	$61.62	$0.42
May-07	$63.27	$0.00
April-07	$64.22	$0.00
March-07	$60.26	$0.38
February-07	$62.93	$0.00
January-07	$66.80	$0.00

Chart 1

1. Determine the stock return of January 2007.

    a. −0.5793%

    b. −5.793%

    c. 0.0615%

    d. 6.15%

    e. None of the above

2. Determine the stock return of December 2007.

    a. −1.87%

    b. −1.54%

    c. −0.923%

    d. 1.56%

    e. None of the above since the real answer is −4.707%.

3. Determine the return of July, 2008.

    a. −3.6%

    b. −2.907%

    c. −0.54%

    d. 0.54%

    e. None of the above

Problems 4–16 rely on the following chart.

	Stock A (%)	Stock B (%)
July-08	−0.5404	−1.9565
June-08	6.4190	7.4866
May-08	3.1250	1.8750
April-08	−0.5217	0.4696
March-08	3.4222	3.7911
February-08	5.3664	6.8129
January-08	1.8689	1.4164

Chart 2

	Stock A (%)	Stock B (%)
December-07	−5.3373	−8.6723
November-07	−0.9226	−2.4917
October-07	3.9435	4.3209
September-07	−0.8067	−2.3294
August-07	7.3256	9.0558
July-07	2.1322	4.9851
June-07	−1.8176	−0.5446
May-07	2.9520	6.1327
April-07	−1.4793	−0.0710
March-07	6.5715	6.2001
February-07	−3.6469	−8.1057
January-07	−5.7934	−11.1108

Chart 2 (*Continued*)

4. Determine the average monthly return of Stock A of Chart 2.

   a. 0.9087%
   b. 1.1716%
   c. 2.7125%
   d. 3.1758%
   e. None of the above

5. Determine the average return of Stock B of Chart 2.

   a. 0.9087%
   b. 1.1716%
   c. 2.7125%
   d. 3.1758%
   e. None of the above

6. Determine the Variance (in terms of percentage squared) of Stock A.

   a. 15.41
   b. 14.6

    c. 0.1541

    d. 0.1460

    e. None of the above

7. Determine the Standard Deviation (in terms of percentage) of Stock A.

    a. .0393

    b. .0382

    c. 3.926

    d. 3.821

    e. None of the above

8. Determine the Variance (in terms of percentage squared) of Stock B.

    a. 3.10

    b. 3.27

    c. 0.31

    d. 0.327

    e. None of the above since the real answer is 32.7 percentage squared.

9. Determine the Standard Deviation (in terms of percentage) of Stock B.

    a. 0.056

    b. 0.572

    c. 5.557

    d. 5.718

    e. None of the above.

10. Assuming you invest all of your money in Stock A or in Stock B, which of the following statements concerning Stock A and B is not true?

    a. Stock B is a riskier stock

    b. Stock B offers a better risk-return than does Stock A.

    c. Stock A offers superior expected return.

    d. All of the above statements are false.

11. Assume you invest 25% of your money in Stock A and 75% of your money in Stock B, the expected average monthly return is:

   a. 0.908%
   b. 0.9744%
   c. 1.1059%
   d. 1.1716%

12. Assume that you have $250,000 to invest in Stocks A and B. You plan to invest $187,500 in Stock A and the remainder in Stock B. What is the expected average monthly return of this portfolio?

   a. 0.908%
   b. 0.9744%
   c. 1.1059%
   d. 1.1716%

13. Determine the Covariance of the returns (in decimal format) of Stocks A and B

   a. 0.002026
   b. 0.002139
   c. 21.39905
   d. 20.260647
   e. None of the above

14. Find the variance of the portfolio as described in Problem 11.

   a. 32.7 percentage squared
   b. 27.38 percentage squared
   c. 18.74 percentage squared
   d. 15.41 percentage squared
   e. None of the above

15. Find the variance of the portfolio as described in Problem 12.

   a. 32.7 percentage squared
   b. 27.38 percentage squared
   c. 18.74 percentage squared
   d. 15.41 percentage squared
   e. None of the above

16. Replicate (in decimal format) the following table. Note that w is the proportion of money invested in Stock A.

w	AR (%)	Variance	σ
0.05	0.9218	0.003158	0.056198
0.1	0.9350	0.003049	0.055219
0.15	0.9481	0.002943	0.054247
0.2	0.9612	0.002839	0.053282
0.25	0.9744	0.002738	0.052325
0.3	0.9875	0.002639	0.051375
0.35	1.0007	0.002544	0.050435
0.4	1.0138	0.002451	0.049503
0.45	1.0270	0.00236	0.048581
0.5	1.0401	0.002272	0.04767
0.55	1.0533	0.002187	0.046769
0.6	1.0664	0.002105	0.045879
0.65	1.0796	0.002025	0.045001
0.7	1.0927	0.001948	0.044136
0.75	1.1059	0.001874	0.043285
0.8	1.1190	0.001802	0.042448
0.85	1.1322	0.001733	0.041626
0.9	1.1453	0.001666	0.04082
0.95	1.1585	0.001603	0.040032
1	1.1716	0.001541	0.039261

17. Assume that the monthly risk free rate earned by holding a 30-day Treasury Bill is .255% and the expected monthly return of the market portfolio is 1%. Let the standard deviation of the market return equal 1%. Assume that you invest $200,000 in the market by borrowing $50,000 by shorting the T-Bill and using your wealth of $150,000. Determine the expected monthly return of this portfolio.

a. 0.5817%

b. 0.6863%

c. 1.3138%

d. 1.4183%

e. None of the above

18. Calculate the variance of the portfolio as described in Problem 17. Assume that the standard deviation of the T-Bill return is zero.

a. 0.6667%

b. 0.75%

c. 1.25%

d. 1.333%

e. None of the above

19. Let the correlation coefficient between the returns of Stock X and Y equal 1. Let the standard deviation Stock X equal 25% and the standard deviation of Stock B be 50%. If the investor invests 40% of her wealth in Stock X and the remainder in Stock Y, then the variance of the portfolio is:

a. 35%

b. 37.5%

c. 40%

d. 1600 percentage squared

e. None of the above

20. Let the correlation coefficient between the returns of Stock X and Y equal −1. Let the standard deviation Stock X equal 30% and the standard deviation of Stock B equal 60%. The proportion of wealth the investor should invest in Λ to obtain a risk-free portfolio is:

a. 1/3

b. .5

c. 2/3

d. None of the above

CHAPTER 4

THE CAPITAL ASSET PRICING MODEL

Introduction

Today is an important day. You took the Path train to the World Trade Center station and as you get off, you ask for directions for the Three World Financial Center. Your smart phone tells you that you have an interview at 10 am for a job at Merrill Lynch in the asset allocation department. As you are about to make your way to the interview, you realize that you are 45 minutes early and you decide to go across the street to a coffee shop. You are worried about the interview because the past few years you have worked as an equity analyst, and you do not have much experience in asset allocation. As you wait in line, you meet your old college buddy. You strike up a conversation, asking how he is doing and fortuitously enough, he works for the bond trading desk at Merrill Lynch. You inform him about your interview and as a good alumnus, he gives you some hints as to what to expect.

"Remember Tzaar, our finance professor? He gave us some difficult exams, but this interview makes him look like a creampuff," he says.

Your friend notices a big drop of perspiration coming off your temple and he states, "Don't sweat it! It is not as if they are going to ask you to derive the Capital Asset Pricing Model!"

After a 30 minute discussion about the Merrill Lynch culture, he wishes you well and you head out for the interview. The interviewer

97

seems to be very nice and asks lots of questions about your experience. You are ready to answer questions about the relevance of your experience and the interview seems to go very well. She then asks, "Can you tell me about what you know regarding the Capital Asset Pricing Model?"

You think to yourself, "At least, she is not asking how to derive the Capital Asset Pricing Model." While you comfort yourself with that thought, the interviewer quickly adds, "And, tell me what you think about the assumptions behind the model!"[1]

What is the Objective of this Chapter?

Now that you have learned how to measure risk and return, it would be interesting to know how the capital markets set the risk-return tradeoff. This discussion began in the mid-1960s, when three famous financial economists, John Lintner, William Sharpe and Jan Mossin, independently developed an economic equilibrium framework to answer this question. But why is this important? Well, if I know the risk-return tradeoff, I might be able to better measure the performance of portfolio managers. I am certain you have seen advertisements that brag about the performance of a particular mutual fund or hedge fund. The objective of the advertisement is to get you to invest with the company behind the advertisement. The advertisement will state that the fund has earned, on average, 12% per annum in the past 5 years. Meanwhile, the Standard and Poor (S&P) 500 Index, a price index meant to proxy the average investment in the equity market, has only earned 9.8% during that same time period. Sounds pretty enticing, does it not? But what if I tell you that the risk of this investment vehicle is twice that of the market? Or, funds with similar risk actually earned 14% during that same period. Would that not take some luster off that claim! Of

---

[1] Of course the story is fictitious. However, you should know that interviewers do ask specific questions to test your knowledge. They do this for two reasons. First, they ask these questions to see if you know the material. Second, they want to see if you know how to communicate with team members and people outside your department.

course it will! Well, you would have to identify funds of equivalent risk to actually determine if the advertisement boast has any merit. But what if there is a model that will tell you how exactly do you measure the risk of a fund and tells you what the average return should have been? That would make your job much easier. This is where the equilibrium model of Sharpe, Lintner and Mossin comes into the picture. We will begin the development of the model by first discussing the assumptions behind the model.

Assumptions

The first assumption is that all investors evaluate securities based upon the expected return and standard deviation. We learned the mathematics of risk and return as well as the role of the correlation coefficient in determining the variance of the portfolio. Let us review.

Consider two stocks A and B. The expected return of Stock A is 20% while the expected return of Stock B is 30%. Let the standard deviation of Stock A be 15% while the standard deviation of Stock B be 30%. Assume that the correlation coefficient equals 1. According to Equation (3.4) of the Risk and Return chapter, the standard deviation of a portfolio of two stocks with a correlation coefficient equal to 1 is given by:

$$\text{Standard Deviation}(R_p) = \sigma_p = w\sigma_i + (1 - w)\sigma_j.$$

According to Equation (3.4) of the Risk and Return chapter is:

$$E(R_p) = wE(R_1) + (1 - w)E(R_2).$$

Note that in this case, the expected return and the standard deviation are simply a weighted average of the expected return and standard deviation of the two stocks. The table below demonstrates this as we vary the w, the percentage invested in Stock A, from 0 to 1. If we were to graph the results of Table 4.1 in Mean and Standard Deviation space, it will look like the line between A and B in Figure 4.1.

Now, let's do the same problem but now, assume that the correlation coefficient is equal to -1. According to Equation (3.10) of the Risk and Return chapter, the standard deviation of the portfolio is

Table 4.1

w	$E(R_p)(\%)$	$\sigma_p\ (\%)$
0	30.00	30.00
0.25	27.50	26.25
0.5	25.00	22.50
0.75	22.50	18.75
1	20.00	15.00

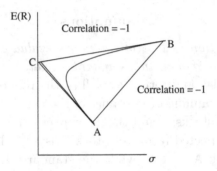

Figure 4.1

given by:

$$\sigma_p = |w^*\sigma_i - (1-w)^*\sigma_j|.$$

Table 4.2 depicts the risk-return relationship of a portfolio consisting of Stocks A and B as we vary w. You can verify that if $w = 0.667$ that the standard deviation will equal zero. We can depict the results graphically, and it is depicted as the lines connecting A, B and C in Figure 4.1. Note that at point C, which represents when $w = 0.667$, $\sigma_p = 0$. As w increases from 0 to 0.667, the standard deviation decreases until it hits zero. This is depicted as line AC. As w increases beyond 0.667, the standard deviation begins to increase. This is depicted as line BC.

What if the correlation coefficient is between 1 and -1? Let us do our example again, but assume that the correlation coefficient is equal to zero. To calculate the standard deviation, we use Equation (3.8)

Table 4.2

w	$E(R_p)(\%)$	σ_p (%)
0	30.00	30.00
0.25	27.50	18.75
0.5	25.00	7.50
0.75	22.50	3.75
1	20.00	15.00

Table 4.3

w	$E(R_p)$ (%)	$\mathrm{Var}(R_p)$ ($\%^2$)	σ_p (%)
0	30.00	900	30.00
0.25	27.50	520	22.81
0.5	25.00	281	16.77
0.75	22.50	183	13.52
1	20.00	225	15.00

of the Risk and Return chapter:

$$\mathrm{Var}(R_p) = w^{2*}\mathrm{Var}(R_i) + (1-w)^{2*}\mathrm{Var}(R_j)$$
$$+ 2^* w^*(1-w)^* \rho_{ij} * \sigma_i^* \sigma_j.$$

Once you calculate the variance, we simply take the square root to find the standard deviation. Table 4.3 summarizes our calculations. Note that the entries for $\mathrm{Var}(R_p)$ are in percentage squared or $\%^2$. Notice that the relationship between the standard deviation and expected return is nonlinear. This is depicted by curve ABC in Figure 4.1. Note also that in our example, the standard deviation of the portfolio for w between 0 and 1 is always less than the weighted average of the standard deviation of the two securities.

Of course, there are many more than two securities in the market place, but the shape of any combination of securities will be identical to that of Figure 4.1, denoted as curve ABC. This is depicted in Figure 4.2. The area shaded with wavy lines in Figure 4.2 represents different portfolios. For example, portfolios c, b, and d may represent portfolios consisting of the banking, oil, and textile sectors, respectively. According to Figure 4.2, these portfolios may not represent

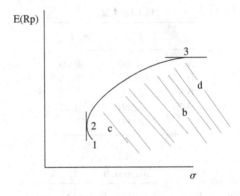

Figure 4.2

the best investment vehicle. For example, note that portfolio c has a greater standard deviation but the same expected return as portfolio 2 which is right on the curve 123. Similarly, portfolio d is inferior to portfolio 3. In fact, the portion shaded represents portfolios or securities that are not efficient in that there are portfolios which are on the curve 123 that have either a higher expected return for a given standard deviation or for a given expected return has a lower standard deviation. In fact, the best investment vehicles are found on the curve between portfolio 2 and portfolio 3. Why not portfolio 1? The answer is very simple. Note that portfolio 2 has both a higher expected return and lower standard deviation than portfolio 1. The portfolios that lie on the curve between 2 and 3 are efficient portfolios and we denote the curve 23 as the risky efficient frontier. The frontier begins at point 2, where the slope of the tangent is equal to infinity and ends at point 3 where the slope of the tangent is equal to zero. How to identify every portfolio on that curve is beyond the scope of this course, but suffice it to say that financial economists have developed mathematical programming that does just that. Furthermore, you will see that for our discussion, it is not too important to know how to identify every portfolio on the efficient frontier.

So let us summarize, the assumption that investors rank portfolios by the expected return and its standard deviation allows us to identify which portfolios offer the best risk-return tradeoff. We are now ready to make our second assumption.

Table 4.4

w	$E(R_p)(\%)$	σ_p (%)
0	4.39	0.00
0.25	5.29	3.00
0.5	6.20	6.00
0.75	7.10	9.00
1	8.00	12.00
1.25	8.90	15.00
1.5	9.81	18.00

Assume that investors can borrow and lend at the risk-free rate. Admittedly, this is a very strange assumption. Lending at the risk-free rate does make sense, after all one can always buy Treasury Securities and that is equivalent to lending to the US government, but borrowing at the risk free rate? Well as of August 28, 2008, the yield of a 30-year Treasury Bond is 4.39%. Thirty-year fixed mortgages rates is currently 6.29%. Recall that unlike the government, you have the right to refinance your mortgage once interest rates dip. This refinancing option is valuable and usually is worth 100 basis points (1% = 100 basis points), implying that if you did not have the option to refinance, then your cost of the mortgage is only 5.29%. Given this assumption regarding the yield of a non-callable mortgage, the difference between lending and borrowing is not that much so the assumption of being able to borrow and lend at the risk free rate may not be so strange after all.

Assuming we accept this new assumption, what does it do for us? Well, assume that the Treasury Rate is 4.39% and portfolio M has an expected return of 8% with a standard deviation of 12%. Note that once you invest in the Treasury security, your return is locked in, implying that its standard deviation is **zero**. Denote the promised rate of return of the Treasury security as R_f. Then the expected return of the portfolio is $E(R_p) = wE(R_M) + (1 - w)R_f$ and the standard deviation of the portfolio is $\sigma_p = w\sigma_M$.[2] Table 4.4 depicts

---

[2]Using Equation (3.8) of the previous chapter, and noting that the correlation coefficient between R_M and R_f is zero and the variance of the risk free rate is zero, the $\text{Var}(R_p) = w^2\sigma_M^2$.

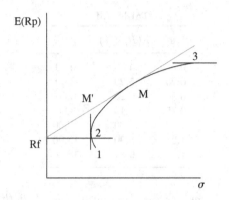

Figure 4.3

the expected return of the portfolio whereby $w\%$ of the wealth is invested in portfolio M and $(1 - w)\%$ is invested in the Treasury security. Note, when $w > 1$, then $1 - w$ is negative implying that we are borrowing from the government. Note also that for every 0.25 increment of w, $E(R_p)$ increases by 0.9% and σ_p increases by 3%, demonstrating the linear relationship between $E(R_p)$ and σ_p. We depict this in Figure 4.3. Consider the line between R_f and portfolio 2. At the Y axis, the individual investor is holding all of her money in the Treasury security, or $w = 0$. The midpoint between R_f and portfolio 2 represents when the investor has half the money in the Treasury and half the money in portfolio 2. At point 2, the investor has all of her money in portfolio 2, or $w = 1$. Any point on the line to the right of 2, is when $w > 1$, implies that the investor is borrowing money to add to her wealth to invest in portfolio 2.

Now consider the line which is tangent to the risky efficient frontier at point M. This line represents combination of investing in risky portfolio M and in the Treasury security. Consider M', consisting of $x\%$ of the investor's wealth invested in portfolio M and $(1-x)\%$ invested in the Treasury security. Note that M' dominates portfolio 2 since it has a higher expected return for the same standard deviation. In fact, one can argue that all portfolios on the risky efficient frontier, other than M, are dominated by a portfolio on the dotted line. The immediate implication of the second assumption is that we should be able to identify the best portfolio in which to invest.

We are now ready for our final assumption. Right now, portfolio M can be different for each individual. It will depend upon the investor's assessment of the expected return and variance of every possible portfolio. If you thought the previous assumption was wild, wait to read the next assumption.

Assume homogenous expectations. In other words, assume that every investor has the same set of beliefs and therefore M is the optimal portfolio for all investors. For now, suspend your disbelief and let us understand the full implication of this strange assumption. Now remember, in equilibrium (yes, you have to remember your economics) supply of each security must equal to its demand. So every security offered by firms must be held. Therefore if M is the optimal risky portfolio for all individuals, then every security in the market place must be in M. Well, there is one such security and that is the market portfolio. Oh, by the way in the real world people do not have the same expectations. But if we were to add up everyone's portfolio holding and average them out, would we not get the market portfolio? So I guess assuming homogenous expectations which leads that people hold the market portfolio is not such a bad assumption!

The Capital Asset Pricing Model

To get a mathematical representation of equilibrium requires some fancy math. Let us avoid that and note that according to the three assumptions, all investors will invest in the Treasury security and the market portfolio. This implies that all securities will be compared to two benchmarks, the rate of the return of the Treasury security and the risk-free rate. The Capital Asset Pricing Model (henceforth, CAPM) of Lintner, Sharpe and Mossin is a mathematical representation of the market equilibrium discussed in the previous subsection. According to this model

$$E(R_I) = R_F + \beta_I[E(R_M) - R_F], \qquad (4.1)$$

where β_I is the beta of security I, and it represents the risk of security I. Note that the expected return of security I is a linear combination of the expected return of the market portfolio, $E(R_M)$, and the risk-free rate. Note that $[E(R_M) - R_F]$ is the average risk premium in the market, since by definition a risk premium is the expected return in excess of the risk-free rate. Hence if beta is equal to two, the stock is said to be twice as risky as the market and therefore the appropriate risk premium for this stock is twice as large as the market.

What is β and what does it mean? If, whenever the market return moves up or down by 10% the individual stock's return moves, on average, by 20%, then we say that the stock is twice as volatile or risky as the market. **The stock is said to have a beta of 2.0 (20%:10%).**

The risk-free rate is usually measured by the annualized yield of a one-month Treasury bill. In August 2008, that annualized yield is 1.67%. $[E(R_m) - R_f]$ is the average risk premium in the market. Generally, the average risk premium in the market is measured by the historical annualized excess return of the market over the return of the 1-month Treasury. That estimate is around 9%.

Now let us consider the advertisement that we discussed on page 98 of this chapter. The advertisement stated that the HOG fund has earned on average 12% per annum in the past 5 years. Meanwhile, the S&P 500 Index, a price index meant to proxy the average investment in the equity market, has only earned 9.8% during that same time period. Now assume that the beta of the HOG fund is 2. According to the CAPM, the return that HOG fund should have earned is

$$E(R_I) = R_F + \beta_I[E(R_M) - R_F]$$
$$1.67\% + 2^*[9\%] = 19.67\%.$$

The CAPM is stating that on average, securities with beta of 2 should earn during this same period 19.67%. Hence, earning only 12% is really not a very good record.

Back to the Interview

After the initial shock wore off, your brain RAM was working fine and you were able to answer the interviewer's question. She then asks, "Did you use the CAPM in your last job and how did you use it?"

Example 1: After careful analysis, you believe that Stock XYZ will pay a dividend of $1.25 per share next year. The growth rate of the dividend is expected to be 3% per annum. Looking at Yahoo Finance, you find that the beta of the stock is 0.85. The current risk-free rate is 2% and the estimated market premium is 9%. What should the price of the stock be?

To answer this question, you must first find the appropriate discount rate for the stock. The CAPM provides an answer since its purpose is to tell you the risk-return tradeoff in the market. Using the CAPM:

$$E(R_I) = R_F + \beta_I[E(R_M) - R_F]$$
$$2\% + 0.85^*9\% = 9.65\%.$$

The 9.65% is what the market is expecting any stock with a beta of 0.85 to earn. If that is so, then the stockholders of XYZ also demand at least a 9.65%. Thus the 9.65% is the appropriate discount rate. Based on the cash flow of the stock, and that the cash dividend is growing at 3% per annum, we can use the dividend growth model to determine the appropriate price.

Price of the Stock XYZ $= \$1.25/(0.0965 - 0.03) = \$18.80$.

Back to the interview: You gave your answer based upon Stock XYZ. The price at the time of your analysis was $24 and you felt that based upon your estimate of 3% growth and the discount of 9.65% derived by the CAPM, the stock price should only be $18.80. As a result, you made a sell recommendation. The interviewer asks if it turned out to be the right recommendation. Ruefully, you say no. It turns out that the firm's earnings grew much faster than expected and the stock price rose to $26.88. The market's assessment of the growth rate was not 3% but rather 5%. The interviewer gave a knowing smile and she then asks if you have any questions.

"Yes, I do. How does your department use the CAPM?" She looks uncomfortable at first and then she gives the perfect repartee.

"I rather hear from you how you would use the CAPM for asset allocation!"

"It will depend upon your expectations of the market," you begin to answer. "If you expect the market to do very well, I would allot more investment to high beta stocks. If you expect the market to do very poorly, then I would allot more money to low beta stocks and Treasuries. Another approach is to actually see which stocks did better than predicted by the CAPM and which stocks did poorly. You allocate more money to those stocks that did better than predicted by the CAPM."

She leans forward and asks, "How do you do that?"

Stock ID	Beta	Annual Return (%)	CAPM Prediction (%)	Prediction Error (%)
1	0.75	4	6.000	−2.000
2	0.89	4.75	6.420	−1.670
3	1.21	7.25	7.380	−0.130
4	0.45	6	5.100	0.900
5	1.375	10.25	7.875	2.375
6	1.06	8.10	6.930	1.170
7	0.98	4.20	6.690	−2.490
8	1.08	7	6.990	0.010
9	1.2	6.79	7.350	−0.565
10	0.59	4.90	5.520	−0.620

"Let me open my laptop and I will show you! Consider the table on the screen. I am sorry, but this information is somewhat proprietary so I am not providing the actual stock identification and I am using numbers to identify the stock. The second column is the beta of the stock. The third column gives the annualized average monthly return for the past 60 months. During the past five years, the average annualized monthly return of the T-bill has been 3.75% while the average annualized excess market return above the market has been 3%. Using the CAPM, one can predict what the return should have been over the past five years. For example, consider Stock 6. According to the CAPM, the return should have been, 3.75% + 1.06*3%, which equals 6.93%. That stock actually earned, on an annual basis, 8.1%. Thus, the stock did 1.17% better than predicted. The last column summarizes who the past winners and past losers were. You can create a portfolio of stocks of winners and invest in that portfolio."

"But this assumes that the past is an accurate guide to the future!" she exclaims.

"That is correct. I am not suggesting that we should only rely on this approach. I am only suggesting it as a possible framework and if we in Wall Street truly believe that the market is so efficient, then none of us would have jobs. Moreover, there is empirical evidence that past winners continue to be winners, at least for the short run. I think this is called momentum strategy. But if you fully believe that the market is fully efficient, implying that the stock price always reflects all available information and that we traders and portfolio managers are wasting our time, then we should offer our clients to invest in an Electronic Trading Fund (ETF) mirroring the market. If the client is risk averse, we put most of the money in the treasury market and some in the ETF. The more aggressive the client, the greater the percentage invested in the ETF."

She stands up and smiles. "We need to negotiate your salary, but first I want you to meet some of my colleagues."

Some Observations: Efficient Markets

Efficient markets: this implies that security prices incorporate information instantaneously. There are three types of efficient markets. The *weak form of market efficiency* implies that there are no statistical trends that can be profitably exploited. The *semi-strong form of market efficiency* states that all publicly available information is impounded in market prices. The *strong form of market efficiency argues that all information is impounded in market prices.*

Empirically, most financial markets are fairly efficient, at least in the weak form and semi-strong form sense. There are several implications for corporate finance managers.

First, the corporate manager can rely on market prices to deduce the required rate of return the market is expecting from the firm. Second, the manager should not use accounting gimmicks that do not increase cash flow of the firm in order to report higher earnings. Third, managers should not seek merger partners that do not increase the cash flow pie.

If markets are so efficient, then why are there so many people making money on Wall Street? It is true that you will find people who can beat the market. However, you do not hear about the millions of experts that do not do well. For example, mutual funds on average do worse than the market. Moreover, investment gurus who tend to do well for a short time find that the law of averages catches up to them. It is also true that there are anomalies that cannot be easily explained by financial experts. For example, positive and negative momentum seems to explain the movements of some securities. In particular, companies who tend to do very well, continue to do so for another year or so. However, they then become laggards. Nevertheless, the fact is that most of us are not very good in predicting market movements. For us, the market efficiency implications hold.

Advanced Topics-Calculating Beta

The mathematical formula for Beta is

$$\beta_i = \text{Cov}(R_i, R_m)/\text{Var}(R_m). \qquad (4.2)$$

Example 2: Consider the following table. The second column gives you the annual return of stock for a given year. The last column gives you the corresponding return for the market during that year.

Year	Stock i (%)	Market (%)
2001	12	18
2002	−7	−16
2003	5	12
2004	6	11
2005	−2	3

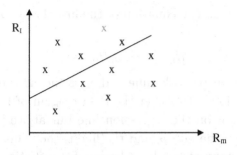

Figure 4.4

Average Annual Return	2.80%	5.60%
Variance	54.70%	174.30%
Standard Deviation	7.40%	13.20%

Please verify that the average return of stock i is 2.8% while the average return of the market for that same time period is 5.6%. Also verify the values of the statistics in the above table. Using the covariance formula (Equation (3.5) of the previous chapter):

$$\text{Cov}(R_i, R_j) = \sum_{t=1}^{n}(R_{it} - \text{AR}_i)(R_{jt} - \text{AR}_j)/(n-1),$$

we can obtain that the covariance is equal to $92.40\%^2$. According to Equation (2), beta is obtained by taking the ratio of the covariance of the returns of stock I with that of the market and the variance of the return of the market portfolio or $92.4/174.3 = 0.5301$.

This is one approach to find the beta of the stock. In actuality, you are using what statisticians call linear regression. Consider the following diagram. The x's in Figure 4.4 represent paired observation of the return of the stock and market for a given period. For example, the bold x represents the monthly return of stock i and the market in March 2008. For that month, the stock had 7% return, while the market return was 5%. Ordinarily, we use 60 month observations and imagine there are 60 of those xs. Linear regression tries to find the best line that fits those points whereby roughly half of the xs will be above the line and the other half will be below the line. The slope of the line is the beta. The equation of the line that is being estimated is given by:

$$R_{it} = \alpha + \beta_i R_m + \varepsilon_{it}. \qquad (4.3)$$

The α is the intercept of the line and ε_{it} is the error term for stock i for the time period t. Consider the bold x again of Figure 4.4. Note that bold x is not on the regression line but above it. The vertical distance between the bold x and the line is the value of ε_{it}.

No doubt, many of you have heard of a statistic called R^2. This statistic measures the goodness of fit for the regression. In a univariate regression such as that is given by Equation (3), one can find the R^2 by finding the correlation coefficient between the returns of the stock and the market. Equation (3.7) of the Risk and Return chapter is the formula for the correlation coefficient:

$$\rho_{ij} = \text{Cov}(R_i, R_j)/\sigma_i \sigma_j$$

In our example, the correlation coefficient is 92.4/[7.4*13.2] = 0.9463. Squaring the correlation coefficient gives us the R^2, which equals 0.8955.

What does this mean? Let us digress just a little. It can be shown that the variance of R_{it} is given by $\beta_i^2 \text{Var}(R_m) + \text{Var}(\varepsilon_{it})$. The first term is the portion of the variance of the stock return that is explained by the variation of the market. We call that component, the systematic risk of the stock. The $\text{Var}(\varepsilon_{it})$ is the portion of the total risk that is unexplained by the market movement. This portion, we call the unsystematic risk. Note that if you computed the following:

$$\beta_i^2 \text{Var}(R_m)/[\beta_i^2 \text{Var}(R_m) + \text{Var}(\varepsilon_{it})] = R^2$$

That is, R^2 is giving us the percentage of the total variation of the stock return, which is explained by the variation of the market. In our case, we have a very good fit. Almost 90% (actually, 89.55%) of the variation of the stock is explained by the market. You should know that for US equities, the typical R^2 is closer to 25%. That means that market movements only explain, on average, 25% of the stock movement. But look at the CAPM! Note that only β matters in determining the risk of the stock and its expected premium. Why does the CAPM ignore the unsystematic risk if it is such a big portion of the risk of the stock?

The answer is simple. Remember the CAPM assumes that you will hold a diversified portfolio. It can be shown, that if you pick one stock with a beta of (let us say) 0.75, the R^2 will be only 30%. But if you create a portfolio of 40 stocks with betas of 0.75, and run the regression of the return of that portfolio with the market, the beta will be 0.75 but the R^2 will almost be 1. Diversification removes the unsystematic risk and since shareholders can remove that risk by holding a diversified portfolio, the market (according to the CAPM) does not reward you for that portion of the risk.

Finally, it can be shown that beta is also given by:

$$\beta_i = \text{Cov}(R_i, R_m)/\text{Var}(R_m) = \rho_{im}^* \sigma_i^* \sigma_m/\text{Var}(R_m).$$

Since $\text{Var}(R_m) = \sigma_m^2$, then $\beta_i = \rho_{im}^* \sigma_i/\sigma_m$.

We can further illustrate how diversification removes the unsystematic risk by going back to the DJIA table from the risk return chapter, which is reproduced below:

Name of the Company	Ticker Symbol	Average Return (%)	Standard Deviation	Beta	R^2
AMERICAN EXPRESS CO	AXP	1.70	13.75	1.5197	0.4799
BOEING CO	BA	1.21	8.56	0.9862	0.5220
CATERPILLAR INC	CAT	1.22	11.61	1.3937	0.5662
CISCO SYSTEMS INC	CSCO	0.20	8.70	0.9459	0.4641
CHEVRON CORP NEW	CVX	0.86	6.01	0.5086	0.2817
DU PONT E I DE NEMOURS & CO	DD	1.26	8.73	1.1747	0.7112
GENERAL ELECTRIC CO	GE	0.46	10.10	1.2179	0.5715
GOLDMAN SACHS GROUP INC	GS	0.37	10.35	1.2142	0.5406
HOME DEPOT INC	HD	2.04	6.87	0.5914	0.2914

(Continued)

(*Continued*)

Name of the Company	Ticker Symbol	Average Return (%)	Standard Deviation	Beta	R^2
INTERNATIONAL BUSINESS MACHS COR	IBM	1.07	5.42	0.5628	0.4238
INTEL CORP	INTC	0.54	7.67	0.7959	0.4235
JOHNSON & JOHNSON	JNJ	0.82	4.44	0.3990	0.3171
JPMORGAN CHASE & CO	JPM	1.14	10.40	1.0396	0.3929
COCA COLA CO	KO	0.78	4.90	0.3200	0.1675
MCDONALDS CORP	MCD	1.04	4.13	0.2446	0.1379
3M CO	MMM	1.12	6.15	0.6838	0.4862
MERCK & CO INC	MRK	0.40	7.07	0.4629	0.1683
MICROSOFT CORP	MSFT	0.53	7.19	0.7002	0.3725
NIKE INC	NKE	1.65	7.42	0.6534	0.3052
PFIZER INC	PFE	0.97	5.85	0.4703	0.2538
PROCTER & GAMBLE CO	PG	0.51	4.76	0.3078	0.1645
TRAVELERS COMPANIES INC	TRV	1.11	5.79	0.4578	0.2457
UNITEDHEALTH GROUP INC	UNH	0.89	9.24	0.7884	0.2860
UNITED TECHNOLOGIES CORP	UTX	0.96	6.39	0.8507	0.6964
VERIZON COMMUNICATIONS INC	VZ	0.85	5.47	0.2582	0.0875
WAL MART STORES INC	WMT	1.00	4.71	0.1470	0.0383
EXXON MOBIL CORP	XOM	0.43	4.92	0.2983	0.1443
Averages		0.93	7.28	0.7034	0.3533
Portfolio Statistic		0.93	4.93	0.7034	0.7989

The last two columns are of interest. The penultimate column labeled beta gives you the beta of each stock on the above list. The last column provides the R^2 for each stock. These statistics were calculated using monthly returns from January 2008 to December

2013. The last row provides the average of the betas and associate R^2's of the 27 stocks. The last column provides the actual Beta and R^2 of an equal-weighted portfolio of the 27 stocks. Note that the average beta and the beta of the portfolio are identical. However, the average R^2 is 35.33% implying that almost 65% of the risk of these stocks is unsystematic. However, when we estimate the actual R^2 of the portfolio, it is 79.89%, implying that only 20% of the portfolio risk is unsystematic. The CAPM defines risk by beta only because by holding a portfolio, one can eliminate all of the unsystematic risk.

Example 3: Assume that Stock j's correlation coefficient with the market is 0.5. Assume that the standard deviation of the market return is 10% and the standard deviation of the Stock j's return is 20%. What is the beta of Stock j?

Since $\beta_i = \rho_{im}\sigma_i/\sigma_m = 0.5(20\%/10\%) = 1$.

Now it is time to test your understanding. Please do the following questions.

CAPM Problems

1. What is the unique risky efficient portfolio? Explain your answer.
2. What will be the correlation coefficient of a portfolio with the market portfolio that is fully diversified?
3. What is the type of risk that is not rewarded according to the CAPM?
4. How would you use the CAPM to evaluate portfolio performance?
5. If the beta of a portfolio is equal to 1, the correlation coefficient of the stock with the market portfolio must be 1. True or False and explain your answer.
6. If the beta of a stock is 1.5, and the correlation coefficient of that stock with the market is 0.5, then:

   (a) Determine the standard deviation of the stock, if the market's standard deviation is 0.3;
   (b) Given your answer to part a, determine the standard deviation of the portfolio, composed of 30% in the stock and 70% in the market.

7. You are considering buying a building. The typical beta of real
   estate companies is 1.2. The current risk-free rate is 6%. The
   expected market risk premium is 8.2%. You expect that the profit
   of the building will be $500,000. You expect the profit to grow
   indefinitely at 4% per annum. What is the maximum price you
   are willing to pay for the building?

Project: Select any 5 stocks other from those listed as components
of the Dow Jones Index. Using http://finance.yahoo.com/, download
the ending monthly price of each stock from January 2009 to December 2013. Using Excel, compute:

  i. The monthly return of each stock.
 ii. The average and standard deviation of each stock.
iii. The beta of each stock.
 iv. The R^2 for each stock.
  v. The average and standard deviation of an equal weighted port-
     folio of these five stocks.
 vi. The beta and R^2 of the portfolio.

Answers to the Problem Set

(1) Assume that investors evaluate all investments based upon the
    expected return and the standard deviation of returns. Further
    assume that investors can borrow and lend at the risk-free rate.
    Moreover, assume that all investors have the same set of beliefs.
    That unique portfolio must contain every stock in the market.
    Hence, the unique optimal portfolio will be the market portfolio.

(2) To be fully diversified, there should be no unsystematic risk.
    That will occur if the correlation coefficient between the invest-
    ment and that of the market is equal to 1. Note that when the
    correlation coefficient is equal to one, the R-square is also equal
    to 1, implying that the total variation of the stock is explained
    by the systematic risk (i.e. variation of the market) and that
    there is no unsystematic risk. Recall the following mathematical

equation to compute R-square:

$$\beta_i^2 \text{Var}(R_m)/[\beta_i^2\text{Var}(R_m) + \text{Var}(\varepsilon_{it})] = \text{R}^2.$$

Note that for R^2 to be equal to one, the unsystematic risk, $\text{Var}(\varepsilon_{it})$, must be equal to zero.

(3) It is the unsystematic risk. Since this risk can be diversified away by holding many different securities. As a result, the market, according to the CAPM, does not offer a risk premium for this type of risk since it can be eliminated.

(4) According to the CAPM, $\text{E}(\text{R}_\text{I}) = \text{R}_\text{F} + \beta_\text{I}\,[\text{E}(\text{R}_\text{M}) - \text{R}_\text{F}]$. First, calculate the beta of the stock, portfolio, and/or hedge fund. Then determine the *ex-post* or actual monthly return of the market portfolio and that of the 30-day Treasury Bill over a sample period. Take the average of these observations and plug the average monthly T-Bill return and market portfolio return into the CAPM. The resulting number is what the CAPM predicts the return should have been. Now compare that prediction to the actual return. If the realized return is better than the predicted return, you have discovered superior performance. On the other hand, if the actual return is lower than the predicted return using the CAPM, then you have inferior performance.

(5) This is false and this can most easily be shown by an example. Assume that stock j's correlation coefficient with the market is .5. Assume that the standard deviation of the market return is 10% and the standard deviation of the stock j's return is 20%. Since $\beta_i = \rho_{im}^* \sigma_i/\sigma_m = 0.5(20\%/10\%) = 1$.

(6) a. Note that beta, which is equal to 1.5 is also given by $\rho_{im}\sigma_i/\sigma_m = 0.5\sigma_i/.3$. Solving for σ_i, we obtain 0.9.
b. We will use:

$$\begin{aligned}
\text{Var}(R_\text{p}) &= w^2\text{Var}(R_i) + (1-w)^2\text{Var}(R_j) \\
&\quad + 2w(1-w)\rho_{ij}\sigma_i\sigma_j \\
&= 0.09(0.81) + 0.49(0.09) \\
&\quad + 2(0.3)(0.7)(0.5)(0.9)(0.3) = 0.1737
\end{aligned}$$

To find the standard deviation, take the square root of the variance term, or .41677 or 41.677%.

(7) To solve this problem, we use the CAPM to find the discount rate. In particular, E $(R_I) = R_F + \beta_I [E(R_M) - R_F] = 6\% + 1.2(8.2\%) = 15.84\%$. Using the growth formula, PV $= CF/(R-g) = \$500,000/(0.1584-0.04) = \$4,222,973$.

CHAPTER 5

CAPITAL BUDGETING
AND COMPANY VALUATION

What is Capital Budgeting?

Capital budgeting is the process that managers use to determine the selection of projects in which the firm should invest in order to maximize the shareholder wealth. In this chapter, we will teach you the basic finance tools used for capital budgeting. We will show you how these tools enable managers to evaluate strategies for expansion, to select equipment for modernization and for increasing manufacturing capacity, and to erect barriers to entry. We will also show how these basic tools can be used to evaluate a firm's asset or stock price. These tools use time value techniques we illustrated in the Time Value chapter.

Some basic financial tools for capital budgeting

The job of the corporation is to take the money entrusted to it by the shareholders and invest it. The stock price will increase only if the investment yields a return greater than what the shareholders can do on their own. How do we differentiate between the good and bad projects? Finance suggests two approaches and both of these approaches rely heavily on the time value of money. The first approach is the Net Present Value (NPV) and the second approach is the Internal Rate of Return (IRR). Both approaches require the manager to forecast future cash flows and to determine how much it costs the firm to raise money.

What is Net Present Value?

Net Present Value is defined as the time value of the cash flows generated by a capital expenditure less the capital expenditure. More formally:

$$\text{NPV} = -I + \sum_{T=1}^{N} \text{CF}_T/(1+R)^T, \tag{5.1}$$

where CF_T is expected cash flow of the project in period T, R is the cost of capital (of funds or the interest cost of raising money from investors), and I is the capital expenditure. The NPV rule states that firms should accept projects with NPV > 0 and reject the project if NPV < 0.

$\sum$ is the Greek letter sigma. In mathematics it represents summation. The subscript letter t in CF_t is a time index. The $T = 1$ below the sigma and N above the sigma implies that you are summing the present value of the cash flows from period 1 to n. Hence, the above equation is telling us to do the following mathematical operations:

$$\text{CF}_1/(1+R) + CF_2/(1+R)^2 + \cdots + CF_N/(1+R)^N. \tag{5.2}$$

Fortunately, we can use the NPV function in excel to find the Net Present Value. Before, we do an example, let us give an economic interpretation for Equation (5.2) which is the second term of the right-hand side of Equation (5.1). In a nutshell, expression (5.2) represents the market value of the asset. For a given interest rate, it represents the maximum price you would pay for the asset. If the market value of the asset is greater than the initial investment, I, then you have yourself a great deal, the NPV is positive and you would accept the project. If you accept the project and the market believes in the firm's projections, then the stock price should increase to reflect the positive NPV. On the other hand, if the market value of the asset is less than I, then the asking price is too high, NPV is negative and you would recommend rejection of the project. Should you accept the project, the stock price should fall!

Interestingly, back in the 1980s, academic research found that whenever oil companies announced major exploration in the continental US, the stock price of that oil company declined at the time of the announcement. What was the stock market telling the managers of the firm? They were saying that given current oil prices and technology for oil extrapolation, these projects had a negative NPV.

Let us do a more concrete example. As an assistant to Mr. Richard Wagoner, CEO of General Motors, you have been asked to analyze a potential new automobile model, Andromeda, and the staff has provided some key estimates. The amount of money GM will have to invest to launch the new brand is $450 million. The marketing staff estimates that the demand is fairly robust, projecting sales of 30,000 cars next year, 45,000 in the following 3 years, 30,000 in year 5 and no more sales thereafter. You estimate a profit of $5,000 per car sold. Mr. Frederick Henderson, Vice Chairman and Chief Financial Officer, tells you that GM's cost of funds is 11%. You must make a presentation to both men in 20 minutes. What do you recommend? First thing is that you do not panic. Your job may depend on this presentation, but you still have your health.

Second, you use the Excel mathematical function that you learned in the time value chapter. Let us illustrate in the table below. In cell A1, we label the column as time and in cell B1 we label the column as the cash flow for each period. The numbers in cells B2 through B7 are in millions of dollars. In cell B2, we enter the initial investment of $450 million. The numbers in cells B3 through B7 represent the profits in each year found by multiplying the level of expected sales in each year by the profit margin of $5,000 per car.

	A	B
1	time	cash flow
2	0	−450
3	1	150
4	2	225
5	3	225
6	4	225
7	5	150
8	PV	=NPV(0.11,B3:B7)

In cell A8, we enter the label of PV and enter the excel function of NPV(0.11,B3:B7) in cell B8. First, recall from the Time Value chapter that the NPV function assumes that B3 is time one, meaning that the nomenclature of NPV is misleading. (Any problem with that should be sent in triplicate form to Bill Gates.) That is why we labeled cell A8 as PV to tell us that the value you get in cell B8 is the market value of the asset. If you were to replicate our table in excel, you will find that the NPV function will yield $719.5 million. Given that you only invest $450 million, you can tell your bosses that this is a good deal and the Net Present Value is $269.5 million.

Step 1	f	clx
Step 2	-450	$g\ \mathbf{CF_0}$
Step 3	150	$g\ \mathbf{CF_j}$
Step 4	225	$g\ \mathbf{CF_j}$
Step 5	3	$g\ \mathbf{N_j}$
Step 6	150	$g\ \mathbf{CF_j}$
Step 7	11	i
Step 8	$f\ NPV$	

Naturally, you can come up with the same answer using your financial calculator. Using the HP-12C, you take the following steps: First, you hit f clx so that you clear your register. Second, you type 450, hit chs to get -450, hit the **g** button and then the $\mathbf{CF_0}$ button. Then you enter the cash flows in Steps 3–6. By entering 11 and hitting the i button, you are telling the calculator that the interest rate is 11%. Now, you need to get into the orange mode (see text in italics in the table above) to get the NPV by first hitting f button and then the **NPV** button. You will get $269.5 million as your NPV.

Internal Rate of Return

It is also possible that either Mr. Wagoner or Henderson would like to know the return on investment. The return on the investment is also known as the internal rate of return or IRR. IRR is found by setting the NPV of Equation (5.1) to zero and solving for the interest rate. More formally:

$$0 = -I + \sum_{T=1}^{N} \mathrm{CF}_T/(1 + \mathrm{IRR})^T. \qquad (5.3)$$

The IRR rule states that firms should accept the project if IRR > R, where R is the cost of funds. Again, the Time Value of Money chapter comes to the rescue. Let us replicate the table once more, but now we label cell A8 as IRR (as in the internal rate of return) and enter the Excel function =IRR(B2:B7). Note that we now include the cell B2 which represents the initial investment of $450 million. The value you will get is 32.25%. That is, the return on investment is 32.25% and the cost of raising funds is 11%. That is not a bad return!

	A	B
1	*time*	*cash flow*
2	0	−450
3	1	150
4	2	225
5	3	225
6	4	225
7	5	150
8	*IRR*	=IRR(B2:B7)

The next table shows you how to obtain the IRR using the HP-12C

Step 1	f	clx
Step 2	−450	**g CF$_0$**
Step 3	150	**g CF$_j$**
Step 4	225	**g CF$_j$**
Step 5	3	**g N$_j$**
Step 6	150	**g CF$_j$**
Step 7	f	*IRR*

What Could Go Wrong?

The big day comes and you make your presentation. Mr. Wagoner smiles benignly and you realize you are in trouble. Anytime you saw that smile, the CEO was about to ask some tough questions to the presenter. You begin to sweat!

"Why do you think that this model will be so popular?" Mr. Wagoner asks.

Not bad, you thought. You were prepared for that one! You answer, "The new model has the best attributes of both an SUV and a compact car. There is room for 6 passengers and it gets 30 miles per gallon on the highway. There are a lot of nice features and our competitors have nothing like it!"

Mr. Hendrickson interjects and asks, "And how long will it take the competitors to mimic this revolutionary product?"

You are not sure how to answer that question but you learned a valuable lesson about capital budgeting. Finding the NPV or IRR is the easy part, but economics and marketing are still the keys to success of such ventures. If Honda is able to replicate the GM product quickly, then competition could eat into sales and the profit margin. You realize that your bosses were asking how does GM stay ahead of the competition to ensure the overall profitability of the new model. Without careful planning, the estimates of NPV and IRR are overly generous. You realize your omission and reply, "Mr. Wagoner and Mr. Hendrickson, I apologize. You are correct. If you give me a second chance, I will prepare a business strategy that incorporates what our competitors might do!"

Now Mr. Hendrickson smiles and says, "Let's have that by the end of this week!"

Will NPV and IRR Always Give the Same Answer?

Generally speaking, whenever NPV > 0, the IRR will be greater than the cost of funds. However, the two approaches do not always agree on which project is best. This is important because many times firms must decide on two different strategies or two different manufacturing processes. In other words, management must decide between two different mutually exclusive projects. It is possible that the NPV and IRR will yield different answers.

Reinvestment rate assumption of NPV and IRR: Consider the following two projects:

Year	Proposal A	Proposal B
0	−$23,616	−$23,616
1	10,000	0
2	10,000	5,000
3	10,000	10,000
4	10,000	32,675
IRR	25%	22%
NPV at 10%	$8,083	$10,347

In this example, we are assuming that the appropriate cost of funds is 10%. Note that IRR says that proposal A is the most profitable since clearly one would like a 25% return on investment rather than a 22% return on investment. The NPV tells us that Proposal B is the better project. This example illustrates that NPV and IRR do not have the same ranking. The reason for this is that NPV assumes that the cash flows of the project, which theoretically belongs to the owners of the firm, can be reinvested at the cost of funds of 10%. On the other hand, IRR assumes that the reinvestment rate for proposal A is 25% and for proposal B is 22%.

Which one is correct? We believe that the NPV is correct. Why? To answer that question, we must understand the true meaning of the cost of funds. When we say that the cost of funds is 10%, we are saying that the owners of the firm are demanding that rate because that is the rate these investors can get in the market without the firm. In essence, if the investors were to receive a $10,000 dividend at time one, they would invest in the market in an investment vehicle of the same risk as the firm yielding 10%.

Independent of scale: Another reason for preferring the NPV approach is because IRR is independent of scale. Consider the following two projects:

Year	Proposal A	Proposal B
0	−$23,616	−$236,160
1	10,000	100,000
2	10,000	100,000
3	10,000	100,000
4	10,000	100,000
NPV at 10%	$8,083	$80,830

Note that proposal B is simply larger than proposal A by a scale of 10. Both projects have an IRR of 25% and clearly both projects are profitable. According to the IRR, the firm should be indifferent between the two projects. The NPV approach says project B is best. Again, the NPV approach gives us the best answer. Why? Think of it this way. If you could earn 25% return on investment and it costs you only 10% to raise funds, how much money would you borrow? Even risk averse business professors will borrow to the hilt. Accordingly, if you have a project that is so profitable that you can replicate 10 times, would you not do so?

What is the message? Another reason why we prefer NPV is that this approach is most consistent with the message of investment bankers and traders who are concerned more about the price. In other words, if you want to know the maximum price one should pay for a particular asset (company), then the NPV appears to be the way to go. If on the other hand, you are a commercial banker interested in the net interest margin, the IRR may be best.

Does NPV Always Work? — Capital Rationing

There are situations when NPV does not rank projects properly. For example consider the last example we used to illustrate the independent of scale problem of the IRR. Project A is one-tenth the size of

Project B. Project A's initial investment is $23,616 and Project B's initial investment is $236,160. Recall that Project A's NPV is $8,083 while Project B's NPV is ten times greater. As long as we can raise $236,160, we should take project B because it has the higher NPV. But what if we cannot raise that amount of money? Then clearly Project A is the better project.

The inability to raise all the money necessary to fund all positive NPV projects is known as capital rationing. In this case, we want to take the portfolio of projects that provide the highest NPV. The Profitability Index (PI) can be used to determine the optimal portfolio of projects. PI is defined as the ratio of the NPV to the Initial Investment or NPV/I. This ratio can help guide the manager in selecting the portfolio of projects that maximizes the NPV. Let us illustrate this with an example.

The table below lists eight projects. The second column delineates the initial investment for each project and the third column gives the NPV for each project. Assume that the manager is told by the CEO that she may not invest more than $11 million. If we were to strictly follow the NPV rule, then we would select projects 4 and 2, yielding an aggregate NPV of $2,460,000.

Project	Initial Investment	NPV	Rank by NPV	PI	Rank by PI
1	$1,000,000	$300,000		0.3	5
2	$5,000,000	$1,200,000	2	0.24	
3	$3,000,000	$810,000		0.27	6
4	$6,000,000	$1,260,000	1	0.21	
5	$2,500,000	$1,000,000		0.4	1
6	$1,500,000	$525,000		0.35	3
7	$2,000,000	$660,000		0.33	4
8	$1,000,000	$390,000		0.39	2

Note you would not be able to take any more projects since you have reached the $11 million limit. Not bad choices! However, if you were to follow the profitability index as depicted in the fifth column, you would select projects 5, 8, 6, 7, 1, and 3. Note that the accumulated investment of these choices is also $11 million and the aggregate NPV is $3,685,000, a much better portfolio choice.

The above is a simple problem, especially constructed to show how the (PI) will lead to a better choice than strictly ranking projects by NPV. The (PI) can be used to find the portfolio of projects that provide the biggest bang for the buck. The above problem becomes more complicated if the capital constraint is $10,000,000 in which case you would take 5, 8, 6, 7, and 2. Note, you are no longer strictly following the PI because if you did, you would violate the capital rationing constraint. Also, capital rationing becomes more complicated if some of the above projects are mutually exclusive. One can use integer programming to solve the capital rationing problem. This is beyond the scope of this chapter. In any case, in a capital rationing environment, you are trying to find the portfolio of projects that maximizes the NPV.

Does NPV Always Work? — Unequal Lives

Assume that you are considering two different projects that are mutually exclusive. One project entails selling off a patent to a company. You estimate that the time to accomplish this task is 2 years and it has an NPV of $1 million. The other alternative is for you to develop and commercialize the patent. This will take 10 years and its NPV is $1.6 million. According to NPV, you will take the second project. But what about the 8 years difference in the lives of these two projects? Could you not invest the proceeds at the end of 2 years and obtain even greater rewards?

The answer in this case is that NPV is correct and no adjustments have to be made. The reason for this is that any profits you make belong to the owners of the firm who could reinvest the proceeds at the going rate, the same rate used for discounting. The NPV of these investments will be zero.

Let us illustrate our argument with the following example. You have developed learning software that has shown in clinical tests to significantly improve learning for learning disabled children. It costs $1 million upfront to develop the various prototypes necessary for commercialization. You can either sell the patent once you have developed the prototypes, or commercialize the product itself. You estimate that you will be successful in selling the patent at the end of the second year for $2.42 million. Assuming that you can borrow and lend at 10%, this will yield an NPV of $1 million. You can find that answer by performing the following excel mathematical function $-1,000,000 + pv(0.1, 2, 0, -2420000, 0)$. Using the financial calculator:

N	i	PV	PMT	FV
2	10	? 2,000,000	0	−2,420,000

Now subtract the $1 million investment and you have a $1 million NPV.

Note that we entered the $2.42 million receipt as a negative entry. The reason why we did that is because we know that the pv excel function and financial calculator function yields an answer in opposite sign to the cash flow entries. Remember, the PV function is telling you how much you must pay to receive that cash flow.

N	i	PV	PMT	FV
10	10	? 2,600,000	−423,138.03	0

If you commercialize the patent, you still have the same $1 million development costs. You expect to generate $423,138.03 per year. The NPV is $1.6 million. You can obtain that answer by performing the following excel function $-1,000,000 + pv(0.1, 10, -423138.03, 0, 0)$ with the financial calculator (see the table above). Now after subtracting out the $1 million investment, we obtain the $1.6 million

NPV. Again, note that we entered negative cash flows in the PV function so that we can obtain a positive PV value. According to the NPV rule, this is the project we should take.

Now that we have a concrete example, let us find what we would obtain if we reinvested all of the income in the market at the going rate. That is we want to find the future value of cash flows generated by each project at time 8. We made sure that the initial investments are the same for each project so we can ignore that part of the problem. The future value of the sold patent can be found using the future value excel function, $=fv(0.1,8,0,-2420000,0)$ which is $5,187,484.92. Using the financial calculator:

N	i	PV	PMT	FV
8	10	−2,420,000	0	?
				$5,187,484.92

Note that we are explicitly taking into account that we are reinvesting the $2.42 million for 8 years at 10%. Now, let us find the future value of the cash flows generated by the commercialization of the patent. This is obtained using $fv(0.1,10,-423138.03,0,0)$. This yields $6,743,730.45.

Using the financial calculator

N	i	PV	PMT	FV
10	10	0	−423,138.03	?
				$6,743,730.45

Again, the commercialization is best. Note that present value fully takes the reinvestment of cash flows into account and therefore whether you use present value or future value, you will get the same ranking.

Let us change the problem wording and assume that you have two strategies as a ship builder. The first choice is to invest $1 million today in equipment that can be used to build yachts. The life of the machine is 2 years. It takes 2 years to build and sell yachts and you expect to receive $2.42 million at the end of the second year. The second choice is to buy $1 million worth of equipment to build row boats. This machine lasts 10 years and you expect to receive an annual income of $423,138.03. Assume that the appropriate discount rate is 10%. Assume that you can only follow one strategy. Either be a yachtsman or the lowly (row) boatman.

Hold on! Is this not essentially the same problem as that of the patent described above? Would not the answer be the same? Clearly, you go for manufacturing the row boats. But in reality, this is a different problem. With the patent situation, once you sell the patent you are out of the picture. The project is done. But now consider the boat problem. Are you going to build the yachts for 2 years and then close up, or are you going to reinvest every 2 years in the equipment to build yachts? If yachts are profitable (and assuming Congress does not pass a luxury tax as it did during President George Bush [1988–1992]), you will continue reinvesting to build more yachts. If that is so, it will be 'unfair' to evaluate the yacht option as if the project only lasts 2 years. In fact, the yacht strategy will cause you to make an investment at five different times before you would invest anew for the rowboats! Accordingly to solve this problem we need to somehow equate the lives of the two projects.

Consider the cash flow tables in an excel sheet for the two projects, assuming that you repurchase the yacht building equipment every 2 years.

	A	B	C
1	year	yacht	rowboat
2	0	−$1,000,000.00	−$1,000,000.00
3	1	$0.00	$423,138.03
4	2	$1,420,000.00	$423,138.03
5	3	$0.00	$423,138.03

(Continued)

(Continued)

	A	B	C
6	4	$1,420,000.00	$423,138.03
7	5	$0.00	$423,138.03
8	6	$1,420,000.00	$423,138.03
9	7	$0.00	$423,138.03
10	8	$1,420,000.00	$423,138.03
11	9	$0.00	$423,138.03
12	10	$2,420,000.00	$423,138.03
13	NPV	$3,540,441.05	$1,600,000.02

In the above table, Excel column B delineates the cash flow for the yacht problem. We are assuming that the cash flow cycle is strictly repeatable. Thus, at the end of year 2, you will receive $2.42 million for the yachts sold but you will need to reinvest $1 million, leaving only $1.42 million cash flow for the owners of the firm. However, also note that now the two projects have equal lives. Cells B13 and C13 yield the NPV for each project. In B13, we enter =npv(0.1,B2:B12) + B1 and in C13 we enter =npv(0.1,C2:C12) + C1. Note that when we equate the lives, the yacht strategy is best. You can also use the cash flow register function to obtain the NPV for each project as well. The inclusion of +B1 or +C1 is because the Excel NPV function does not include the initial investment at time zero. Thus, the addition of these terms is to allow us to calculate NPV, after deducting the cost of the investment at time 0.

How Do We Find the Cost of Funds?

According to NPV (Equation (5.1)) and IRR (Equation (5.3)) approaches to evaluate projects, we still need to know the interest rate that is used to either discount the future cash flows or the benchmark that is used for comparison against the IRR. In corporate finance, that interest rate has many names. It has been called the discount rate, the cost of funds or the cost of capital. For the most part, we will use the latter name.

From where does the firm raise the necessary capital funds to invest in its projects? The firm raises its funds from two sources of capital (although we will expand on that later in this chapter as well as on the Financing Decision chapter). Sometimes the capital for investments comes from stockholders and sometimes it comes from debt. Actually, it usually comes from both, and for this reason we need to know how to calculate the cost of capital when it comes from *both* equity and debt. It also turns out that the path that we are about to embark on is the capital budgeting approach that is easiest to apply. For now, let us look at the mechanics of the approach and read about the other approaches later on in the chapter.

Essentially, the discount rate we use is called the After-tax Weighted Average Cost of Capital (ATWACOC). Its formal definition is:

$$\text{ATWACOC} = \text{L } R_d(1 - T) + (1 - \text{L})R_e, \qquad (5.4)$$

where L is the percentage of debt financing that is used by the firm; R_d is the yield of the firm's debt outstanding; T is the corporate tax rate; $(1 - \text{L})$ is the percentage of equity financing used by the firm; and R_e is the yield of the firm's equity. Note that we multiply the yield of debt by one minus the tax rate to account for the tax deductibility of the interest payments. Note that we do not do the same for yield of equity because dividend payments are not tax deductible.

How do we find L? We define the value of the firm as the value of the firm's assets. From accounting we know that Assets must equal the sum of the liabilities and owners' equity. In finance, the value of the firm's assets equals the market value of the firm's debt and equity. Accordingly, L represents the proportion of the firm's value that is debt. Let S be the market value of equity which is defined as the price per share times the number of shares outstanding. Let D be the market value of debt outstanding which equals the price per bond times the number of bonds outstanding. Then $\text{L} = \text{D}/(\text{S}+\text{D})$. We do not use book value because it represents an historical value, the amount of proceeds the firm obtained when it first issued the securities. Rather, we will use wherever possible market value because this reflects the market's current assessment of the firm's prospect and risk.

We use the excel function, Rate (nper, pmt, pv, fv, type) to find the yield or cost of debt. We cannot use the Rate function to find the yield or cost of equity because we cannot set nper to infinity, the expected maturity of common stock. Instead, we can use the dividend growth model. Recall that the present value of cash flows growing at a constant rate is given by:

$$\text{Price} = (\text{Expected Dividend at } t = 1)/(\text{K} - \text{G}),$$

where K is the cost of capital. We can solve for K, assuming we know the price per share of the common stock and we have an estimate of the growth rate, G. In that case:

$$\text{R}_e = (\text{Expected Dividend at } t = 1)/\text{Price} + \text{G}. \qquad (5.5)$$

Example 1: Here is a simple example of determining the ATWA-COC. ACME has outstanding long-term debt with a book value of $50 million. ACME also has outstanding common stock with a book value of $100 million. The firm also has $75 million in retained earnings.

What does the book value of common stock mean in our example? At one time in the market, the firm raised $100 million in common stock. However, common stock does not necessarily have the same value today. Why not? Recall our previous discussion that accepting positive NPV projects raises the stock price, but what happens if the projects turn out badly and the actual return on investment is below the cost of funds? In that case, you would expect the value of the stock to fall. Whenever you see that the market value of equity is below its book value of equity it is because the market does not anticipate the firm to earn sufficient return to cover previously "bad" investment decisions.

And, what are Retained Earnings? Retained Earnings are the cumulative earnings of the firm that have not been paid out in dividends. What is the market value of Retained Earnings? Their value, if any, should be incorporated into the expected future dividends that determine the market price of equity.

With this background, let us continue with the above example. Consider the following information.

	Book Value (mm)	Price Per Share	Units Outstanding	Coupon Rate
Long-Term Debt	$50	$1000	50,000	10%
Common Stock	100	$40	3.75 mm	—
Retained Earnings	75	—	—	—

In addition to the book values listed previously, we also give you the market price per unit so that we can calculate the market values of debt and equity. We also give you the coupon rate of the debt so that we can calculate the yield of debt. Assume that the maturity of the debt is 10 years. Further assume that T, the tax rate, is 45%, and that the firm is expected to pay a $4.40 dividend per share beginning next year. The dividend is expected to grow at 10% per year. We now have enough information to calculate the ATWACOC.

Let us revisit our formula: $ATWACOC = L\,R_d(1-T)+(1-L)R_e$. Note that the market value of debt is $50 million (the product of the price per bond and the number of bonds outstanding). The market value of equity is $150 million (the product of the price per share and the number of shares outstanding). Hence, debt represents 25% of the total value of the firm and equity represents 75% of the value of the firm. So now we have values for L and $(1 - L)$. To find R_d, note that nper is 10, pmt is the coupon rate times the $1000 face value or 100, pv is −1,000, fv is 1,000 and type is zero. Plugging these values in the excel finance function =Rate(10,100,−1000,1000,0), we obtain an answer of 10%.

Or, you can use the financial calculator:

N	i	PV	PMT	FV
10	?	−1,000	100	1,000
	10			

Next, we calculate the cost of equity using the dividend growth model R_e = (Expected Dividend at $t = 1$)/Price + G or \$4.40/\$40 + 0.1 = 0.21 or 21%. Thus, our ATWACOC = 0.25(10%)(0.55) + 0.75(21%) = 17.125%.

Security Class	Market Value (mm)	Proportion	Cost of Capital	Contributing Costs (%)
Debt	\$50	0.25	10%(0.55)	1.375
Equity	\$150	0.75	21%	15.75
Total	\$200	1		17.125

The table above summarizes our calculations. The first column, labeled Security Class, lists the different sources of financing, which in our case are Debt and Equity. The second column gives you the market value of each security class. The third column labeled Proportion derives the proportion of each security class. The fourth column provides the Cost of Capital as obtained earlier. Note that we are multiplying the cost of debt by $(1 - T)$ or 0.55 to account for the tax deductibility of interest payments. The 5th column, labeled Contributing Costs is obtained by taking the product of the proportion value and the corresponding Cost of Capital. The last row, labeled Total, simply sums up the entries above. Hence, under the column labeled Market Value, the entry for Total is the sum of the values of debt and equity. The entry for Total in the Proportion column is the sum of all the proportions which should add up to one. The entry for Total in the Contributing Costs column will give us the ATWACOC.

It is simple to use Excel to calculate the ATWACOC and it is very useful since the firm can actually have many more classes of debt and equity.

Capital Asset Pricing Model

In the above, we assume that the firm pays out dividends so that we can estimate a cost of equity, but there are plenty of stocks that do not pay dividends. For example, Ebay Inc. (EBAY:Nasdaq), Mirant Corp (MIR: NYSE), Xerox (XRX:NYSE) and Yahoo Inc. (YAHOO:Nasdaq) do not pay dividends. How do we calculate their cost of equity?

There is another way to calculate the cost of equity that relies on the **Capital Asset Pricing Model (CAPM)**. This model says the risk premium of equity is related to how the stock varies with the market. This volatility is measured with beta, β, which is obtained by mathematically comparing the volatility of the return of an individual stock with the volatility of the return of the whole market. In case you do not want to do the calculation, you can obtain beta by looking it up on Yahoo Finance.

For example, if you go to http://finance.yahoo.com/ and enter XRX in the top left window that states **Enter Symbol(s)**. Go to the blue panel on the left side and click on **Key Statistics** under Company Profile. You will find the panel **Trading Information** on the right-hand side. The very first statistic is Beta, which for Xerox is 1.32.

What does beta mean? If, whenever the market return moves up or down by 10% the individual stock's return moves by 20%, then we say that the stock is twice as volatile or risky as the market. **The stock is said to have a beta of 2.0 (20%:10%)**. The CAPM states that the expected return from the stock will depend on its beta, and can be calculated using the following relationship:

$$E(R) = R_f + \beta[E(R_m) - R_f].$$

E(R) is the expected return of the stock required by the market. Hence, we can interpret E(R) to be the cost of equity. **R_f** is the risk-free rate. The risk-free rate is usually measured by the annualized yield of a one-month Treasury bill. $[E(R_m) - R_f]$ is the average risk premium in the market.

Generally, the average risk premium in the market is measured by the historical annualized excess return of the market over the return of the 1-month Treasury bill. That estimate is around 9%. So, if the beta of Xerox is 1.32, and the current risk-free rate is 5%, then according to the CAPM, the cost of equity is given by $E(R) = R_f + \beta[E(R_m) - R_f] = 5\% + 1.32(9\%) = 16.88\%$.

More Complicated ATWACOC

Most firms have multiple types of debt and equity. Consider ACME, a manufacturer of glue and other binding products. ACME has two types of bonds outstanding: Senior Bonds, which have a first mortgage on the firm's tangible assets; and Junior Bonds, or debentures, which are held by general creditors who have no liens (collateral) on specific assets. The company also has two types of equity outstanding: preferred and common stock. Preferred stock is similar to a bond in that it has a coupon rate. The coupon rate multiplied by the par value of the preferred stock is its annual dividend. Preferred stock has an indefinite life, but its dividend payments are not tax deductible, while interest payments on debt are. Consider the information given to you in the following table.

	Book Value (mm)	Unit Price	# of Units	Coupon (%)	Maturity (years)
Bonds	$20	$1,000	20,000	9	10
Debentures	40	875	40,000	8	10
Preferred Stock	20	75	200,000	10	—
Common Stock	100	40	3 mm	—	—
Retained Earnings	100	—	—	—	—

Assume that next year's dividend of $4 is expected to grow at 5% per year in perpetuity and the tax rate is 40%. What's the ATWACOC? Let us reconstruct the tabular format you can replicate on Excel.

Security Class	Market Value	Proportions	Cost of Capital	Contributing Costs
Bonds				
Debentures				
Preferred Stock				
Common Stock				
Total				

The first step is to find the market value of each class by taking the product of the price per unit and the amount of units outstanding. For example, the market value of Bonds is obtained by multiplying the price of each bond, $1,000, by the number of bonds outstanding, 20,000. This yields $20 million. We follow a similar procedure to obtain the market values of Debentures, Preferred Stock, and Common Stock. Thus, the table will now look as:

Security Class	Market Value (mm)	Proportions	Cost of Capital	Contributing Costs
Bonds	$20			
Debentures	35			
Preferred Stock	15			
Common Stock	120			
Total	$190			

According to the table above, the total value of the firm is $190 million. Next, we calculate the proportion of each security class to the total value of the firm. This is found by taking the ratio of the market value of a particular class to the total value of the firm. For example, the proportion of debentures is found by dividing the market value of debentures, $35 million, by the total value of the firm, $190 million, yielding 0.184. The table will now look like the following.

Security Class	Market Value (mm)	Proportions	Cost of Capital	Contributing Costs
Bonds	$20	0.105		
Debentures	35	0.184		
Preferred Stock	15	0.079		
Common Stock	120	0.632		
Total	$190	1.00		

Then, calculate the yield of each security class. Let us discuss each class in turn.

Bonds: Please observe that book value and market value of the bonds are identical. This is equivalent to saying that the price of the debt security is equal to par. Whenever this is the case, the yield of the bond is automatically equals the coupon rate of the bond. Since interest payments are tax deductible, we multiply the yield by one minus the tax rate. In this case, we multiply the 9% by $(1 - T)$, where $T = 40\%$. Hence, the after-tax yield of the bond is 5.4%.

Debentures: The book value of the junior bonds does not equal its market value. So the coupon rate should not equal the bond yield. We must calculate the bond yield using the Excel function =rate(nper, pmt, pv, fv, type). In our example, nper = 10 since the maturity of the debenture is 10 years (we are assuming annual payments in this example). Pmt is found by multiplying the coupon rate by the par value of the bond, which is always $1,000. Given a coupon rate of 8%, then pmt equals 80. The price of the bond is $875, so pv = −875. Par value is $1,000 and therefore fv = 1,000. Since we are assuming that the payments are made at the end of the period, then type = 0. Accordingly, =rate(10,80,−875,1000,0), which yields 10%. Multiplying the yield of debentures by one minus the tax rate, we obtain the after tax yield of debentures, 6%.

Similarly, you can use the financial calculator:

N	i	PV	PMT	FV
10	?	−875	80	1,000
	10			

Preferred Stock: The maturity of preferred stock is infinite. Accordingly, we must use the dividend growth model to find the yield of the preferred stock. To find the annual dividend payment, we multiply the stock's coupon rate by its par value. Typically, the par value of preferred stock is $100. It can also be found by taking the stock's aggregate book value divided by the number of shares outstanding. Given that the book value of preferred stock is $20 mm and there are 200,000 preferred shares outstanding, the par value of preferred stock of this example is $100. Since the coupon rate is 10%, then the annual dividend payment is $10. Since the maturity of preferred stock is indefinite, we can use the dividend growth model setting g = 0. Accordingly, the yield of preferred stock is found by Dividend/Price = $10/$75 or 13.33%.

Common Stock: Finally, we find the yield of common stock. Again, because we assume that dividends are growing at a constant rate, we can use the dividend growth model. $R_e = E(Div_1)/Price + G$ or $4/$40 + 0.05 = 0.15$ or 15%.

Now once we enter these values into the table immediately above, our table will look like:

Security Class	Market Value (mm)	Proportions	Cost of Capital (%)	Contributing Costs
Bonds	$20	0.105	5.4	
Debentures	35	0.184	6.0	
Preferred Stock	15	0.079	13.33	
Common Stock	120	0.632	15	
	$190			

The final step is to calculate the contributing costs. To calculate the contributing costs, we take the product of the cost of capital and its relevant proportion. Hence, the contributing cost of preferred stock is $0.079 \times 13.33\% = 1.053\%$. You should do the same for the other cells in the last column. After entering the contributing cost values for each security class, we sum these numbers to get the ATWACOC. The final look of the table is given below.

Security Class	Market Value (mm)	Proportions	Cost of Capital (%)	Contributing Costs (%)
Bonds	$20	0.105	5.4	0.567
Debentures	35	0.184	6.0	1.104
Preferred Stock	15	0.079	13.33	1.053
Common Stock	120	0.632	15	9.48
	$190			WACOC = 12.2

How Do We Define Cash Flows?

In the last section, we learned about ATWACOC. This represents the blended required rate of both stockholders and bondholders. This is the discount rate that we will use for the typical capital budgeting project. To compute the NPV of the project, not only do we need a discount rate but we also need the project's cash flow. For the project to be profitable, the project must generate sufficient cash flows to both stockholders and bondholders so that the project earns a return greater than the ATWACOC. How do we define this cash flow? It is defined as:

$$\text{Cash Flow}_U = \text{Sales} - \text{Costs} - \text{Long-Term Investment}$$
$$- \text{Change in Working Capital}$$
$$- \text{Tax Rate}(\text{Sales} - \text{Costs} - \text{Depreciation}).$$

$$(5.6)$$

Sales include all items that the accountants record as sales, whether or not the firm was paid or for which an accounts receivable was created. **Cost** does not include depreciation expense since the only impact depreciation has upon cash flow is to reduce the tax liability. You will see that we include depreciation expense only when calculating the tax liability.

Working capital is the difference between current assets and current liabilities. **Current assets** are short-term assets that can be converted into cash in less than a year. These include: *cash and marketable securities* that can be quickly deployed to make purchases for the project; *accounts receivables* which are monies owed by customers who buy goods on credit; and *inventory*, which is the raw materials and finished goods stored in warehouses to ensure smooth production and distribution. **Current liabilities** are obligations that come due within a year such as an account payable incurred when the firm buys production inputs on credit.

The change in working capital represents the net money the firm has invested to finance short-term investments. For example, assume that the firm sold $10 million of goods for credit out of inventory. Although, this transaction represents $10 million in sales, it has no cash flow implications, as accounts receivable (A/R) has increased but inventory has decreased, leaving current assets unchanged. However, if the firm replenishes its inventory, say, by $10 million, then the change in working capital is $10 million, implying that the firm has expended $10 million cash. In essence, change in working capital is a fudge factor, that translates the accrual basis of accounting to the cash basis of accounting.

Depreciation is the annual depreciation expense. Tax laws in the US and in most other countries allow firms to reduce their tax liability by incorporating (as a cost) the money needed to purchase a long-term investment. US tax codes delineate the percentage of the investment which may be expensed over time. To make things easier for this course, we will always assume straight line depreciation. That is, if a firm spends $5 million on new equipment and the life of the new equipment is 5 years, then the firm will be allowed to depreciate $1 million per year for 5 years. The effect of depreciation expense is to reduce the tax liability and increase overall cash flow. Note that in our cash flow equation, depreciation expense is found in the computation of the tax liability, defined as the Tax Rate (Sales − Costs − Depreciation). Mathematically, cash flow of the project increases by the Tax Rate * Depreciation.

We do not account for interest expenses because we use the ATWACOC as our discount rate. Recall that this discount rate represents the minimum required return of both stockholders and bondholders. Thus, the cash flow we use in our NPV formula is the cash flows available to both stockholders and bondholders (we are using bondholders interchangeably with lenders, including banks, debenture, and subordinated debenture holders). Since interest expense is simply a transfer of funds from the stockholders to the bondholders, there is no difference as far as the cash flow is concerned. Furthermore, the tax deductibility of interest is already accounted for in the ATWACOC since we multiply the yields of all debt by one minus the tax rate. Because we ignore the interest expense in Equation (5.6), we will refer to such cash flow as the cash flow of the unlevered firm and we denote the cash flow as Cash Flow$_U$.

Sometimes cash flow is defined based upon EBIT, earnings before interest and taxes. EBIT is defined as Sales − Costs − Depreciation. We can algebraically manipulate the above cash flow equation and redefine the cash flow as $(1 - T)$ EBIT + Depreciation − Change in Working Capital − Long Term Investment.

Another popular cash flow definition used by Wall Street is Free Cash Flow. This is defined as net income plus amortization and depreciation minus long term investment, change in working capital and dividends. This represents the money still available to stockholders. However, since we are concentrating on the use of the ATWA-COC for discounting, Free Cash Flow is not useful to us (at least not in this chapter).

Let us do an example. Assume you want to expand the firm's warehouse capability. You estimate that initial costs to build the expansion will be $500,000. You expect the firm will save on storage fees of $100,000 per year over the next 20 years. Assume that the salvage value of this building after 20 years is zero. Annual maintenance expense will be $60,000. Annual depreciation expense is $25,000 per annum. You expect no change in working capital requirements. Let the tax rate equal 40% and assume that ATWACOC is 12%. Should you expand?

According to our cash flow definition, the annual cash flows per year for years 1–20 are:

$$
\begin{aligned}
\text{Cash Flow}_U = {}& \text{Sales} - \text{Costs} - \text{Long-Term Investment} \\
& - \text{Change in Working Capital} \\
& - \text{Tax Rate (Sales} - \text{Costs} - \text{Depreciation)} \\
= {}& \$100,000 - \$60,000 - 0 - 0 \\
& - 0.4(\$100,000 - \$60,000 - \$25,000) \\
= {}& \$34,000.
\end{aligned}
$$

The NPV = −$500,000 + pv(0.12,20,−34000,0,0) = −$246,039. Since the project has a negative NPV, we should recommend not expanding the warehouse facilities.

Incremental Cash Flows

The cash flows of the project are not necessarily the total cash flows of the project, but rather its incremental cash flows. Let us illustrate this idea with an example.

Overextended Inc. has an old piece of equipment that the firm can either keep or replace. The machine still has seven more good years, during which it should produce annual sales of $5 million. Costs are expected to be 60% of sales. The current book-value of the equipment is $3 million. If sold today, the equipment would fetch $1.8 million. Alternatively, one can replace the equipment with a $12 million new machine that also has a life of 7 years. This new machine will increase sales starting next year by 10% and reduce annual costs to 50% of sales. Assume (again for simplicity) straight-line depreciation. If you purchase the new equipment, the firm will need to increase its inventory immediately by $500,000. Once the new equipment is retired, inventory levels will go back to original levels prior to the purchase of the new machine. Assume no salvage value at year 7 for either machine. Assume an ATWACOC of 16.87% and a tax rate of 40%. Which machine would you choose?

Essentially, we want to determine the NPV by finding the annual incremental cash flow. We achieve this by asking the following question: How much better off are you with the new than with the old machine? We analyze the cash flow for each period below.

At $t = 0$, if the firm undertakes the investment and purchases new equipment, as a result, it has to lay out $12 million. However, it will now sell the old equipment for $1.8 million. The net investment is therefore only $10.2 million. Note that the book value of the old equipment is $3 million. Consequently, if we sell the old equipment for $1.8 million, the tax authorities recognize a loss of $1.2 million. This loss can be used to reduce the tax liabilities incurred by the firm for other projects. Since the tax rate is 40%, the tax liability is reduced by 0.4($1.2 million) or $480,000. Essentially, the firm will be able to record this loss as a depreciation expense of $1.2 million. The firm will need to increase its inventory by $500,000. Hence, the change in working capital is $500,000. Letting T denote the tax rate, the table below summarizes our discussion. Note that the cash flow at time zero if we undertake the project is −$10.22 million.

	$t = 0$	$t = 1\text{--}6$	$t = 7$
Sales			
− Costs			
− Long-term Investment	($10.2 mm)		
− Change in Working Capital	($500,000)		
− T(Sales-Costs −Dep)	$480,000		
Total	**($10.22 mm)**		

Now consider the cash flows at time 1. The new equipment will increase annual sales by $10%. That is if we keep the old equipment, sales will be $5 million, but with the new equipment, sales will be $5.5 million. Consequently, in terms of sales, the firm is better offer with the new equipment compared with the old equipment by only $500,000.

The problem also states that there is a cost reduction with the new equipment. The production cost to the firm if it retains the old equipment is 60% of the old sales, or $3,000,000. The cost of production with the new equipment is 50% of total sales, or 0.5($5.5 million) = $2,750,000. Thus, if the firm replaces the old equipment and purchases the new equipment, Overextended, Inc. will be better off by $250,000.

Now we must calculate the tax liability of the project. Note that Sales − Costs equals $750,000. Thus to find the total taxable income, we need to calculate the *incremental* depreciation expense of the project. Recall that we assumed straight line depreciation so the depreciation expense of the old machine is $3 mm/7 or $428,571 per annum for 7 years. The new machine's depreciation expense is

$12 mm/7 or $1,714,285 per annum for 7 years. Consequently, if the firm takes the new project, the firm will enjoy an increase in annual depreciation expense of $1,285,714. The tax liability of the project is the tax rate times (Sales − Costs − Depreciation) = 0.4($500,000 + $250,000 − $1,285,714) = −$214,286. This project then reduces the total tax liability of the firm by $214,286 per annum for 7 years. If the firm has no taxable income, then the firm will simply not pay any taxes. In this example, we are assuming that Overextended, Inc. has other profitable projects. If Overextended takes this project, the new machine will allow the firm to reduce its taxes by $214,286 per annum.

Let us our cash flow formula to calculate the *incremental* cash flow at time 1. More formally,

Sales − Costs − Long-term Investment − Change in Working Capital − T(Sales − Costs − Depreciation) = $500,000 + $250,000 − 0 − 0 − 0.4($500,000 + $250,000 − $1,285,773) = $964,286.

Note, that we expect this cash flow in every year from 1 to 6. We will get to year 7 in a moment. We can now reproduce our cash flow table.

	$t = 0$	$t = 1$–6	$t = 7$
Sales		$500,000	
− Costs		$250,000	
− Long-term Investment	($10.2 mm)		
− Change in Working Capital	($500,000)		
− T(Sales-Costs − Dep)	$480,000	$214,286	
Total	**($10.22 mm)**	**$964,286**	

In year 7, the cash flow should be identical to that of year 6 except for an additional lump sum cash flow of $500,000. Once the project is over, the firm no longer needs to keep an investment of $500,000 in inventory. The liquidation of such inventory, results in a reduction of working capital of $500,000. This amount represents an added cash flow. The completed cash flow table is presented below:

	$T = 0$	$t = 1$ to 6	$t = 7$
Sales		$500,000	$500,000
− Costs		$250,000	$250,000
− Long-term Investment	($10.2 mm)		
− Change in Working Capital	($500,000)		$500,000
− T(Sales-Costs − Dep)	$480,000	$214,286	$214,286
Total	**($10.22 mm)**	**$964,285**	**$1,464,286**

We can now calculate the NPV of the project using Excel:

	A	B
1	*time*	*cash flow*
2	0	−$10,220,000
3	1	$964,286
4	2	$964,286
5	3	$964,286
6	4	$964,286
7	5	$964,286
8	6	$964,286
9	7	$1,464,286
10	NPV	−$6,255,537.33

The NPV entry in cell B10 is obtained by entering =npv(0.1687, B3:B9) + B2. The final conclusion is that since the NPV is negative, the old machine should not be replaced.

Case Study-Firm Valuation

Karl Ikan has hired you to evaluate the Carob Inc. The company has been in existence since 1978. It is a telecommunication firm that specializes in using internet protocols for business communications. Its stock is currently traded on the NYSE. The original founder of the company, Ms. CPU, recently retired and she owns 5% of the shares outstanding. Management owns another 5%. You observe the following information regarding its capital structure.

Security	Coupon Rate	Bk. Value	Maturity	Market Price	Units Outstanding
Senior Bonds	8%	$ 30,000,000	10 years	$1,000	30,000
Debentures	9%	$ 30,000,000	10 years	950	30,000
Pref. Stock	12%	$ 50,000,000	—	100	500,000
Comm. Stock		$100,000,000	—	40	4,000,000
Retained Earnings		$ 75,000,000	—	—	—

All interest and dividends are paid annually. The expected common stock dividend is $6 per share in perpetuity. Assume a tax rate of 40%. You estimate that if Mr. Ikan is able to take control of the firm, Carob Inc.'s profitability will dramatically improve. In particular, you estimate that beginning next year, the firm will enjoy sales of $150 million. Costs are expected to be 40% of sales. To continue the profitability of the company, the firm must maintain a continuous long-term investment in R&D (net of taxes) equal to 10% of sales, and investment in working capital (equivalent to change in working capital) of 5% of sales. The firm has very few tangible assets and therefore its annual depreciation expense is minimal. You believe the firm's sales growth is 6% per annum. What is the maximum stock price you recommend that Mr. Ikan should offer?

Solution for Case Study

First, please understand that this case study is an over-simplification of the real world. The study is written so

that a better understanding of corporate finance application is achieved while minimizing the amount of computation needed. Obviously, evaluating a company requires more in-depth analysis than that presented here. However, the purpose is to show that the traditional capital budgeting techniques may be used to evaluate firms. With this understanding, let us begin presenting the solution.

To solve this case, one must recognize that acquiring a company is no different, conceptually speaking, than any other capital budgeting project. The main difference here is that we are looking for the price we can afford to pay as opposed to the NPV. Hence, we can use the capital budgeting methodology employed in this chapter. Namely, we will calculate the ATWACOC and the cash flows, and use the ATWACOC to discount the cash flows to calculate the value of the firm. ("Hold on!" you say, "We do not want the value of the firm! We want the value of the common stock!" Be patient, and I will get to that as well.)

First let us calculate the ATWACOC using the tabular form we used in the lessons. In particular, we determine the market value of each security class by multiplying the price of each security by the number of outstanding units. This is summarized in the second column of the table below. In the third column, we calculate the proportions. This is found by taking the total value of each security class and dividing it by the total value of the firm. The cost of capital is summarized in the fourth column. In particular, since price = par for senior bonds, the yield of senior bonds equals its coupon rate. Multiplying the coupon rate by one minus the tax rate yields 4.8%. The price is not equal to par for debentures. In this case, we calculate the yield, using the excel function rate(nper, pmt, pv, fv, type). Multiplying the yield by one minus the tax rate yields 5.9%. Price is equal to par value for preferred stock. Hence, its yield is its coupon rate. Finally, under current management, the dividend of common stock is not expected to grow. Hence the yield of equity is dividend over price or 15%. The last column is the product of the proportion and cost of capital for each security class.

Adding up the entries of the last column yields an ATWACOC of 12.34%.

Security Class	Market Value (million)	Proportion	Cost of Capital (%)	Contributing Costs (%)
Senior Bonds	$30	0.112	4.8	0.538
Debentures	$28.5	0.106	5.9	0.625
Preferred Stock	$50	0.186	12	2.232
Common Stock	$160	0.596	15	8.94
Total	$268.5		ATWACOC =	12.34

We now estimate the cash flows of the firm under the new management, using the following formula:

Sales – Costs – Long-term Investment – Change in Working Capital – Taxes.

Next year sales are expected to be $150 million. Costs are expected to be $60 million. Long-term Investment is 10% of sales or $15 million. Change in working capital is $7.5 million. Finally, the tax liability is the tax rate times (Sales – Costs) or $36 million. Hence, the expected cash flow is $31.5 million. The case study expects the growth rate of sales to be 6% per annum. Given our simplistic assumptions that all the cash flow components are a percentage of sales, the appropriate cash flow growth rate is also 6%. Using the dividend growth model, the value of the firm is given by:

$$31.5 \text{ mm}/(0.1234 - 0.06) = \$496.85 \text{ mm}.$$

The firm under Karl Ikan is worth approximately $496.85 million. Why is the firm worth so much more than the $268.5 million obtained in our ATWACOC calculation? One answer is that Karl Ikan is a better manager, who is able to achieve 6% growth while the current management is not expecting any growth. Or, it might simply be hubris and Karl Ikan's team is overly optimistic. In any case, let us use the above numbers.

To find the value of common stock, we need to subtract out the values of the bonds, debentures and preferred stock. According to our ATWACOC table that figure is $108.5 million. Hence, the value of common stock is $388.35 million. Dividing the aggregate value of equity by the number of common stock shares outstanding yields a $97 share price. Given that the current stock price is $40, it looks like you should recommend to Mr. Ikan to make a tender offer.

Capital Budgeting Appendix

There are other capital budgeting techniques that are used to calculate the NPV or IRR. Each of these approaches uses a different definition of cash flow other than the one described in the previous sections. You will learn these other techniques so you can better understand the implicit assumptions you are making when you use a constant discount rate to calculate either NPV or IRR.

BTWACOC: This approach uses the Before-Tax Weighted Average Cost of Capital (BTWACOC) as the discount rate. The only difference between BTWACOC and the ATWACOC is that we no longer multiply the cost of debt by $(1 - T)$. In particular:

$$BTWACOC = L\,R_d + (1 - L)R_e. \qquad (5.7)$$

Recall the ATWACOC table, which began on page 138:

	Book Value (mm)	Unit Price	# of Units	Coupon (%)	Maturity (years)
Bonds	$20	$1,000	20,000	9	10
Debentures	40	875	40,000	8	10
Preferred Stock	20	75	200,000	10	—
Common Stock	100	40	3 mm	—	—
Retained Earnings	100	—	—	—	—

Note that when we found the yields of the Bonds and Debentures, they were 9% and 10%, respectively. The ATWACOC table is replicated below:

Security Class	Market Value (mm)	Proportion	Cost of Capital (%)	Contributing Costs (%)
Bonds	$20	0.105	5.4	0.567
Debentures	35	0.184	6.0	1.104
Preferred Stock	15	0.079	13.33	1.051
Common Stock	120	0.632	15	9.48
	$190			WACOC = 12.2

Note that the entries for the cost of Bonds and Debentures are 5.4% and 6.0%, respectively since we multiplied the before tax yields of 9% and 10% by $(1 - T) = 0.6$ since the assumed tax rate is 40%. To calculate the BTWACOC, we use the before tax yields of the bonds and debentures. In other words:

Security Class	Market Value (mm)	Proportion	Cost of Capital (%)	Contributing Costs (%)
Bonds	$20	0.105	9.0	0.945
Debentures	35	0.184	10.0	1.84
Preferred Stock	15	0.079	13.33	1.051
Common Stock	120	0.632	15	9.48
	$190			WACOC = 13.32

Note that the BTWACOC is higher than the ATWACOC and is equal to 13.32%.

Cost of Equity: This approach uses the cost of the common stock as the discount rate to calculate the NPV or as a comparison to the IRR.

Do the Various Capital Budgeting Approaches Yield Identical NPVs?

Of course they do! You might ask how is that possible if we are using different discount rates? The answer is that we use different definitions of cash flows for the different types of discount rates. However, the cash flows for each of the approaches must be set such that the leverage is held constant throughout the life of the project.

Let us begin by describing the cash flows to stockholders. For our examples, henceforth, we will assume that the firm does not finance its operations with preferred stock. The cash flow to stockholders is defined as:

$$CF_s = \text{Sales} - \text{Costs} - \text{Change in Working Capital}$$
$$- \text{Equity Investment} - \text{Interest Expense}$$
$$- \text{Principal Repayment}$$
$$- T(\text{Sales} - \text{Costs} - \text{Interest Expense} - \text{Depreciation}).$$
$$(5.8)$$

Note that Equation (5.8) differs from the unlevered cash flow of Equation (5.6) in several ways. First, we use the Equity Investment instead of the Long-term Investment. That is we only include that portion of the investment financed by the stockholders. Equity Investment is defined as Long-term Investment — New Debt Financing. When you use the cost of equity as your discount rate, the cash flow definition that you use is the cash flow to stockholders as given by Equation (5.8).

Before we introduce the cash flow associated with the BTWA-COC, note that the cash flow to bondholders of the firm is given by:

$$CF_B = \text{Interest Expense} + \text{Principal Payment}$$
$$- \text{New Debt Financing.} \qquad (5.9)$$

Note that our definition of cash flow to bondholders includes the net proceeds that the firm receives from selling new bonds. If we add Equations (5.8) and (5.9), together we get the levered cash flow of the firm or

$$\text{Cash Flow}_L = \text{Sales} - \text{Costs} - \text{Long-Term Investment}$$
$$- \text{Change in Working Capital}$$
$$- \text{Tax Rate (Sales} - \text{Costs}$$
$$- \text{Interest Expense} - \text{Depreciation).} \qquad (5.10)$$

Equation (5.10) is the cash flow used when using the BTWACOC as the discount rate. By the way, Equation (5.10) can be simplified further. Note that Cash Flow$_U$ = Sales − Costs − Long-Term Investment − Change in Working Capital − Tax Rate [Sales − Costs − Depreciation] (recall, Equation (5.6)). Then Cash Flow$_L$ = Cash Flow$_U$ + T(Interest Expense).

An Example: Consider a firm with a before tax cost of debt equals 10% and a cost of equity of 12%. Let the tax rate equal 40% and the market value of the debt is 40% of the total value of the firm. The ATWACOC is 9.6% as summarized by the table below:

Security Class	Market Value (mm)	Proportion	Cost of Capital (%)	Contributing Costs (%)
Debt	$40	0.40	6.0	2.4
Common Stock	60	0.60	12	7.2
	$100			WACOC = 9.6

The firm is contemplating a new project with an initial investment of $10 million. The project will generate in perpetuity annual sales of $25 million. Assume that costs are 80% of sales. Assume no investment in working capital or depreciation expense. (The problem is greatly simplified to make it easier to understand the concepts.) To find the NPV of the project, we must first find the cash flows of the project. Consider the following table:

	$T = 0$	$t = 1 - \infty$
Sales		$25,000,000
− Costs		$20,000,000
− Long-term Investment	($10.00 mm)	
− Change in Working Capital		
− T(Sales-Costs − Dep)		($2,000,000)
Total	**($10.00 mm)**	**$3,000,000**

The NPV of the project is

$$\text{NPV} = -\$10 \text{ mm} + \$3 \text{ mm}/0.096 = \$21.25 \text{ mm}.$$

Note that the maximum price or amount of investment you will be willing to pay for this project is $31.25 million (i.e., $3 mm/0.096). Hence, if the firm is to maintain 40% leverage, the total amount of debt the firm uses to finance the project must be equal to 0.4*$31.25 million or $12.5 million. That is, the project allows the firm to borrow an additional $12.5 million. Note also, that since we are assuming the cash flows are perpetual, the firm will have a permanent increase in its debt capacity of $12.5 million. This means that the debt is effectively never repaid. Given this, we know that the firm will carry an incremental interest expense of 10% of $12.5 million, or $1.25 million per year in perpetuity.

Now let us find the NPV using the BTWACOC. First, let us calculate the BTWACOC and as summarized by the table below it is equal to 11.2%.

Security Class	Market Value (mm)	Proportion	Cost of Capital (%)	Contributing Costs (%)
Debt	$40	0.40	10.0	4.0
Common Stock	60	0.60	12	7.2
	$100			WACOC = 11.2

The cash flow table is now set up to find the levered cash flow, taking into account that the firm has increased its debt by $12.5 million and is now incurring an additional annual interest expense of $1.25 million:

	$T = 0$	$t = 1 - \infty$
Sales		$25,000,000
− Costs		$20,000,000
− Long-term Investment	($10.00 mm)	
− Change in Working Capital		
− T(Sales-Costs − Interest − Dep)		($1,500,000)
Total	**($10.00 mm)**	**$3,500,000**

Note that the cash flow for $t \geq 1$ is $500,000 greater than what we obtained using the unlevered cash flow. However, also recall that Cash Flow$_L$ = Cash Flow$_U$ + T(Interest Expense) and that 0.4*$1.25 million of interest expense equals $500,000. Now using the BTWACOC, the NPV is given by:

$$\text{NPV} = -\$10 \text{ mm} + \$3.5 \text{ mm}/0.112 = \$21.25 \text{ mm}.$$

Now let us use the cost of equity approach. In this case, we know that the cost of equity is 12%. The cash flow table is now:

	$T = 0$	$t = 1 - \infty$
Sales		$25,000,000
− Costs		$20,000,000
− Equity Investment	$2,500,000	
− Change in Working Capital		
− Interest Expense		($1,250,000)
− Principal Payment		
− T(Sales-Costs − Interest − Dep)		($1,500,000)
Total	**$2,500,000**	**$2,250,000**

Note that now the cash flow at time 0 is actually positive. Why is that? The reason is that the project is so profitable that the firm is able to carry an additional $12.5 million of debt. The firm is then able to make the $10 million investment and give out an extra dividend of $2.5 million. Also, note that we include an interest payment of $1.25 million for years $t \geq 1$. The NPV of the project is therefore:

$$\text{NPV} = \$2.5 \text{ mm} + \$2.25 \text{ mm}/0.12 = \$21.25 \text{ mm}.$$

Note that all three approaches gave you identical answers, but that only happened because we ensured that all three capital budgeting approaches assumed identical leverage assumptions.

An Even More Complicated Example: Let us retain the identical cost of capital assumptions of the previous example. This time, however, assume that the initial investment is $10 million and the unlevered cash flow of the project is $2.5 million per year for 10 years. Using the ATWACOC as your discount rate, the NPV of the project is equal to -$10mm + PV(0.096, 10, −2500000,0,0) = $5,628,969.59. The market value of the project (the maximum price one would pay to acquire this project is $15,628,969.59. Assuming, we maintain a 40% leverage ratio, the amount of debt the firm will raise is 40% of $15,628,969.59 or $6,251,587.84. However, the value of the project will decline through time. For example, after 1 year, the maximum price you would pay for the project is simply the present value of

Time	CFu	Market Value	Debt	Interest	CF$_L$	Principal	CF$_S$
0	($10,000,000)	$15,628,969.59	$6,251,587.84		-$10,000,000.00	($6,251,587.84)	($3,748,412.16)
1	$2,500,000	$14,629,350.67	$5,851,740.27	$625,158.78	$2,750,063.51	$399,847.57	$1,725,057.16
2	$2,500,000	$13,533,768.34	$5,413,507.33	$585,174.03	$2,734,069.61	$438,232.94	$1,710,662.64
3	$2,500,000	$12,333,010.10	$4,933,204.04	$541,350.73	$2,716,540.29	$480,303.29	$1,694,886.27
4	$2,500,000	$11,016,979.07	$4,406,791.63	$493,320.40	$2,697,328.16	$526,412.41	$1,677,595.35
5	$2,500,000	$9,574,609.06	$3,829,843.62	$440,679.16	$2,676,271.66	$576,948.01	$1,658,644.49
6	$2,500,000	$7,993,771.53	$3,197,508.61	$382,984.36	$2,653,193.74	$632,335.01	$1,637,874.37
7	$2,500,000	$6,261,173.59	$2,504,469.44	$319,750.86	$2,627,900.34	$693,039.17	$1,615,110.31
8	$2,500,000	$4,362,246.26	$1,744,898.50	$250,446.94	$2,600,178.78	$759,570.94	$1,590,160.90
9	$2,500,000	$2,281,021.90	$912,408.76	$174,489.85	$2,569,795.94	$832,489.74	$1,562,816.35
10	$2,500,000	$0.00	$0.00	$91,240.88	$2,536,496.35	$912,408.76	$1,532,846.71

the 9 remaining unlevered cash flows of $2,500,000 or pv(.096, 9, $-2500000,0,0$) = $14,629,350.67. Hence, to maintain 40% leverage, the amount of debt outstanding must decrease from $6,251,587.84 to 40% of $14,629,350.67 or $5,851,740.27. Note, this implies that the firm must pay a principal payment at $t = 1$ equal to $6,251,587.84 − $5,851,740.27 or $399,847.57. The table below summarizes the unlevered cash flow, the levered cash flow and the cash flow to stock holders. Your job is to replicate the table and show that each of the capital budgeting approaches yield identical NPVs.

Capital Budgeting Problems

Here are some review questions! The correct answer is in bold font.

1. Assume that the expected dividend for KalTest in year 1 is $1.25. The current stock price is $25. The growth rate of the dividend is 8%. The cost of equity is:

   a. 8.05%

   b. 13%

   c. 16%

   d. None of the above

2. The beta of Tzar is 1.35. The risk free rate is 7% and the market premium is 9%. The cost of equity is:

   a. 10.4%

   b. 14%

   c. 19.15%

   d. None of the above

3. Assume that the initial investment is $500,000. Assume that the project has an expected cash flow of $25,000 at time 1, $75,000 per year from time 2 until time 8 and $25,000 at times 9 and 10. Assume that the appropriate discount rate is 14%. The NPV of the project is:

   a. −$181,513.56

   b. $188,257.16

   c. $313,313.41

   d. None of the above

4. Assume that the initial investment is $500,000. Assume that the project has an expected cash flow of $25,000 at time 1, $75,000 per year from time 2 until time 8 and $25,000 at times 9 and 10. Assume that the appropriate discount rate is 14%. The IRR of the project is:

   a. 2.876%

   b. 3.636%

   c. 14.12%

   d. None of the above

5. Assume that the Elimelech Company has outstanding Debt of $40 million. The yield of the debt is 12%. Further assume that this firm has $60 million of equity outstanding. Assume that the yield of equity is 18%. Let the tax rate equal 40%. Then the ATWACOC is:

   a. 15.6%

   b. 14.25%

   c. 13.68%

   d. None of the above

6. The price of the bond is $785. The coupon rate of the bond is 5%. The face value of the bond is $1000. Assuming annual interest payments and a bond maturity of 10 years, the yield of the bond is:

   a. 6.37%

   b. 8.24%

   c. 9.12%

   d. 10.25%

7. Firm XYZ is considering the following two mutually exclusive investments (The table below describes the relevant cash flows:

Time	Project A	Project B
0	−$250,000	−$2,500,000
1	$100,000	$1,000,000
2	$100,000	$1,000,000
3	$100,000	$1,000,000
4	$100,000	$1,000,000

The ATWACOC is 25%. You would:

a. **Reject both projects because NPV for each is negative**

b. Prefer project B because it has a higher NPV

c. You are indifferent between the two projects because they have identical IRRs

d. None of the above

8. Firm ABC is considering purchasing new die cutting equipment. The purchase price of the equipment is $2,000,000. The purchase of this equipment would necessitate buying $1,000,000 of raw materials (inventory) at time 0 but you are able to liquidate the inventory at the end of the 10th year. The life of the equipment is 10 years. Assume that there is no salvage value at time 10. Assume that the corporate tax rate is 40%. Further assume that annual sales during the life of the equipment are $4,000,000 and costs (other than interest and depreciation) are 60% of sales. Further assume straight line depreciation. The cash outlay at time 0 is:

a. $2 million

b. **$3 million**

c. Not enough information to do this problem

d. None of the above

9. Given the information in problem 8, the expected cash flow at time 1 is:

a. **$1.04 million**

b. $1.21 million

c. $1.6 million

d. Not enough information to do this problem

10. Assume that the ATWACOC of firm ABC of problem 9 is 9%. Further assume that the firm will have no inventory for this project at the end of time 10. The NPV of project described in problem 8 is:

a. $2.143 million

b. $3.674 million

c. $4.097 million

d. None of the above

More Advanced Capital Budgeting Problem

1. Determine the feasibility of the following project. You may assume that the project is slightly more risky than your usual project. The following information is available:

Investment Cost..$10,000,000

Tax Rate..48%

Depreciation Expense per Year ....$1mm (10 years)

Periods	Sales (mm)	Costs (mm)	Cash (mm)	A/R (mm)	Inventory (mm)	A/P (mm)
1–5	10	7	0.5	1.5	2	3
6–10	8	6	0.3	3	2	3
11	0	2	0	0	0	0

A/R is the accounts receivable. The above table is indicating that in years 1–5, the level of accounts receivable for this project is $1.5 million. A/P is the accounts payable. Costs include Depreciation Expense, but do not include Interest Expense. Included in the cost for years 1–11 is the project's allotted $500,000 annual maintenance expense for the plant. Assume that the firm's total maintenance expense (including the project's allotted share) will not change whether or not the firm undertakes the above project.

Balance Sheet

Security	Coupon (%)	Book Value ($)	Price per Unit	Outstanding Units	Maturity (years)
Sr. Debt	7	10 mm*	$1000	10,000	10
Jr. Debt	9	40 mm	1020	40,000	15
Pref. Stock	12	100 mm	75	1,500,000	—
Com. Stock	—	250 mm	50	7,000,000	—
Ret. Earn.	—	500 mm	—		—

*mm = million.

Assume that the expected dividend on common stock is $8 per share and the perpetual growth rate is 4%. Assume that coupon payments are paid once a year.

Solution to Problem Set

(1) Find the cash flows. The table below summarizes the cash flows for each period. The first row of the table below is simply our cash flow formula. Since the initial investment is $10,000,000, the cash flow at time 0, CF_0 is $-$10$ million. Note that although the problem stated that in year 1, the expense is $7 million, our solution reduces cost amount by $1.5 million. The reason for that is that costs of our formula should not include depreciation expense of $1 million and there is $.5 million sunk costs. The latter requires a little more explanation. Note the problem allocated $500,000 in maintenance expense for the project, but stated that this maintenance expense will be there regardless of whether or not the firm took the project. Hence, this maintenance expense is not incremental. Accordingly, the costs for years 1–10 is $1.5 million less than what is recorded in the problem. The working capital for the firm at time 1 equals to cash+A/R +Inventory − A/P. This equals $1 million. Taxes are computed as 0.48*(Sales − Costs − Depreciation expense) or 0.48*($10 mm − $5.5 mm − $1 mm) = $1.68 mm. Note that the cash flow at time 2 is the same as the cash flow of time 1, except for there is no change in working capital. According to the problem, the working capital remains at $1 million in each year for years 1–5. Hence, the

CF	=	Sales	− Costs	− Chg. Working Capital	− Long Term Investment	− Taxes	=	Sum
CF_0	=				($10,000,000)			
CF_1	=	$10,000,000	($5,500,000.00)	($1,000,000)	−0	($1,680,000)	=	$1,820,000
CF_{2-5}	=	$10,000,000	($5,500,000.00)	0	−0	($1,680,000)	=	$2,820,000
CF_6	=	$8,000,000	($4,500,000)	($1,300,000)	−0	($1,200,000)	=	$1,000,000
CF_{7-10}	=	$8,000,000	($4,500,000)	0	−0	($1,200,000)	=	$2,300,000
CF_{11}	=	0	($1,500,000)	$2,300,000	−0	$720,000	=	$1,520,000

change only occurs at time 1. CF_{2-5} is the cash flow per year for years 2–5. At time $= 6$, we see investment in current assets and liabilities has changed. In particular, the working capital is now equal to $2.3 million. Thus, at time 6 working capital increases by $1.3 million. This is working capital until time 10. Thus, there is no change in working capital for years 7–10. Finally, note that at year 11, the solution reduces costs by only $500,000, the allotted maintenance expense. There is no depreciation expense at time 11. Working capital goes to zero, so the change in working capital is now $-$2.3 million resulting in a positive cash flow of that amount. Finally, the taxes equal $-0.48(-$1.5$ million) resulting in a rebate of $720,000.

	Market Value (mm)	Proportions	Costs	Contributing Costs (%)
Senior Debt	$10	0.019	3.64%	0.069
Junior Debt	40.8	0.079	4.55%	0.360
Preferred Stock	112.5	0.219	10.67%	2.337
Common Stock	350	0.683	20.00%	13.660
	$513.3			16.43

The next step is to find the ATWACOC. The calculations are summarized in the table above. The second column is obtained by taking the product of the price per unit and the number of units outstanding. The third column is obtained by taking the market value of a security class by the total value of the firm, which equals $513.3 million.

The fourth column represents the after-tax cost of capital for each security class. Senior debt is priced at par; hence, the before-tax yield is 7%. Multiplying 7% by $(1 - $ Tax Rate$)$ or (0.52) 7%, which equals 3.64%. Junior debt is not priced at par. Using the financial calculator, one can obtain a before tax yield of 8.76%. See below!

N	i	PV	PMT	FV
15	? 8.76%	−1,020	90	1,000

Multiplying the before tax rate (8.76%) by (1 − Tax Rate) yields an after tax cost of debt of 4.55%.

The cost of preferred stock is obtained by noting that the par value of Preferred Stock is the total book value of preferred stock divided by the number of units outstanding. That is, $100 mm/1.5 mm = $66.67. The coupon rate is 12%. The preferred stock dividend is (0.12)*$66.67 or $8. Using the dividend growth model, the cost of preferred stock is simply the ratio of the dividend and price yield a cost of preferred stock of 10.67%. Finally, we can use the dividend growth model to find the cost of common stock. That is Div/Price + G or $8/$50 + 0.04, which equals 20%. The last column is found by taking the product of the cost of capital with the proportions. Summing up the contributing costs, yield an ATWACOC of 16.43%. Since this project is slightly more risky than the usual project, then we need a discount rate greater than 16.43%. We will use 16.75% as the discount rate.

We find the NPV using excel. The figure below depicts an Excel Sheet

	A	B
1	time	Cash Flow
2	0	−$10,000,000
3	1	$1,820,000
4	2	$2,820,000

(*Continued*)

(Continued)

	A	B
5	3	$2,820,000
6	4	$2,820,000
7	5	$2,820,000
8	6	$1,000,000
9	7	$2,300,000
10	8	$2,300,000
11	9	$2,300,000
12	10	$2,300,000
13	11	$1,520,000
14	NPV	$1,393,051

Cell B14 is found using the excel function =NPV(0.1675,B3: B13) + B2. Since NPV > 0, we should accept the project.

CHAPTER 6

THE FINANCING DECISION

What is the Financing Decision?

Firms must often raise capital to finance their capital budgeting decisions. For example, the firm's management wants to buy a building with a $23 million price tag for office use. Where does the firm get the money to purchase the building? If the firm has sufficient profits, it can use that money to pay for the building, but remember, the profits do not belong to the firm's management. The profit belongs to the owners of the firm, the stockholders. Thus, using the profits of the firm is equivalent to using equity financing. If the firm does not have sufficient earnings, it will have to raise money externally. Should the firm borrow money from a bank? How about issuing public debt and using the proceeds to pay for the building? Or perhaps the firm should issue new common stock and use the proceeds from the sale of that stock to pay for the building! This is a brief description and introduction to the financing decision.

In reality, the financing decision is even more complicated than what is described above. For example, if the firm decides it should borrow, then it must decide the maturity of the loan. This is no different for a new homeowner who must decide whether to take out a 15-year mortgage or a 30-year mortgage on his prime residence. The firm has many more options than a typical consumer. For example, firms can borrow from foreign banks whereby the loans are denominated in a foreign currency. There are loans that have an equity kicker, where under certain circumstances the lender can convert the bond into an equity position.

We cannot even begin answering the more complicated issues of financing unless we understand the basics as to whether it makes a difference to borrow money, use internal profits or issue new common stock. To understand what factors determine the optimal financing decision, we will begin by calculating again the After-tax Weighted Average Cost of Capital (ATWACOC) of a fictitious firm first introduced in the Capital Budgeting chapter. Consider again the following information:

	Book Value	Price Per Share	Units Outstanding	Coupon Rate
Long-Term Debt	$50 mm	$1,000	50,000	10%
Common Stock	100 mm	$40	3.75 mm	—
Retained Earnings	75 mm	—	—	—

Assume that the maturity of the debt is 10 years. Further assume that T, the tax rate, is 45%, and that the firm is expected to pay a $4.40 dividend per share beginning next year. The dividend is expected to grow at 10% per year. We then produced a table that we used as a template to calculate the ATWACOC. Let us reproduce that template below:

Security Class	Market Value (mm)	Proportion	Cost of Capital (%)	Contributing Costs (%)
Debt	$50	0.25	10 (0.55)	1.375
Equity	$150	0.75	21	15.75
Total	$200	1		17.125

As reproduced, the ATWACOC of our firm is 17.125%. Why begin here? Good question, chap! Recall that in our Capital Budgeting Decision chapter, you were hired to evaluate Carob Inc. We essentially used a capital budgeting procedure to calculate the value of the firm. We estimated the future cash flows and discounted these cash flows by the ATWACOC. We made the problem simple by assuming that the cash flows would grow at a constant rate. Thus, we found that the value of the firm's assets by using the following formula:

$$V = CF/(ATWACOC - G). \qquad (6.1)$$

Remember, for capital budgeting purposes, our cash flow definition does not include any debt payments. So if we were to change the capital structure mix by having more or less debt financing, CF would not change. Since G is tied to CF, G also does not change. The only possibility left is that if we change the financing mix, then ATWACOC could change. With this background, please answer the following question.

What would happen to the ATWACOC if the firm chose a debt-equity ratio of 1, where now 50% of the financing is done with debt and 50% done with equity? It would be wrong to just change the weights and simply do a recalculation without changing the cost of equity since as leverage increases so will the cost of equity. The reason for this is that leverage increases the volatility of earnings to stockholders. As you increase the volatility or risk of the earnings to stockholders, you would expect the required rate of return to stockholders should also increase. By just changing the weights, you are only getting part of the picture because the cost of equity should be greater than 21%!

Please do not be so impatient and ask how much greater will the cost of equity increase as leverage changes as we will get to that later in this chapter. But first how do we know that earnings volatility increases with leverage? Consider two firms are identical in every way except that one firm has used debt financing for its operations and the other firm has not. Table 6.1 summarizes the income statement of Firm A with three different sales assumptions. Let the last

Table 6.1

	Firm A		
Sales	$900,000	$1,000,000	$1,100,000
− Costs			
Fixed	$100,000	$100,000	$100,000
Variable	$540,000	$600,000	660,000
EBIT	$260,000	$300,000	$340,000
− Interest Expense	0	0	0
EBT	$260,000	$300,000	$340,000
− TAX	$104,000	$120,000	$136,000
Net Income	$156,000	$180,000	$204,000

Table 6.2

	Firm B		
Sales	$900,000	$1,000,000	$1,100,000
− Costs			
Fixed	$100,000	$100,000	$100,000
Variable	$540,000	$600,000	660,000
EBIT	$260,000	$300,000	$340,000
− Interest Expense	$100,000	$100,000	$100,000
EBT	$160,000	$200,000	$240,000
− TAX	$64,000	$80,000	$96,000
Net Income	$96,000	$120,000	$144,000

year's sales of Firm A equal $1 million. This year, we are expecting either an increase or decrease in sales of 10%. Firm A has fixed costs of $100,000. Variable costs are 60% of Sales. Finally, let the tax rate be equal to 40%. Accordingly, if sales increase or decrease by 10%, net income to shareholders will increase or decrease by 13.333%.

Now consider Firm B which is identical in every way to Firm A except that this firm is carrying $100,000 interest expense. The calculations for its net income under varying sales assumptions are given below. Note that in this case, if sales increase or decrease by 10%, net income to shareholders will increase or decrease by 20%.

Note, that financial leverage increases the volatility of earnings which in turn should increase the required rate of return to stockholders.

OK! If financial leverage increases the volatility of stock, then why should a firm ever borrow? We are going to get more theoretical in a moment. However, a simple answer is that by borrowing, the amount of equity capital required decreases. In other words, shareholders might be willing to take on more risk if they can invest less. Having said that, we now want to turn to the important question of whether and how debt financing impacts upon the value of the firm. Based upon Equation (6.1), we know that the optimal financing mix of debt and equity is the one that minimizes the ATWACOC since both the expected unlevered cash flow and its associated growth rate do not change.

Operating versus Financial Leverage

Before we proceed with theory, we should first understand how leverage affects profits. **Leverage** increases the sensitivity of profits to change in sales due to the firm's fixed costs. There are two types of leverage. **Operating Leverage** measures the change of earnings before interest and taxes (EBIT) as a response to changes in sales. With no fixed operating costs, there is no operating leverage. This means that we will find when there are no fixed operating costs, a percentage change in sales results in an equal percentage change in EBIT. The formula to determine the *degree of operating leverage* (*DOL*) is given by:

$$DOL = \% \text{ change in EBIT}/\% \text{ change in Q(unit sales)}$$
$$(Sales - Variable\ Costs)/(Sales - Variable\ Costs - Fixed\ Costs).$$
$$(6.2)$$

Example 1: Firm A has no fixed costs. Note that when the firm has no fixed costs, DOL = 1. Costs are 60% of Sales. Assume that last year, sales of Firm A were $20 million. If sales are expected to increase by 10%, then EBIT will increase by 10%. To see this consider the following table. The second column presents the calculation of EBIT when the original Sales figure is $20,000,000. The third column summarizes the calculation of EBIT when Sales increases by 10% to $22 million.

Sales	$20,000,000	$22,000,000
− Variable Costs	−$12,000,000	−$13,200,000
− Fixed Costs		
= EBIT	$8,000,000	$8,800,000

It can also be shown that the percentage change of EBIT is directly related to DOL as given by the following formula:

NOTE THAT Δ%EBIT = DOL(%ΔSALES).   (6.3)

In the above example, since DOL = 1, then Δ%EBIT = DOL (Δ%SALES) = 1(10%), which equals 10%. However, with fixed operating costs, the degree of Operating Leverage is greater than one. As a result a percentage change in sales results in a greater percentage change in EBIT. Moreover, the more fixed costs the greater the magnification.

Example 2: Firm B has fixed costs of $6,000,000. Variable costs are 60% of Sales. Assume that last year, the sales of Firm B were $20 million again. Using Equation (6.2), the DOL is given by ($20 mm − $12 mm)/ ($20 mm − $12 mm − $6 mm) which equals to 4. Again assume that sales are expected to increase by 10%. According to our formula, Δ%EBIT = DOL (Δ%SALES). Accordingly, the percentage increase in EBIT is 4(10%) implying that EBIT is expected to increase by 40%. We can verify the calculation based upon the table below.

Sales	$20,000,000	$22,000,000
− Variable Costs	−$12,000,000	−$13,200,000
− Fixed Costs	−$6,000,000	−$6,000,000
= EBIT	$2,000,000	$2,800,000

Financial Leverage measures the percentage change to earnings per share (EPS) in response to changes in EBIT. As with Operating Leverage, if there are no fixed financing costs, (i.e., interest expense) then there is no financial leverage. In this case, a percentage change in EBIT results in an equal percentage change in EPS.

Example 3: Consider Firm B of Example 2. Assume that Firm B has 1 million shares of equity outstanding and no debt. Assume a tax rate of 50%. In which case, with sales of $20 million, earnings before taxes (EBT) are the same as EBIT or $2 million. After taxes, the net income is $1 million, implying an EPS of $1. If sales increase by 10%, then EBIT increases by 40%. Note that EBT will also increase by 40% to $1.4 million. EPS will also increase by 40% or to $1.40.

However, with fixed financing cost, there is financial leverage. As a result a percentage change in EBIT results in a greater percentage change in EPS. That is, *the more fixed financing costs the greater the magnification.*

Example 4: Consider, once again, Firm B. Assume now that Firm B has an annual interest expense of $200,000. In this case, with sales of $20 million, EBT will equal $1.8 million. With a 50% tax rate, the net income is $900,000. Assuming 1 million shares of equity outstanding, EPS is $0.90. Now consider the same calculations with an increase in sales of 10%. The calculations are summarized in the following table. Note that EPS increased by 44%.

Sales	$20,000,000	$22,000,000
− Variable Costs	−$12,000,000	−$13,200,000
− Fixed Costs	−$6,000,000	−$6,000,000
= EBIT	$2,000,000	$2,800,000
− Interest Expense	−$200,000	−$200,000
= EBT	$1,800,000	$2,600,000
− Taxes @ 50%	$900,000	$1,300,000
= Net Income	$900,000	$1,300,000
EPS	$.90	$1.30

The above examples can be generalized by the following formulas:

$$DFL = \% \text{ change in EPS}/\% \text{ change in EBIT}$$
$$= EBIT/ (EBIT - Interest) \qquad (6.4)$$

and

$$\Delta\%EARNINGS = DFL(\Delta\%EBIT). \qquad (6.5)$$

The DFL of Firm B with interest expense of $200,000 is given by:

$$EBIT/(EBIT - Interest) = \$2 \text{ million}/(\$2 \text{ million} - \$200,000)$$
$$= 1.1111.$$

Recall that for a 10% increase in sales, EBIT jumped by 40%. We can demonstrate that EPS will increase by 44.44% if the interest expense is $200,000 using the formula:

$$\Delta\%EARNINGS = DFL(\Delta\%EBIT) = 1.1111^*(0.4) = 0.4444.$$

Finally, the total risk can be measured by the degree of total leverage (DTL) or:

$$DTL = \% \text{change in EPS}/\% \text{ change in Q} = DFL * DOL \quad (6.6)$$

and

$$\Delta\%EARNINGS = DTL(\Delta\%SALES). \qquad (6.7)$$

Example 5: Consider Firm B of Examples 3 and 4. Recall that DOL = 4 and DFL = 1.1111. The product of the two yields a DTL = 4.4444. This implies that a 10% increase in sales, increases EPS by DTL ($\Delta\%SALES$) = (4.4444)*(0.1) = 0.4444.

Question: What Happens to EPS as Leverage Changes?

Consider a firm that has sales of $20 million. Operating fixed costs are $6 million and variable costs are 60% of sales. Assume that there are 10 million shares of common stock outstanding and the current stock price is $10 per share. Currently the firm has no debt outstanding and the corporate tax rate is 40%. What is the EPS? We know that

EPS = NET INCOME/ # SHARES. Accordingly,

= [SALES − VAR. COSTS − FIXED COSTS]$(1 − T)$/# SHARES

= [20 mm − 12 mm − 6 mm](0.6)/10 mm = \$0.12 (per share).

Assume now that the firm raises \$5 million in debt and buys back 500,000 shares. Assume that the coupon rate of the debt is 6%. What is the new EPS?

$$EPS = \{[SALES − VAR.\ COSTS − FIXED\ COSTS$$
$$− INT.\ EXPENSE](1 − T)\}/\#\ SHARES$$

or

$$= (20\ mm − 12\ mm − 6\ mm − 0.3\ mm)0.6/9.5\ mm = \$0.107.$$

Now let us determine the breakeven sales for the two financial scenarios (i.e., so that both financial schemes will have identical EPS). We solve for Sales in the following equation.

$$\frac{(SALES − 0.6\ SALES − 6\ mm)0.6}{10\ mm}$$
$$= \frac{(SALES − 0.6\ SALES − 6\ mm − 0.3\ mm)0.6}{9.5\ mm}.$$

SALES = \$30 million. That is, if Sales are greater than \$30 million, then the leveraged firm will have the higher EPS. Otherwise the firm without debt will have the higher EPS. This does not mean that if the firm has reasonable expectations that sales will be greater than \$30 million, then it is optimal to have debt and that otherwise, we are better off without debt. The above analysis ignores both the tax benefit of debt and the cost of bankruptcy. However, it is a useful tool to assess the impact of leverage upon earnings.

What Are the Factors that Determine the Optimal Financing Mix?

We would expect that since common stock holders are paid only after the debt holders are completely satisfied, that common stock holders bear more risk than do the debt holders. Certainly, the required rate of return demanded by stockholders should reflect that extra risk and consequently, the required rate of return demanded by shareholders should be greater than that of bondholders. Not only that, but if markets efficiently price all securities, we would expect a definitive relationship between the required rate of return of the debt and equity securities issued by a firm. This means that as the firm borrows more, the cost of equity should increase in an exact fashion that reflects the extra financial risk borne by the stockholders.

In 1958, Modigliani and Miller published an important paper that made a very controversial point in the *American Economic Review*. To understand their point, consider the claims that the stockholders and debt holders have on the firm. Essentially, they have dibs on the firm's profits. The profits are shared among the two set of claimants. Now, if the financing mix does not affect the level of profits then the financing decision becomes irrelevant. On the other hand, if it affects the level of profits, there should be an optimal financing mix.

In their 1958 paper, Modigliani and Miller made two very strange assumptions. They assumed no taxes and no risk of default. OK, STOP ROLLING YOUR EYES AND SAYING TO YOURSELF "*THAT IS STUPID!*" Please go with the flow for a little while longer. You will see that there are some benefits in making such weird assumptions. Moreover, both Modigliani and Miller received Nobel prizes in Economics for this work, so it must have some merit.

Consider the following example. Firm XYZ has an expected EBIT of $1 million. In a world of no taxes, interest expense does not affect how much money the firm can distribute to its claimants. If firm XYZ owes $250,000 in interest, and assuming no principal payment is due, then XYZ will distribute $250,000 to its lenders and $750,000 in dividends to its stockholders. The amount of money it can distribute is still $1 million. Let us call the firm XYZ with debt outstanding Leveraged XYZ. Should XYZ have no debt obligations, (aka Unleveraged XYZ) then it can distribute the entire $1 million to shareholders in the form of dividend payments. Again, the total distribution is still $1 million. Since the expected distributions are the same under both scenarios, the total market value of the Leveraged XYZ securities must be identical to the value of the equity of Unleveraged XYZ. Note that the financing decision does not affect

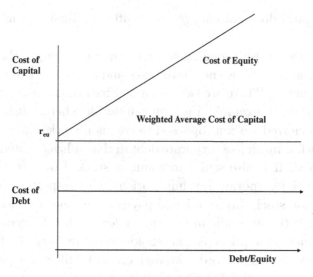

Figure 6.1

firm value. This implies that the cost of equity will increase as leverage increases at a rate which would keep the weighted average cost of capital unchanged. This concept is illustrated above.

In Figure 6.1, the X–axis represents the debt-equity ratio. The further to the right you go, the greater the leverage of the firm is. The Y-axis represents the cost of capital. Note the bottom line, whose intercept is labeled Cost of Debt. The figure tells us that the cost of debt does not change as we take on more debt. This is so only because Modigliani and Miller assume no risk of default. Now please note the two lines that intersect at r_{eu}. The intersection represents the cost of equity of an unlevered firm. The line with zero slope is the after-tax weighted average cost of capital and the line that is sloped represents the values of the cost of equity of a levered firm as the firm increases leverage. The figure is simply summarizing Modigliani and Miller's finding that the value of the firm is independent of the firm's financing decision because the financing mix does not affect the total amount of money that can be distributed among the various claimants of the firm. If this is correct, then the cost of equity increases at such a pace so that the overall after tax weighted average cost of capital does not change as we alter the financing mix of the firm.

OK, why are we spending so much time on a paper that is not possibly relevant. Do we not have taxes and do we not know of spectacular defaults? There are two answers. First, their assumptions are not so weird. For example, the firm can decide whether it is optimal to issue preferred stock as opposed to common stock. Note that preferred stock is much like corporate debt in that it has a stated coupon that is fixed. It is also senior to common stock. However, there are no differential corporate tax implications with respect to preferred and common stock. Both dividend payments are not tax deductible. Moreover, if the firm fails to pay the preferred stockholders its dividend payment, the preferred shareholders cannot force the firm into bankruptcy. In other words, Modigliani and Miller are predicting that there is no optimal equity mix!!!!

Second, by understanding the classical example, we can identify the two important economic forces that can affect the financing mix: taxes and the risk of default. Let us begin with taxes.

In 1963, Modigliani and Miller published a correction to their paper and incorporate the reasonable assumption that interest expenses are tax deductible. (AUTHOR'S SIDE NOTE: IF WE REGULAR ACADEMICIANS MAKE A MISTAKE IN OUR PAPERS, WE DO NOT GET TENURE OR PROMOTED. MODIGLIANI AND MILLER EACH GET NOBEL PRIZES IN ECONOMICS. GO FIGURE!)

Consider the following situation. You are about to start your own business and you need $100,000 capital. You can lend yourself the money at 10% interest rate and call yourself the bondholder entrepreneur. Or you can invest in the company and call yourself the shareholder entrepreneur. Assume that the return on assets before taxes is 10%. Therefore, you expect that your EBIT will be $10,000. Let the tax rate equal 40%. Should you lend yourself the money, your EBIT is $10,000 but your earnings before taxes is zero. Uncle Sam gets nothing from you and you take home $10,000. But if you are the shareholder entrepreneur, your EBIT and earnings before taxes are $10,000. Uncle Sam takes $4,000 and you get to take home $6,000.

Which do you think is the best financial strategy? Clearly borrowing money is the better choice.

Now before you do this at home, note that the IRS is familiar with Modigliani and Miller and they do not consider lending yourself money as true debt deserving of interest expense tax deductibility, but the point is that by borrowing the capital, the firm can promise more money to its claimants. And the more debt you borrow, the greater is the cash flow. Hence, Modigliani and Miller conclude that the optimal financing mix is all debt. We can now redraw Figure 6.1. Since the stockholders received the tax benefits of debt (i.e., a tax liability reduction), the cost of equity of the levered firm will not increase as fast as depicted in Figure 6.1. Hence, the after-tax weighted average cost of capital will decrease as leverage increases. Also see Figure 6.2 on page 187.

Now we know that firms do not just borrow money to finance their operations. Clearly they use internal sources (profits or retained earnings) and issue new common stock from time to time. Hence, if taxes are a positive force to increase debt, what is the countervailing force? We will now relax the assumption of no risk of default.

There are three types of costs that a firm incurs when it cannot meet its debt obligations. The first type is the *Direct Costs of Bankruptcy*. These costs are the legal and administrative cost incurred during bankruptcy. They also include the loss of interest tax shelters and the liquidation costs when the firm goes bankrupt.

What are liquidation costs? Imagine a bank recognizes that one of its clients will never earn enough money to pay off a $100,000 loan. The loan was collateralized by three printing presses located on the 26th floor of a building located in downtown New York City. Although a new printing press costs $40,000 each, and even though the client's three printing presses are relatively new, there is no way that the bank can seize those assets and sell them for anywhere near the $100,000 obligation. Why? Have you ever seen these giant printing presses? Let us say the bank finds a buyer who happens to be on the third floor of a building located in the Midwood section of Brooklyn. How do you get those printing presses over there? You cannot take the printing presses out of the window nor through the door. No, you are going to have to disassemble the printing presses, bring down the pieces via the freight elevator, load them on the truck, bring them to the location in Brooklyn and reverse the process. By that time, it would cost $70,000 to make the transfer. Consequently, the $120,000 printing press is only worth $50,000. In fact, the bank might be better off settling for a little over 50 cents on the dollar than going through all this.

The problem is that legal and liquidation costs may equal a large percentage of the assets of a small enterprise. But these expenses are generally a much smaller percentage of the assets of large publicly held firms. In which case, the direct costs of bankruptcy will not be a sufficient countervailing force against the corporate tax advantage of debt. However, there is a second type of bankruptcy costs, namely the *Indirect Cost of Bankruptcy*. These are costs associated with the disruption of normal business relationships during bankruptcy proceedings. After passing this course, you decide to go on a vacation to Tahiti and there are several airlines that you are considering using. However, just before you pick Tahiti Express, you read in the *Wall Street Journal* that the company is having financial difficulties and may file for bankruptcy. Chances are, even at a 20% discount, you would choose another airline since you are not sure the company will be still there when you are ready to fly. Note, that the company lost business simply because of bad financial press. These costs can be huge especially for manufacturers of durable goods since their warranties become suspect.

The third type of bankruptcy costs are known as *Agency Costs*. These costs arise from a conflict of interest between stockholders and bondholders. Think about this ridiculous example. You owe $100,000 to a disreputable lender. He tells you, if you do not pay by tomorrow, both kneecaps will be shot. You only have $10,000 to give him. Do you wait until the next day and give him $10,000 and beg for mercy? Or do you go to Las Vegas and play roulette and hope for the best? Most people will consider doing the latter and this is also true for firms as well. Back in the early 1980s, the Savings and Loan industry of Texas was in serious trouble. The banks overextended themselves by lending at fixed rates to homeowners in the previous decade. At that time interest rates were fairly low, around 6–8%. These banks financed these loans through demand deposits which promised very low interest rates. But by the 1980s, interest rates were high and the banks were borrowing at a higher rate than the return they were getting from older loans. In essence, their net interest margin was negative. The Texas banks began advertising higher than industry average certificate of deposit (CD) rates to attract liquidity. People were willing to invest in these CDs since they were insured by FSLIC and Federal Deposit Insurance Corporation (FDIC). But, now the banks were borrowing money from these investors at rates higher than the current mortgage rate. To make money they had to take greater risks. With this example we can see how leverage increases the appetite of corporate management to take on more risk because limited liability reduces their loss exposure and the higher upside potential that goes with the risk might bail them out of any trouble.

Now how do agency costs affect the profitability of firms. Lenders fully understand the risk incentive of leverage. As the firm borrows more, the lenders assume the worst of the borrower and begin charging an interest rate not appropriate for the current risk level of the firm but the potential risk appetite of the firm. This increases interest expense and further reduces the profitability of the firm. Ultimately, it is the stockholders who bear the agency costs.

The point is that there exists an interior optimal capital structure. In essence, there is a tradeoff between the tax benefit of debt and the costs of financial distress. Can we model this so you can actually come up with the optimal debt-equity ratio? Of course we can! But only if you are willing to make some assumptions such as the probability distribution of cash flows of the firm over the next umpteen years or what the interest rates will be during this period. In addition, we have to make assumptions as to how much the debt holders and bankers will be able to collect if the firm does go bankrupt. Academicians do this all the time! OK, so you are not an academician. What should you do instead?

First, the CFO should know how his firm's financial decision compares to that of the firm's competitors. Hopefully, you learned about financial ratios in the in an accounting course. The purpose of financial ratios is to allow the investigator to determine the strengths and weaknesses of the firm vis a vis its competitors. If the firm's financial ratios are different from those of its competitors, then the question must be asked as to why. If the deviation from the industry norm can be explained, then it is not a problem, but if not, then the firm must conform to the industry average. There are several relevant financial ratios: times interest earned, fixed coverage ratio, and debt-equity ratio.

Once you compute these ratios for your firm and your competitors', then you must be able explain the deviation. Here are some questions:

(a) **Does your firm have a different tax rate than your competitors?** Remember that the deductibility of interest becomes more important the higher is the tax rate. If your tax rate is higher, then that fact might explain why your firm has a higher degree of leverage. If not, perhaps you need to reduce your leverage exposure.

(b) **Is the operating or business risk of the firm different from the competitors?** If the firm has a greater level of operating fixed costs than its competitors, then the firm must have more sales to break even than its competitors. If you have insufficient sales, you may not have enough money to pay even the interest expense. Your firm is riskier and therefore should carry less debt on its balance sheet. If you have less fixed costs, then your firm might be able to carry more debt than its competitors. In other words, the greater is the DOL, the less financial leverage (DFL) should be employed to finance operations.

(c) **How dependent is your future profitability upon continuing the planned investment strategy?** The more dependent the firm is upon discretionary investment, investment activity that can easily be altered, the more risky the firm's future profits are for bondholders. When a firm becomes financially strapped, it can easily cut down its R&D or maintenance program. Doing that hurts the future profitability of the firm and value of existing assets that may have been used for collateral.

If so, the firm should reduce its level of debt compared to its competitors.

There are other qualitative factors that affect the financing decision of the firm. One factor is the managerial ownership of the firm. Assume you own 45% of the outstanding equity. You need to raise additional money for a project. If you issue new equity, your ownership stake falls to 32% of the firm while if you issue debt, your stake remains at 45%. Your sister owns another 6% of the firm so that if you issue equity, family ownership falls below 50% and your firm can be taken over by the dreaded corporate raider. But if you issue debt, then the firm is safely in your hands. Just remember your sister's birthday that will take place one week from now!

But there is a cost to this decision to issue debt to avoid loss of control. Most likely, you do not have a diversified portfolio and as the firm takes on more leverage, your personal exposure to risk becomes greater. The lack of diversification becomes especially important for managers who do not own a great stake in the firm and if the firm does poorly, that manager can be scapegoated and can be thrown out easily. Remember, most of the manager's wealth is tied to the firm he is running since a big part of his wealth is based upon the compensation he receives and/or will receive.

Or, you could change the equity structure of the firm, where you own all of the class B stock which has more voting rights than the class A common stock. You could confer with the Schulzberger family that controls the New York Times that has done just that. Such strategy hurts the value of the stock since managers who control the firm via class B stock are totally inured from market control forces which generally force management to value maximize the stock.

Another important factor is the confidence of the management. The more confident the management is about the firm's future the more likely it will prefer the use of debt over new equity. Why? Remember in the beginning of the chapter when we found that for an equal percentage increase in sales will result in a greater percentage increase or earnings per share for a levered firm than for an unlevered firm. The more confident is the management the more it will discount the possibility of a sales decrease. So for the confident management, the downside risk of leverage becomes less important.

The stock market fully understands this motivation. A manager who relies on new equity is basically admitting that he or she has no confidence in the firm's future. The market understands that and will therefore punish the stock as the market's expectations of the firm's potential decreases. In fact, the market may even take a dim view of firms issuing equity since this may signal that the earnings were not as high as was expected. This observation explains a common practice by corporate management. The firm uses retained earnings first to finance its operations. If the firm does not have enough earnings (remember, the firm is very reluctant to cut back its dividends), it will then use debt. Once it uses up its debt capacity, then and only then will the firm issue new equity. Another observation is that when the firm does issue new equity, the stock price drops. In fact, the stock falls so much that on average the loss of the equity value is approximately one-third of the total proceeds of the new equity issue. What has been just described is known as the *Pecking Order Theory of Finance.*

Let us sum up! Management should first use financial ratios to get a picture of the financial health of the firm. If the firm's leverage is significantly different from that of its competitors, it must have a good explanation. Is it more risky? And if so, what should the firm do about it! Does it have more leverage because the firm's management wants to retain control of the firm? If so, what mechanisms does the management have in place to ensure stock value maximization! And you thought finance was only about numbers. Finance has strategic implications as well.

Cost of Capital and Leverage

Figure 6.2 suggests that leverage impacts the cost of capital. Modigliani and Miller (1963) derive the relationship between cost of capital and leverage in the absence of default risk. Why should we care? After all, that is not a good assumption. However, one can use this relationship (a) to understand how leverage can benefit

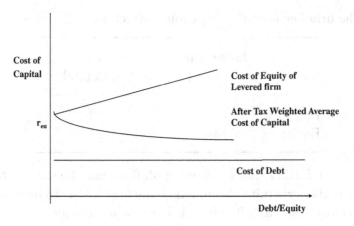

Figure 6.2

shareholders and (b) to determine the maximum benefit of taking on more debt. We will also talk about how to calculate the new cost of capital when you allow for default risk. But let us do one step at a time. According to Modigliani and Miller, the relationship between leverage and the after-tax weighted average cost of capital, ATWACOC, is given by:

$$ATWACOC = R_{EU}(1 - TL), \qquad (6.8)$$

where R_{EU} is the cost of equity of an unlevered firm, T is the corporate tax rate and L is the leverage ratio defined as the ratio of the market value of debt to total value of the firm. The relationship between the cost of equity and leverage is given by:

$$R_{EL} = R_{EU} + (1 - T)(R_{EU} - R)D/S, \qquad (6.9)$$

where

R_{EL} = cost of equity of levered firm;

R_{EU} = cost of equity to unlevered firm;

R = pre-tax cost of debt;

D = Market value of debt;

S = Market value of equity.

An example: Assume that firm XYZ has a debt/equity ratio of 1/3.

The firm has the following capital structure

Security	Market Value (million)	Coupon Rate or Cost of Capital (%)
Debt	$100	12
Equity	$300	24

Assume further that the firm's cash flows may be represented as a (constant) perpetuity. Assume that the firm wishes to increase the debt/equity ratio to 1.0, which is equivalent to assuming that the new leverage ratio is 0.5. Determine, assuming a corporate tax rate of 34%:

(A) The new ATWACOC.
(B) The New R_{EL}.
(C) The New Value of the Firm.
(D) The New Level of Debt and Equity.

Solution:

(A) *Step* 1: First, find the current ATWACOC. Note that debt currently represents 25% of the firm and equity is 75% of the firm. Thus, the current ATWACOC is given by:

$$ATWACOC = (1/4)(0.66)(12\%) + (3/4)(24\%) = 19.98\%.$$

Step 2: Second, using the equation (6.8), find R_{EU}. Note that L is equal to 25%.

$$R_{EU} = ATWACOC/(1 - TL)$$
$$= 19.98\%/(1 - 0.34(0.25))$$
$$= 21.84\%.$$

Note that the cost of equity of the unlevered firm is 21.84%. This number is less than the current cost of equity. This makes sense since the cost of equity of the unlevered firm represents the cost of capital of a firm that has no debt and we know that as leverage increases, the risk to stock holders increase and so does the cost of equity.

Step 3: Find the new ATWACOC based upon R_{EU} of 21.84% and the new leverage ratio of 0.5. That is, re-using Equation (6.8) and substituting for our values of R_{EU} and L, the new ATWACOC is:

$$ATWACOC = R_{EU}(1 - TL)$$
$$= 21.84(1 - (0.34)(0.5)) = 18.12\%.$$

Note that the new ATWACOC is lower than what it is currently. Why is that? The reason for this is that according to Modigliani and Miller, there are no bankruptcy costs. If so, the firm should have 100% debt, since as leverage increases, the ATWACOC should decrease. Modigliani and Miller also assume that the cost of debt does not change as leverage increases. How do we know that? Well let us first continue with the problem and then we will deal with this question.

(B) Using Equation (6.9), we can find the new cost of equity. Note that if the new leverage ratio is 0.5, then D/S = 1.

$$R_{EL} = R_{EU} + (1 - T)(R_{EU} - R)D/S$$
$$= 21.84\% + (0.66)(21.84\% - 12\%)1$$
$$= 28.33\%.$$

Note, this could have been obtained using the definition of the ATWACOC. That is:

$$ATWACOC = LR(1 - T) + (1 - LR_{EL}),$$
$$18.12\% = 0.66(12\%)(0.5) + 0.5R_{EL}.$$

Solving for R_{EL}

$$R_{EL} = (18.12\%) - (0.66)(12\%)(0.5))/0.5$$
$$= 28.32\%.$$

(Difference is due to rounding error.) Note, we obtain identical answers for the cost of equity only because we (these models) are assuming no change in the risk of default and therefore no change in the cost of debt. We will discuss below what to do if there is a change in the risk of default.

(C) To find the new value of the firm, we must determine the level of the unlevered cash flows. Recall, the value of the firm (refer to Equation (6.1) of this chapter) is the present value of the unlevered cash

flows discounted by the ATWACOC. Recall that the current value
of the firm (before the change in leverage from 25% to 50%) is $400
million. The problem also assumes that the cash flows are perpetual
with no growth. Hence, using Equation (6.1) with g = 0, we have:

$$V = CF_U/ATWACOC,$$
$$400 = CF_u/0.1998,$$
$$CF_U = \$79.92 \text{ million}.$$

Now the new value of the firm is the discounted value of $79.92
million per year in perpetuity but now we use the new ATWACOC
of 18.12%.

$$V_{new} = 79.92/0.1812 = \$441.06 \text{ million}.$$

Hence, the firm's value has gone up by $41.06 million. Note that this
represents the maximum increase, since we have not accounted for
any change in the risk of default.

(D) The new level of debt is $220.5 million and the new level of
equity is $220.5 million. Let us go back to the videotape. Note that
originally, the value of the debt was $100 million and the value of
equity was $300 million. Hence, if debt increased to $220.5 million,
the firm raised $120.5 million in debt and bought back $120.5 million
of equity. If so, then the new level of equity should be approximately
$179.5 million. Yet, we see that the new value of equity is $220.5
million, meaning that the entire increase of $41 million in the value
of the firm accrues to the stockholders.

Now consider the following two scenarios. The first scenario
involves a CEO who owns 30% of the firm and his loyal wife owns
another 10%. All of his money and wealth is essentially tied to the
firm. He wants to buy back stock to ensure that no one can take over
the firm. If he borrows like suggested above, his firm will be over-
leveraged compared to his rivals, but if he finances with equity, he no
longer has assurance that someone cannot buy enough of the remaining equity to force him out. Chances are, he will elect to use more debt
to buy back stock, because he and his wife can gain 0.4(41) = $16.4
million, more than enough to compensate for the extra risk under-
taken. Now, consider the second scenario: a CEO who owns only 2%

of the outstanding shares. She knows that increasing the leverage will increase the risk of the firm and thereby her undiversified portfolio becomes more risky. Buying back stock does not improve her position in the sense that the firm can still be bought out. Chances, are increasing the leverage will be too risky for this CEO.

But let us assume that the CEO is totally altruistic and is not worried about control of the firm or even the risk of the portfolio. The analysis suggests that the firm would increase in value by $41 million. Now does this mean the firm should automatically increase its leverage? Not necessarily! Remember that this exercise assumed that the risk of default did not increase significantly. If it did, then the assumption of the cost of debt not changing as leverage increases is a very bad assumption. Let us propose an approach to find the new ATWACOC if there is a change in the cost of debt as leverage changes. Assume that an investment banker of the firm in the above example, tells the CEO that if the firm increases its leverage from 25% to 50%, the cost of borrowing would increase from 12% to 14%. In this case, Equations (6.8) and (6.9) would not be correct since these equations both assume that the cost of debt would not increase as the firm takes on more leverage.

So what do we do? Here is an ad hoc solution. Start as before by finding out the current ATWACOC. In the above example, it is 19.98%. Then find the cost of equity of the unlevered firm, exactly the same way we did before. Recall that number is 21.84%. But now, when we want to find the new ATWACOC, we do not use Equation (6.8) but rather use the *ad hoc* Equation proposed below:

$$R_{EL} = R_{EU} + (1 - t)(R_{EU} - R)D/S + \Delta R. \qquad (6.10)$$

Note that we added a new term, ΔR, to the Equation (6.9). Consider the previous example, but assume that the cost of debt increases by 200 basis points (from 12% to 14%). It is therefore logical that the cost of equity will increase beyond what Modigliani and Miller proposes (as given by Equation (6.9)) by at least 200 basis points. Recall that without ΔR, the cost of equity of our example increased to 28.33%. Thus, our ad hoc approach states that if the cost of debt goes from 12% to 14% when leverage increases from 25% to 50%, then the new cost of equity will be 30.33%. Now ,we use the definition of ATWACOC to find the new ATWACOC. That is:

$$ATWACOC = LR(1 - T) + (1 - L)R_E$$
$$= 0.5(14\%)(0.66) + 0.5(30.33\%) = 19.79\%.$$

Note that the ATWACOC decreased but not by much. The new value of the firm will be $79.92 mm/0.1979 = $403.84 million. Not much of an increase. Now imagine if you are the CEO and you own only 10% of the company. Your equity will increase by $384,000 but the risk of your wealth portfolio has also significantly increased. Will you increase the level of debt ? Chances are you will not.

In sum, the financing decision must take into account how the firm differs from the industry average. If the firm is significantly different, then management must be able to explain why. We also showed how one might be able to guess as to how the value of the firm will change as you take on more debt. But, again, this is an art form. One must consider the assumptions behind the model and use it as a guide as to what to do.

Financing Decision Problems

1. Assume that Firm XYZ has a debt/equity ratio of 1/3. The firm has the following capital structure:

Security	Market Value (million)	Coupon Rate or Cost of Capital (%)
Debt	$100	12
Equity	$300	24

The 12% cost of capital for Debt is the yield of the debt. Assume further that the firm's unlevered cash flows may be represented as a (constant) perpetuity. Assume that the firm wishes to increase the debt/equity ratio to 1.2 and assume no change in the probability of default. Assuming a corporate tax rate of 34%:

(a) Find the new ATWACOC.

(b) Find the New Cost of Equity.

(c) Find the new Value of the firm.

(d) Find the new levels of debt and equity.

(e) Find the expected price per share, assuming that there are currently 5 million shares outstanding.

2. Assume that the sales of the firm in Problem 1 are $100 million before the recapitalization. Hence assume that the level of debt is still $100 million. Fixed operating costs are $20 million and variable costs are 50% of sales.

(a) Determine the operating, financial and total degree of leverage.

(b) Determine the expected percentage decrease in earnings for a decrease of 25% of sales.

3. Firm of Problems 1 and 2 is considering raising $50 million of debt and it will use the money to retire an equivalent amount of common stock. Again do this problem assuming that the debt level is $100 million. Determine the break-even sales point in terms of EPS between the level of debt financing in Problem 1 and the new level of debt financing. Do not assume any valuation effect of debt (such as was calculated in Problem 1).

Solution to the Financing Decision Problem Set

Question 1:

(A) *Step* 1: First, find the current ATWACOC. Note that debt currently represents 25% of the firm and equity is 75% of the firm. Thus, the current ATWACOC is given by:

$$\text{ATWACOC} = (1/4)(0.66)(12\%) + (3/4)(24\%) = 19.98\%$$

Step 2: Second, using the Equation (6.8), find R_{EU}. Note that L is equal to 25%.

$$R_{EU} = \text{ATWACOC}/(1 - \text{TL})$$
$$= 19.98\%/(1 - 0.34(0.25))$$
$$= 21.84\%.$$

Step 3: Find the new target leverage ratio. The target debt-equity ratio is 1.2. This means that for every $1 of equity outstanding, there will be \$1.20 of debt outstanding. In other words, if the total value of the firm is \$2.20, there will be \$1.20 of debt and \$1 of equity. Hence, L = \$1.20/\$2.20 or 0.5455. (In general, L = D/S/[1+D/S] where D/S is the debt-equity ratio. Hence, we can find the new ATWACOC based upon R_{EU} of 21.84% and the new leverage ratio of .5455. That is, re-using Equation (6.8) and substituting for our values of R_{EU} and L, the new ATWACOC is:

$$\text{ATWACOC} = R_{EU}(1 - TL)$$
$$= 21.84(1 - (0.344)(0.5455)) = 17.786\%.$$

(B) Using Equation (6.3), we can find the new cost of equity. Note that if the new leverage ratio is 0.5455, and the new D/S = 1.2.

$$R_{EL} = R_{EU} + (1 - T)(R_{EU} - R)(D/S)$$
$$= 21.84 + (0.66)(9.84)(1.2)$$
$$= 29.63\%.$$

(C) To find the new value of the firm, we must determine the level of the unlevered cash flows. Recall, the value of the firm (refer to Equation (6.1) of this chapter) is the present value of the unlevered cash flows discounted by the ATWACOC. Thus, the current value of the firm (before the change in leverage from 25% to 50%) is \$400 million. The problem also assumes that the cash flows are perpetual with no growth. Hence, using Equation (6.1) with g = 0, we have:

$$V = CF_U/\text{ATWACOC},$$
$$400 = CF_u/0.1998,$$
$$CF_U = \$79.92 \text{ million.}$$

Now the new value of the firm is the discounted value of \$79.92 million per year in perpetuity but now we use the new ATWACOC of 17.789%.

$$V_{new} = 79.92/0.17789 = \$449.27 \text{ million.}$$

(D) The new level of debt is 54.55% of the new value of the firm or \$245.08 million and the new level of equity is \$204.21 million.

(E) Note that the value of the firm increased by \$49.27 million. We know from our notes that the existing stockholders get that increase.

Given that there are 5 million shares outstanding, the new price of the stock will increase by $49.27/5 = \$9.85$. Hence, the new price of the stock is \$69.85.

Note further that rebalancing to the new Leverage ratio involves issuing debt and retiring equity. How many shares are retired? If we consider that the debt raised is used to retire equity, then we can see that:

ΔDebt = Debt$_{\text{NEW}}$ − Debt$_{\text{OLD}}$ = \$245.08 million − \$100 million = \$145.08 million. The number of shares retired is equal to:

$$\#\text{Shares Retired} = \Delta\text{Debt}/P_{\text{NEW}}$$
$$= \$145.08 \text{ million}/\$69.85$$
$$= 2,077,022 \text{ Shares.}$$

And, #Shares Remaining = Original #Shares − #Shares Retired = 5,000,000 − 2,077,022 = 2,922,978 Shares. Thus the #Shares Remaining times the new Price per Share equals the new value of Equity, which matches our result from (D), above (give or take minor rounding differences). That is, $V_{\text{E-NEW}}$ = 2.923 million shares * \$69.85/share = \$204.2 million.

Question 2:

First, we find DOL, which equals (Sales-Variable Costs)/(Sales-Variable Costs − Fixed Costs) or (\$100 million − \$50 million)/ ((\$100 million − \$50 million − \$20 million) = 1.667. Next, we find DFL, which equals (EBIT/EBIT − Interest Expense) or \$30 million/(\$30 million − \$12 million) = 1.667. Now TDL = DOL*DFL or 1.667*1.667 = 2.78. Since %ΔEarnings = %ΔSales*DTL or 2.78*(−0.25) = −0.6944, we expect a decline of 69.44% in earnings.

Question 3:

To solve this problem, we equate the EPS assuming there is 100 million debt outstanding to the EPS assuming there are \$150 million debt outstanding. EPS is given by:

$$\text{EPS} = [(\text{Sales} - \text{Variable Costs} - \text{Fixed Costs}$$
$$- \text{Interest Expense})(1 - \text{T})]/\#\text{of shares outstanding}$$

With $100 million debt outstanding, the interest expense is 12% (the cost of debt) times the debt outstanding or $12 million. In this case:

$$EPS = [(Sales - 0.5 \text{ Sales} - \$20 \text{ million} - \$12 \text{ million})]/5 \text{ million}. \tag{A}$$

With $150 million debt outstanding, the interest expense is now 12% of $150 million or $18 million. The problem tells you to assume no change in the valuation of the firm. Thus, if the firm raises $50 million of debt to repurchase stock, the number of shares repurchased will be $50 million/$60 or 833,333 shares. As a result there are now 4,166,667 shares outstanding. In this case:

$$EPS = [(Sales - 0.5 \text{ Sales} - \$20 \text{ million} - \$18 \text{ million})]/4,166,667. \tag{B}$$

Equating Equations (A) and (B) and solving for Sales, we find that the break-even sales is $135.88 million.

Advanced Financing Decision Problems

1. Find the ATWACOC of the following firm:

Security Class	Book Value (mm)	Price per share	# of Units	Coupon (%)	Maturity (years)
Senior Debt	$20	$1,000	20,000	9	10
Junior Debt	40	875	40,000	8	10
Preferred Stock	20	75	200,000	10	—
Common Stock	100	40	3,000,000	—	—
Retained Earn.	100	—	—	—	—

The expected dividend at time 1 is $4 and is expected to grow at 5.1% thereafter. Tax rate is 40%. Assume that the par value of the bonds is $1,000 and for preferred stock it is $100.

2. The above company is considering buying die cutting machinery for $10 million. The machinery will produce annual sales of $20 million for 10 years. Costs are 70% of sales and working capital is 50% of sales. Assume straight-line depreciation. Find the NPV of this project.

3. Assume that the price of your common stock is $50. Your computer company XYZ is worth $100 million and is composed of 50% debt and 50% equity. Assume that the debt is riskless and has a yield of 10%. Your company is considering investing in the container ship industry. Companies of the container ship industry have an average common stock dividend yield of 15%. That is, the current dividend to current stock price is equal to 15%. On average, the expected dividend growth rate is 10.41%. The typical leverage structure is 70% debt and 30% equity. Assume that the debt in the container ship industry is also riskless. Assume further that the marginal tax rate is 50% for all companies. You plan to finance this project on the basis of your firm's present capital structure — i.e., 50% debt and 50% equity. Given the following information below, would you buy this project? (Assume a Modigliani–Miller Leverage Framework).

Initial Investment	$20 million
Sales Per Year (1–10)	25 million
Costs	15 million
W/C	50% of Sales
Depreciation Expense	$1 million

4. Firm XYZ currently has a capital structure of 30% debt and 70% equity. The cost of debt is currently 6% and the cost of equity is 12%. The value of debt is $300 million and the value of equity is $700 million. Let the tax rate equal 34%. An investment banker tells the CFO of the company that if the firm increases its leverage ratio, the cost of debt will increase according to the following schedule:

Percentage Debt (%)	Percentage Equity (%)	Cost of Debt (%)
30	70	6
40	60	7
50	50	9
60	40	12

Assume that the cash flow of the firm may be represented as a perpetuity. Determine the ATWACOC for each debt level. Determine the value of the firm for each firm level. Determine the optimal level of debt.

Solution to the Advanced Financing Decision Problem Set

Problem 1:

Security Class	Market Value	Proportion	Cost of Capital	Contributing Cost
Senior Debt	20,000,000	0.105	5.4%[A]	0.567%
Junior Debt	35,000,000	0.184	6.02%[B]	1.108%
Preferred Stock	15,000,000	0.079	13.33%[C]	1.053%
Common Stock	120,000,000	0.632	15.1%[D]	9.543%
Total	190,000,000		ATWACOC =	12.27

[A] Since price = par, the coupon rate is the yield. The after tax cost of debt is the coupon rate times $(1 - T)$.

[B] Using the financial calculator. $N = 10$, $PV = -875$, $PMT = 80$, $FV = 1,000$. The financial calculator tells us that the yield is equal to 10.04%. After multiplying the yield by $(1 - T)$, we obtain 6.02%.

[C] Cost of preferred is found by taking the ratio of Dividend to Price or $10/$75. Dividend is obtained by recognizing that the par value is $100 and the coupon rate is 10%.

[D] Using the dividend growth model, the cost of common stock is $4/$40 + 0.051.

Problem 2: We use the following cash flow formula:

Cash Flow =	Sales	− Costs	− Long Term Investment	−Δ Working Capital	− T(Sales − Cost − Dep)
CF_0			−$10,000,000		−$10 mm
CF_1	$20,000,000	−$14,000,000	0	−$10,000,000	−$2,000,000	−$6 mm
CF_{2-10}	$20,000,000	−$14,000,000	0	0	−$2,000,000	$4 mm
CF_{11}				$10,000,000		$10 mm

Note, the change in working capital occurs at times 1 and 11. This is because working capital is 50% of sales. Hence, the investment in working capital occurs at time one when there are sales. Working capital remains at that level through year 10 since annual sales remain constant. In year 11, when sales equal zero, the working capital is zero, implying a decrease in working capital of $10 million. The table below summarizes the NPV calculation:

	A	B
1	Time	Cash Flow
2	0	−$10,000,000
3	1	−$6,000,000
4	2	$4,000,000
5	3	$4,000,000
6	4	$4,000,000
7	5	$4,000,000
8	6	$4,000,000
9	7	$4,000,000
10	8	$4,000,000
11	9	$4,000,000
12	10	$4,000,000
13	11	$10,000,000
14	NPV	$6,245,795.10

The NPV obtained in cell B14 by using the excel function =npv(0.1227, B3:B13) +B2. The 0.1227 is the ATWACOC obtained in Problem 1.

Problem 3: Note that you cannot use your ATWACOC because that project is of another risk class (industry). Nor can you use the ATWACOC of the container ship industry because the leverage decision of your company differs from that of the container ship industry. Hence, we must adjust the ATWACOC of the container ship industry for the new leverage.

Let R_{EL} denote the cost of equity of a levered firm. Let R denote the (pre-tax) cost of debt. Let R' denote the after-tax cost of debt. Let ATWACOC denote the after-tax weighted average cost of capital. Let R_{EU} denote the cost of equity of an unlevered firm.

STEP 1: Find the WACOC of the container ship industry.
Using the dividend growth model, we can estimate the cost of equity.

$$R_{EL} = \mathrm{Div}_1/\mathrm{P} + g$$
$$= [\mathrm{Div}_0(1+g)]/\mathrm{P} + g$$
$$= 15\%(1.1041) + 10.41$$
$$= 26.97\%,$$
$$R = 10\%,$$
$$R' = 5\%,$$
$$\mathrm{ATWACOC} = \mathrm{LR}(1-\mathrm{T}) + (1-\mathrm{L})R_{EL}$$
$$= 0.7(5\%) + 0.3(26.97\%)$$
$$= 11.59\%.$$

STEP 2: Find the R_{EU} of the container ship industry

$$R_{EU} = \mathrm{ATWACOC}/(1-\mathrm{TL}) = 11.59\%/(1-0.5(0.7))$$
$$= 17.83\%.$$

STEP 3: Find the new ATWACOC

$$\mathrm{ATWACOC} = R_{EU}(1-\mathrm{TL}) = 17.83\%(1-0.5(0.5))$$
$$= 13.37\%.$$

STEP 4: Find the cash flows and NPV

Cash flow	Sales	− Costs	− LTI	ΔWC	− Taxes	=
CF_0			−20 mm			−20 mm
CF_1	25 mm	−15 mm	0	−12.5 mm	−4.5 mm	−7 mm
CF_{2-10}	25 mm	−15 mm	0	0	−4.5 mm	= 5.5 mm
CF_{11}	0	0	0	12.5 mm	0	= 12.5 mm

The table below simulates the excel sheet with the NPV calculation.

	A	B
1	Time	Cash Flow
2	0	−\$20,000,000
3	1	−\$7,000,000
4	2	\$5,500,000
5	3	\$5,500,000
6	4	\$5,500,000
7	5	\$5,500,000
8	6	\$5,500,000
9	7	\$5,500,000
10	8	\$5,500,000
11	9	\$5,500,000
12	10	\$5,500,000
13	11	\$12,500,000
14	NPV	\$1,525,953

The NPV obtained in cell B14 by using the excel function =npv(0.13377, B3:B13) +B2.

Problem 4: Step 1: Find the current ATWACOC. Recall that

$$\text{ATWACOC} = L\,R(1-T) + (1-L)R_E$$
$$= 0.3(6\%)0.66 + 0.7 * (12\%) = 9.588\%.$$

Step 2: Find R_{EU}, which equals ATWACOC/(1 − TL) = 9.588%/(1 − 0.34(0.3)) = 10.677%.

Step 3: Find the CF_U. Assuming a perpetual cash flow, the value of the firm, V, is given by the expression, $V = CF_U/ATWACOC$. Since V is the sum of the value of Debt and Equity outstanding, V = \$1,000 million and CF_U = \$95.88 million.

Step 4: We use the modified Modigliani–Miller formula for R_{EL} as given by Equation (6.10) in the notes, or:

$$R_{EL} = R_{EU} + (1 - t)(R_{EU} - R)D/S + \Delta R. \qquad (6.10)$$

Note that ΔR is R_{NEW} − the current cost of debt. The current cost of debt is 6%. Applying Equation (6.10), we can calculate the new cost of equity. This is summarized in the table below.

L	(1 − L)	ΔR (%)	R (%)	R_{EL} (%)
0.3	0.7	0	6	12.00
0.4	0.6	1	7	13.73
0.5	0.5	3	9	16.76
0.6	0.4	6	12	21.31

For example, when L = 0.5, then D/S = 1 (or L/(1 − L)) and ΔR = 3%. According to Equation (6.10), R_{EL} = 10.677%+0.66*(10.677% − 6%) + 3%, which equals 16.76%. The new ATWACOC is found by applying ATWACOC = L R(1 − T) + (1 − L)R_E but using the new values for R and R_E for each leverage ratio. Finally, we find the new value of the firm by taking the cash flow from Step 2, \$95.88 million divided by the new ATWACOC. The table below summarizes the results:

L	(1 − L)	ATWACOC (%)	V
0.3	0.7	9.59	\$1,000.00
0.4	0.6	10.09	\$950.29
0.5	0.5	11.35	\$844.62
0.6	0.4	13.28	\$722.27

Hence, it is optimal not to increase the leverage ratio beyond L = 0.3.

CHAPTER 7

LEASING VERSUS BUYING OR IS IT LEASING VERSUS BORROWING?

Introduction

You heard from your mechanic and he tells you that your 1994 Pontiac with 122,000 miles has had it. It is time for you to get another car. You have owned this car for more than 6 years and it seems that you have to go to your mechanic every 3–4 weeks costing you several hundred dollars to fix what is wrong. No more, you decide. You do not want to buy another used car. That is it! You want a new car! After all, you are starting a new job in a few days. It pays an annual salary of $72,000 and you deserve it.

You go online and look at prices of new cars. You prefer a Toyota Camry but the list price is $25,000. Last time you checked your savings account, it looked ugly. (Not to mention that you have $33,000 in outstanding education loans!) Despondent, you begin thinking about taking public transportation to and from Lancaster, Pennsylvania where you go once a month for a weekend to visit your parents and friends. Jersey City is nice but there is something about home.

Just then your eye catches an advertisement. The advertisement proclaims that you can purchase your dream car from Toyota in

Lansing, Pennsylvania. And you have two options! Neither option requires any down payment. The first option allows you to borrow the money to purchase the $25,000 Camry at an annual rate of 12%. Of course, you must make monthly payments for the next 48 months. The second option allows you to lease the car for $421 per month for 36 months. After that, you have the option of giving back the car or buying it from the dealer for $17,633.85. Implicitly, there is a third option. You can buy the car for $25,000, but your bank account tells you otherwise.

Using your financial calculator, you find that the borrowing option will result in a monthly payment of $658.35. But after 4 years, the car is yours!!!!! On the other hand, paying a lease payment of $421 per month will help your bottom line and you can use the 3 years to save money to purchase the car from the dealer.[1]

Your corporate finance notes come in handy. You reason that by leasing you save on the purchase price. Hold on! But you were not paying $25,000 for the car. You are borrowing the money. Then you picture your old professor (white male, almost white beard, definitely overweight, and fairly bald). You remember him saying that purchasing the asset and borrowing the money to pay for the asset are really the same thing. After all, what is the present value of the loan payments if it is not equal to the amount borrowed, which is in your case, $25,000.

OK, you are convinced that if you lease the car, you save $25,000 up front. Instead, you will pay $421 per month and buy the car at the end of 3 years for $17,633.85. You take the present value (PV) of the lease payments. Using your calculator ($N = 36$, with an annual rate of 12%, the monthly rate, i, is 1%, PMT = $421, FV = $17,633.85), you find that the PV is equal to $25,000. Naturally, you say to yourself, the dealer is not planning to lose money on the deal.

---

[1] Author's note: Actually, you get married and have triplets by the end of the third year of the lease, and your bank account will look even bleaker. But the triplets are great source of joy in your life. But I digress!

But you go with the lease, since it helps your budget in the short run, and if the car is a lemon, the dealer owns it.

N	I	PV	PMT	FV
36	1	? −25,000	421	17,633.85

Leasing for Corporations

Leasing is a form of financing. The choice that the firm makes is either to purchase the asset and finance it through normal means (e.g., debt, retained earnings, new equity financing) or by leasing. Intuitively, you choose to lease the asset instead of purchasing if and only if the cost of leasing is lower than the cost of buying.

To evaluate the lease, one must understand the tax implications of the lease. There are two types of lease arrangements as far as the internal revenue service (IRS) is concerned. The lease is classified as a *true lease* if (1) the life of the lease is less than 80% the life of the asset and (2) that the user (lessee) does not have the right to purchase the asset at the end of the life of the lease at a significantly lower price than the prevailing market price. Otherwise the lease is classified as an *installment sale*. If the lease is a true lease then the lease payment is tax deductible to the lessee and the lessor receives the tax benefits of depreciation.

In this chapter, we will evaluate the benefits of leasing by taking the present value of the incremental cash outflow of leasing compared to buying. That is, we want to know how much better off is the firm to lease the asset instead of buying it. To determine whether leasing is beneficial, we want to determine the difference in the cash flows if the firm leases the assets as opposed to buying them.

The main benefit of leasing is that the firm does not have to pay the purchase price for the asset. Let us denote the purchase price of the asset as I (which we have used before as the initial investment).

The firm pays the lessor lease payments (which we will assume for now are constant through the life of the asset). However, if the lease is a true lease, the lease payments are tax deductible. Let Lease represent the periodic lease payment and T denote the tax rate, then the periodic incremental after-tax cash outflow is Lease (1 − T). Furthermore, the lessee no longer can claim as a tax deduction the depreciation expense of the asset. Again, assuming straight line depreciation, the incremental cost of the lease of losing the tax benefits of depreciation is T*Dep, where Dep is the annual depreciation expense. In addition, the lessee does not have rights to the salvage value of the asset as it belongs to the lessor.

However, there is another incremental cash flow impact of leasing that we have not yet considered. To understand that impact, let us step back a bit. When we determine the NPV of the project, we use the formula, NPV = −I + PV(CF), where I is the initial investment. We normally use the After-Tax Weighted Average Cost of Capital (ATWACOC) to calculate the NPV. Assume that the unlevered cash flows of the project may be represented as a perpetuity. Then the NPV is equal to −I + CFu/ATWACOC, where CFu is the unlevered cash flow. We have learned in the capital budgeting chapter that when we use the ATWACOC we are making an assumption regarding the amount of debt used to finance the project. That amount of debt is equal to the leverage ratio (L) times the market value of the asset or L*CFu/ATWACOC. Consequently, since leasing is a form of borrowing, when you consider the incremental cash flow of leasing, you must take into account that leasing reduces the debt capacity of the firm. In fact, by leasing you are financing this project by 100% debt financing but usually you only finance it by L%. The impact of the reduction of the debt capacity is that the firm cannot borrow as much for other projects, and therefore the tax benefits of debt normally borrowed to finance the project is no longer available to those projects. Hence, we must include as an incremental cost of the lease the cash flow implications of that reduction in debt capacity. The incremental cost is the lost tax benefit of debt, which may be defined as $T * R*$ Debt Displaced.

Consequently, the incremental benefit of leasing compared to purchasing is obtained by taking the PV of the incremental cash flows of the lease. If that PV > 0, leasing is beneficial, and if PV < 0, then leasing is not beneficial. More formally, the profitability of leasing is given by:

Incremental Benefit of Leasing

$$= I - \sum [\text{Lease}(1 - T) + T * \text{Depreciation}$$
$$+ T * R * \text{Debt} * \text{Displaced}] / (1 + K_1(1 - T))^t$$
$$- \text{After-Tax Salvage Value} / (1 + K_2)^n.$$

This leaves us with two questions. What is K_1 and what is K_2? Let us start with K_1. You have the following choices. Is it

(a) The before tax cost of debt?
(b) The after-tax cost of debt?
(c) The cost of equity of the levered firm?
(d) The cost of equity of the unlevered firm?
(e) The after-tax weighted average cost of capital?
(f) The before-tax weighted average cost of capital?

Let us reason this out together. Note that the cash flows discounted by K_1 are generally lot less risky than the typical cash flows of a project. For example, once you sign the lease contract, you must pay the lease payment. It is like debt! And of course the lost tax benefits of debt displaced has the word debt in it! You also know that the tax laws require you to lose the tax benefits of depreciation which are valuable only as long as you are solvent. And the term solvent is debt-like. Thus, K_1 should be related to the cost of debt.

But do we really want to figure out the amount of debt displaced? Of course not! Now, we know from capital budgeting that one may either account for the tax benefits of debt in the cash flow (i.e., the levered cash flow) and use a before-tax cost of capital or account for the tax benefits of debt in the discount rate using an after-tax cost of capital to discount the unlevered cash flow. We will use the latter approach and therefore we can rewrite our formula as:

Incremental Benefit of Leasing

$$= I - \sum_{t=1}^{n} (\text{Lease}(1 - T) + T * \text{Depreciation})/$$

$$(1 + R(1 - T))^t$$

$$- \text{After-Tax Salvage Value}/(1 + \text{ATWACOC})^n.$$

where R is the cost of debt and n is the life of the lease. Note that we are using the after-tax cost of debt to account for the impact of debt displacement upon the cash flows. Also, we snuck in the ATWACOC as our discount rate for salvage value. This is not necessarily correct. The point that is being made is that generally the estimate of the salvage value is far less certain than the lease payment or the depreciation benefit. We need another discount rate for that part of the formula. Instead of making one up, we are using the ATWACOC which is certainly greater than the after-tax cost of debt. Naturally, the more confident you are about the estimate of the salvage value, the closer K_2 should be to the after-tax cost of debt.

An Academic Example: As the CFO of Mantle Inc., you are considering whether or not you should purchase or lease an asset that will increase your firm's sales. Assume that the ATWACOC of your firm is 12% and your cost of borrowing is 8%. You are considering purchasing an asset for $1 million. The asset has a 5 year life and the depreciation expense is $200,000 per year. The expected incremental annual sales are $1.15 million per annum and the incremental costs are 74% of sales. There is no working capital associated with the project. Assume that the salvage value of the asset is zero at the end of the fifth year. Alternative to purchasing the asset, you may lease the asset for $230,000 per year for 5 years. Let the tax rate equal 34%. Assume that the IRS is generous and it allows us to treat the lease as a true lease so that the lease payments are tax deductible to your firm. This means that should you lease the asset, you will not be able to take tax deductions for the depreciation expense. (In reality, this lease should be treated as an installment sale which has different tax implications. But the true lease assumption is a useful pedagogical framework that will enhance, hopefully, your understanding of the lease versus buy decision. Later on in the chapter you will learn more about the cash flow implications of an installment sale.) Should you lease, buy or reject the project?

We begin the solution by first finding the NPV of the project without the lease option. Why do we do that? Let us leave that question open for now and we will answer that question fairly soon. The following table summarizes the cash flows for the project:

Table 7.1

	$t = 0$	$t = 1–5$
Sales		$1,150,000
− Costs		−$851,000
− Long Term Investment	−$1,000,000	
− T(Sales-Costs-Dep)		−$33,360
= Total Cash Flow	−$1,000,000	$265,340

The NPV of the project is given by $-\$1,000,000 + \$265,340*$ $A_{5,12\%} = -\$42,508.68$. Recall that $\$265,340*A_{5,12\%}$ is equivalent to using your financial calculator by using the following inputs: $N = 5$, $i = 12\%$, and PMT $= 265,340$. If we were still in the capital budgeting chapter, you would reject the project. However, you have the option to lease the asset for $230,000 per annum. Recall that the incremental benefit of the lease is given by:

$$I - \sum_{t=1} (\text{Lease}(1 - T) + T * \text{Depreciation})/(1 + R(1 - T))^t$$

$$- \text{After-Tax Salvage Value}/(1 + \text{ATWACOC})^n.$$

We can plug into the above formula, noting that $I = \$1$ million, Lease $= \$230,000$, Depreciation $= \$200,000$, $T = 0.34$, and $R = 8\%$. In other words, the incremental value of this lease is given by:

$$\$1,000,000 - [\$230,000(0.66) + 0.34(\$200,000)]A_{5,5.28\%} = \$55,702.$$

This means that leasing is better than buying by $55,702. Hence, if we were to lease the asset, the true Net Percent Value (NPV) is

Table 7.2

	$t = 0$	$t = 1-5$
Sales		$1,150,000
− Costs		−$851,000
− Lease Payment		−$230,000
− Long Term Investment	$0	
− T(Sales-Costs-Lease)		−$23,460
	$0	$45,540

−$42,508.68 + $55,702 = $12,193.32. In other words, the lease terms were so generous; it made an unprofitable project profitable.

What if the incremental value of the lease was equal to $35,000? Leasing would be preferable to buying, but in reality not profitable enough to make the NPV of the project to be greater than zero. In this case, you would have rejected the project.

To understand this better, consider the incremental cash flows of the project had you leased the asset. First at time zero, the incremental cash flow would be zero because if you lease the asset, we assume that there is no down payment. Second, your costs would increase by the annual lease payment or in our example, $230,000. Finally, you would not be able to use the tax deduction associated with the annual depreciation expense. The incremental cash flows would then be as is described in Table 7.2.

Now note what we did to find the NPV of the project with the lease option. In particular, we added the incremental value of the lease to the NPV of the project without the lease option. That is:

$$-\$1,000,000 + \$265,340 * A_{5,12\%} + \$1,000,000$$
$$-[\$230,000(0.66) + 0.34(\$200,000)]A_{5,5.28\%}.$$

The sum of the first two terms is the NPV of the asset without any lease arrangement. The sum of the last two terms is the incremental value of the lease. Notice that the first term and the third term cancel out. Is that not equivalent to having no incremental cash flow at time zero as in the just previous table? Note also, that the $265,340 of the second term representing the annual cash flow of the project as summarized in Table 7.1 is obtained without including as part of costs the lease payment and using the $200,000 depreciation expense in calculating the tax liability of the firm. Note that the fourth term of the above equation implicity reduces the overall cash flow by the after-tax lease payment and the loss of the tax benefit of depreciation expense. Thus, in essence, Table 7.2 represents the cash flow if we were to sum the cash flows of the project without the lease option and the incremental cash flows of the lease option.

We now have one important question to answer. Why not simply discount the cash flows of Table 7.2 to find the answer? There are two reasons why this would be wrong. First, we need to separately calculate the NPV of the cash flows as summarized by Table 7.1 because it is possible that the incremental value of the lease is negative but the NPV of the project without the lease option is positive. In this case, the firm should purchase and not lease the asset. There is no way of seeing that by taking the present value of the cash flows as depicted in Table 7.2 since those cash flows include the incremental cash flows of assuming the investment is leased and not purchased. Second, if we were to simply discount the cash flows as depicted in Table 7.2, what discount rate would you use, the ATWACOC or the after-tax cost of debt? Take a closer look at the last equation, copied below for your convenience.

$$-\$1,000,000 + \$265,340 * A_{5,12\%} + \$1,000,000$$
$$-[\$230,000(0.66) + 0.34(\$200,000)]A_{5,5.28\%}.$$

Note that the second term and the fourth term use different discount rates. The second term uses the ATWACOC but the last term uses the after-tax cost of debt. That is, we are not *using* a single discount rate to evaluate the lease versus buy decision. Consequently, we break the lease versus buy decision into two parts. The first part is to find the NPV of the project without the lease option. Then we consider the incremental value of the lease. If the incremental value of the lease is positive, we sum the NPV of the project without the lease option and the incremental value of the lease. Finally, consider the case that the NPV of the project were positive but the incremental value of the lease is negative. Remember, leasing is an option. No one is putting a gun to your head to take a lease. Thus in this case, you

Table 7.3

$V_p > 0$	$V_{\text{lease}} > 0$		Lease
$V_p < 0$	$V_{\text{lease}} > 0$	$V_p + V_{\text{lease}} > 0$	Lease
$V_p > 0$	$V_{\text{lease}} < 0$		Purchase
$V_p < 0$	$V_{\text{lease}} > 0$	$V_p + V_{\text{lease}} < 0$	Reject

would purchase the asset but not lease it. Let V_p denote the NPV of the project without the lease option and V_{lease} denote the incremental value of the lease. Then Table 7.3 summarizes our decision rule.

Further Interpretation: Recall that the incremental value of the lease of the previous example is $55,702. This implies that leasing is better than purchasing the equipment outright by $55,702. Why is leasing preferable in this case? We are saying that the PV of the total payments accruing to the lessor is less than what the firm would pay to acquire the asset. In a sense, the firm is saving $55,702 by leasing as opposed to purchasing.

Another interpretation may be given if we thought of the lease contract as another form of borrowing. Now recall you are paying the lessor [$230,000(0.66) + 0.34($200,000)] or $219,800 per year. This payment of $219,800 that is going to the lessor could be used to support debt. What is the equivalent amount of debt we can borrow assuming that the total after-tax payments we can afford to pay each year for 5 years is $219,800? The table below demonstrates the calculation.

Time	0	1	2	3	4	5
Payment to Lessor		$219,800	$219,800	$219,800	$219,800	$219,800
Principal Balance	$944,298.23	$774,357.17	$595,443.23	$407,082.63	$208,776.60	$0.00
Principal Repayment		$169,941.05	$178,913.94	$188,360.60	$198,306.04	$208,776.60
Interest Payment		$75,543.86	$61,948.57	$47,635.46	$32,566.61	$16,702.13
Interest Tax Shield		$25,684.91	$21,062.52	$16,196.06	$11,072.65	$5,678.72
After-tax Payment		$219,800.00	$219,800.00	$219,800.00	$219,800.00	$219,800.00

To find the principal balance in any period we find the PV of the payments to lessor discounted by the after-tax cost of debt. In our example, the discount rate is 5.28%. At time 0, the Principal Balance is $944,298.23. Thus, if the firm were to borrow to finance the purchase and were to have the same after-tax payments in each year as implied by the lease contract (i.e., $219,800) the firm will be only able to borrow $944,298.23. In essence, traditional financing will not be sufficient to acquire the assets. But leasing allows you to purchase a $1million asset by borrowing only $944,298.23.

To complete this interpretation, we can go into more detail regarding how the numbers in the table are obtained, which represents the amortization of the $944,298.23 loan. The row Principal Balance is obtained by finding the present value of the remaining payments. At time 1, there are four remaining payments of $219,800. The present value using the 5.28% after-tax cost of debt discount is $774,357.17. The row, principal repayment is calculated by finding the difference in the principal balance of two consecutive periods. For example, the principal payment at time 1 is obtained by taking the difference of the principal payment at time zero, $944,298.23, and the principal balance at time 1, yielding $169,941.05. The interest payment is simply the before-tax interest rate of 8%. Hence, the interest payment at time 1 is the product of 8% and $944,298.23. Finally, the tax credit received for paying $75,543.86 interest at time 1 is the product of the 34% tax rate and the interest payment. Finally, if you were to sum the principal payment and interest payment and subtract out the tax credit, you will find the after tax payment of this loan is $219,800, the equivalent after-tax payment given to the lessor. Consequently, we can express that the equivalent loan of the lease is $944,298.23, since the amortization of the $944,298.23 loan would be such that the after-tax payment of the loan equals the after-tax payment of the lease for every period.

The problem becomes more complicated if there is a salvage value. We will examine two different assumptions. The first situation is when the firm would normally sell the asset it purchases at the equivalent time of the end of the lease. The second situation is when the firm would normally hold onto the asset until the end of the life of the asset. We will describe the appropriate formula for the incremental value of the lease for each scenario without regard to the NPV of the project without the lease option. Clearly that NPV will be different if we assume that we normally hold onto the asset for, say 5 years (the life of the lease) and for, say 10 years (the life of the asset).

Consider the first situation. Assume that the purchase price of the asset is $10,000 and the life of the asset is 5 years. Let the tax rate equal 34%. The ATWACOC is 12% and the pre-tax cost of debt is 8%. Let us begin by assuming that you lease the asset for 3 years, paying $2,300 per annum. Let the salvage value equal $6,000. Assume further that ordinarily the firm would junk the asset if purchased after 3 years. As a result, if the firm leases the asset it loses the Salvage Value of the asset at the end of the lease since it does not own the asset. Then the formula becomes:

Incremental Benefit of Leasing

$$= I - \sum(\text{Lease}(1 - T) + \text{TDepreciation})/$$
$$(1 + R(1 - T))^t$$
$$- [\text{Salvage Value} - T(\text{Salvage Value} - \text{Book Value})]/$$
$$(1 + \text{ATWACOC})^n.$$

The complication is that if the salvage value is different from the book value, there are additional tax implications. In our example, the book value of the asset is $4,000. Consequently, the firm is making a $2,000 gain if it owned the asset and sold it. Hence, the after-tax salvage value that the firm gives up when it leases is [$6,000 − 0.34*($6,000 − $4,000)] = $5,320. In this case, our incremental value of the lease is

$$\$10,000 - [\$2,300(0.66) + 0.34(\$2,000)]A_{3, 5.28\%}$$
$$- \$5,320/(1.12)^3$$
$$= \$258.90.$$

The problem is even more complicated under the second situation. In this case, the firm would normally hold onto the asset for its full life. However, because it leases the asset, it has to repurchase the asset either from the lessor or from the used or secondary market. Assume that the repurchase price is $6,000. Assuming the firm leases the asset, at the end of the third year, the firm reacquires the asset for $6,000. As a result, the firm is able to depreciate that asset over the next two year period. But note that in this case the $6,000 is not certain, it is only an estimate and therefore the tax benefits of depreciation here will also be discounted by the ATWACOC because the tax benefits of depreciation are based upon the estimated salvage value. But in this scenario, by leasing, the firm is really giving up the original tax benefits of depreciation over the entire life of the asset.

The incremental benefit of leasing formula becomes even more complicated. Let us make some simple assumptions. We will assume that the lease payment is constant and straight line depreciation. Let n be the life of the lease and k be the life of the asset. Now the formula becomes:

Incremental Benefit of Leasing

$$= I - \text{Lease}(1 - T)A_{n,r(1-T)} - (TI/K)A_{k,r(1-t)}$$
$$- \text{Repurchase Price}/(1 + \text{ATWACOC})^n$$
$$+ T[\text{Repurchase Price}/(K - N)]A_{k-n,\text{ATWACOC}}/$$
$$(1 + \text{ATWACOC})^n.$$

The first term in the above formula is the purchase price that is saved at time zero by leasing the asset as opposed to purchasing it. The second term is the present value of the after-tax lease payment during the n-year period the firm leases the asset. The third term is the present value of the tax benefit of the depreciation expense based upon the life of the asset, which is k years. The fourth term is the repurchase price the firm has to pay to obtain use of the asset after the expiration of the lease. The fifth term is the present value of the tax benefits of the depreciation (assuming straight line) as a result of the asset being repurchased at the end of the life of the lease. In our new example, the incremental benefit of leasing is now:

$$\$10,000 - \$2,300(0.66)A_{3,5.28\%} - 0.34 * \$2,000A_{5,5.28\%}$$
$$-\$6,000/(1.12)^3 + 0.34(\$3,000)A_{2,12\%}/(1.12)^3.$$

The incremental benefit of leasing in this case is -$77.38. In this last case, we would prefer not to lease.

True Lease or Installment Sale

We have been analyzing the lease from the perspective of the lessee assuming that the IRS treats the lease arrangement as a true lease as opposed to an installment sale. Let us understand the IRS. Consider what happens if a firm borrows an asset for its own use. Who owns the asset? If the lender owns the asset, then the lender should get the tax benefits of the depreciation. If the borrower owns the asset, then the borrower should get the tax benefits of the depreciation. According to the IRS, if you give back the asset to the lender with a significant remaining life, then the asset belongs to the lender. Otherwise, the asset should belong to the borrower. Of course, in the real world, you cannot borrow the asset for free. Actually, you make a (lease) payment. If the asset belongs to the lender, then the lease payment is like an interest payment which is completely tax deductible. If it belongs to the borrower, then the lease payment is like a partial payment to pay down what the borrower owes.

The IRS would consider the lease to be a true lease if (a) the life of the lease is less than 80% of the life of the asset, and (b) the lessee does not have the right to buy the asset at the end of the lease for a song (way below its expected market value). For this chapter, if at the end of the lease, the asset still has value, we will consider the lease as a true lease. In this case, the IRS considers that the owner of the asset is the lender or what we call the lessor. If there is no salvage value, then the IRS views the owner of the asset as the user (borrower or lessee). In this case, the IRS views the lease as an installment sale.

We should note again that in our original academic example whereby the life of the lease equals that of the life of the asset violates the IRS rules regarding a true lease. In actuality, the IRS would consider the lease contract to be an installment sale. In this case, the tax authorities view the asset to be owned by the lessee regardless of what the legal contract might state. As far as taxes are concerned, the lessee gets to depreciate the asset and not the lessor. Moreover, only the interest portion of the lease is tax deductible to the lessee.

Accordingly:

Incremental Benefit of Leasing

$$= I - \sum [\text{Interest portion of the lease}(1 - T)$$
$$+ \text{principal portion of the lease}]/(1 + R(1 - T))^t$$
$$- \text{After-Tax Salvage Value}/(1 + \text{ATWACOC})^n.$$

Let us go back to the original example. We will make one simplifying assumption. We will assume that the depreciation, the interest portion and principal portion of the total lease payment are amortized on a straight line basis. That is, the difference between the lease payment and the normal depreciation rate is the interest portion of the lease payment and the remainder is the principal. (Actually, if the contract does not state what proportion is interest and what proportion is principal, the IRS would require the determination of the interest basis using the scientific amortization basis. We show this in the advanced problems section of this chapter.)

Let us restate the original example. You are considering purchasing an asset for $1 million. As an alternative to purchasing the asset, you may lease the asset for $230,000 per year for 5 years. Let the tax rate equal 34%. Note that over a 5-year period, the firm will pay out a total of $1,150,000 in lease payment. The lessor, who is really the seller of the asset as far as the IRS is concerned, is lending you $1,000,000. Thus, if you are paying $1,150,000 in aggregate, it means that $1,000,000 is principal and $150,000 is interest. If we were to amortize these two numbers on a straight-line basis, the firm is paying a principal payment of $200,000 and $30,000 in interest. Thus, the incremental benefit of leasing is now:

$$\$1,000,000 - [\$200,000 + 0.66(\$30,000)]A_{5,5.28\%} = \$55,702.$$

Why is there Leasing?

Let us move to the lessor's perspective. In essence whatever benefits the lessor is a cost to the lessee and vice versa. Thus, the incremental benefit of leasing (assuming a true lease) to the lessor is given by:

$$\sum (\text{Lease}(1-T) + \text{TDepreciation})/(1 + R(1-T))^t$$
$$+ \text{After-Tax Salvage Value}/(1 + \text{ATWACOC})^n - I.$$

Note that the incremental benefit of the lease to the lessor is the mirror image of the incremental benefits to the lessee. The trick here is to note that R in this equation is identical to the R in the equation for the lessee. Why? The reason is that the lessor is lending money to the lessee. The risk concerning the lessee making that payment is equal to the risk of default of the lessee's bonds. Hence, R of the lessee is appropriate for the lessor's incremental value of the lease. However, the Tax rate, T, should reflect the tax rate of the lessor. Hence, note if both lessor and lessee have identical T, R, and after-tax salvage value, then any lease deal that makes the lessee better is a bad deal for the lessor, and vice versa. Thus for a lease deal to work, we need a win–win situation. This will happen if either the tax rates of the lessor and lessee are different, or the estimates of the salvage value are different. It can be shown that a lease deal can be structured so that both the lessor and lessee benefit as long as the tax rates are different. Many text books assert that the lessor must have the higher tax rate, but this is not true. However, taxes do not play the most important role. Rather, the difference in the opinion of the value of the salvage value is the more important economic reason for leasing. The more optimistic is the lessor relative to the lessee regarding the salvage value, the lower the lease payment the lessor would charge the lessee and therefore the more likely the deal can be structured even if the tax rates of the lessee and lessor are identical.

Subsidized Loans

As the CFO of Windmill Energycorp, you are considering investing $1 billion in windmills in Kansas. The windmills would be used to generate "green" electricity so coveted by the Obama administration. Recognizing that the US has become too dependent upon oil, President Obama has received authorization from Congress to advance loans to companies such as Windmill Energycorp at below market rates. You estimate that if you borrowed \$450 million in long-term secured bonds, as was originally intended, the cost of borrowing would be 9.5% because of the speculative credit grade rating the company has received from Moody's. The government is willing to lend Windmill Energycorp \$250 million at 4.5%. The terms of the loan is that the firm will pay down 20% of the original amount of the loan each year. As the CFO, you recognize that this will provide a tremendous savings but you are not sure how much. Given current electric rates, you estimate that the NPV of the windmill project is −\$12,379,418. Will the subsidy be enough? The tax rate of the firm is 34%.

Discussion: The question we must ask ourselves is how is this form of financial arrangement different from the Installment Sales contract? The installment sales contract that we learned about in the previous section is profitable only if the implicit borrowing rate of the contract is below the normal borrowing rate. Thus, it should not be surprising that we can use a very similar formula to discern the profitability of a subsidize loan as the formula we used to find the incremental value of the lease that is deemed by the IRS as an installment sale. Recall that the incremental benefit of leasing when the lease is deemed an installment sale is given by:

Incremental Benefit of Leasing

$$= I - \sum [\text{Interest portion of the lease } (1 - T)$$
$$+ \text{principal portion of the lease}]/(1 + R(1 - T))^t$$
$$- \text{After-Tax Salvage Value}/(1 + \text{ATWACOC})^n.$$

The incremental benefit of the subsidized loan is very similar. Note that instead of I, the initial investment, we will use "The Amount Borrowed". Additionally, we do not have to worry about the salvage value since the asset (in our example the cost of the windmill project) belongs to the firm. Hence, the formula is now:

Incremental Benefit of a Subsidized Loan

$$= \text{Amount Borrowed} - \sum [\text{Interest portion of the loan } (1 - T)$$
$$+ \text{principal portion of the loan}]/(1 + R(1 - T))^t$$

Note that R is the normal borrowing rate of the firm. Now, let us solve the windmill problem. The cash flow of the subsidized loan is given by the following table.

Time	Principal Balance	Interest Payment	Principal Payment	After Tax Payment
0	$250,000,000.00			
1	$200,000,000.00	$11,250,000.00	$50,000,000.00	$57,425,000.00
2	$150,000,000.00	$9,000,000.00	$50,000,000.00	$55,940,000.00
3	$100,000,000.00	$6,750,000.00	$50,000,000.00	$54,455,000.00
4	$50,000,000.00	$4,500,000.00	$50,000,000.00	$52,970,000.00
5	$0.00	$2,250,000.00	$50,000,000.00	$51,485,000.00

To use the above formula, we find the PV of the cash flows of the last column, using the after-tax cost of borrowing of $R(1 - T) =$ 9.5% * 0.66. The present value of the cash flows in the last column is $228,463,233.64. Accordingly, Amount Borrowed ($250,000,000) − $\sum$ [Interest portion of the loan $(1 - T)$ + principal portion of the loan]$/(1 + R(1 - T))t$ ($228,463,233.64) = $21,536,766.36. Note that the NPV without the special financing arrangement is −$12,379,418. Consequently, the loan saves the project.

Bond Refunding

The windmill project has become extremely profitable. Oil prices went through the roof and demand for the electricity from non-fossil fuel sources has soared. The technology to store and transmit electricity has decreased costs for Windmill Energycorp and as a result, the company now enjoys a AAA (triple A) rating. The company now has $150 million of debt outstanding. The stated coupon rate is 9.5%. The bond matures in 12 years. The interest rate for similar triple A rated bonds is now 6.25%. As the CFO, you see that there is a tremendous opportunity to refinance and save a bundle for the company. Maybe, by refunding, you will save so much that your bonus will be enough for you to buy that $1 million home that you and your spouse want. The question is how much money will you save?

Before answering this question, we should explore how a firm can retire and refund outstanding debt. Consider the above situation. You would expect that if the yield of the Windmill Energycorp debt has decreased from 9.5% to 6.25%, the value of those bonds has increased. We can use present value to determine the new value. Using our financial calculator:

n	i	PV	PMT	FV
12	6.25	? −$190,316,838	$14,250,000	$150,000,000

Hence, the value of the debt is $190,316,838. If you announced your intention to purchase back the debt, no doubt the debt holders would hold out for full value of the securities. What then does the firm gain? However, many debt securities have a call feature. The call feature enables the firm to call the bond at a pre-specified price set in the bond indenture agreement. Generally speaking, the call feature allows the firm to buy back the debt at face value plus an amount equal to or less than one year's interest.[2] In our case, the call feature will be set at 109.5. This means that for each debt with a face value of $1,000, the firm can call the bond back at $1,095. The debt holders will not see the value of their bonds rise to $190,316,838 or $1,268.78 per debt with face value of $1,000 because new holders know that the firm has every incentive to call the bonds at $1,095. But if you retire the existing debt, how much money can you raise to pay for the cost of retiring, which should include the payment of the call premium (i.e., $95 per $1,000 face value debt)? Additionally, it usually costs money to float new debt. Assume that the investment banker tells you that it would cost the firm $7.5 million to float new debt to retire the existing debt.

---

[2]It is more complicated than that. The call price declines as the maturity of the debt declines. A full description of these types of bonds is beyond the scope of this chapter.

There are two answers to this question. One approach is to find the amount of debt you can raise that would have the identical after-tax cash flow stream as the currently outstanding debt. In this approach, the profit of retiring the debt is given by:

$$\sum [\text{Interest portion of the loan}(1-T)$$
$$+ \text{principal portion of the loan}]/(1 + R(1-T))^t$$
$$- \text{Face Value of the Loan} - \text{Call Premium}(1-T)$$
$$- \text{Transaction Costs of New Debt}(1-T).$$

The summation term represents the after-tax payment you will no longer have to make if the bond is retired. These payments are discounted by the after-tax cost of new debt. But to have that benefit, you must pay the aggregate face value of the bond, the call premium and the transaction costs associated with refinancing. Note that both the call premium and transaction costs are assumed to be tax deductible.[3] In our example, assuming the outstanding debt is a bullet loan whereby the principal is paid at the end of maturity of the loan (12 years), the annual interest portion of the loan is $14.25 million. The principal of $150 million is first paid in year 12. The face value of the loan is $150 million. The call premium equals $95*150,000 units of debt outstanding or $14,250,000. The transaction costs equal $7.5 million. Finally, the R in the above equation is the current cost of debt or 6.25%. Consequently, the profit of retiring the bond is now:

$$\$14.25 \text{ million}(0.66)A_{12,6.25\%*0.66} + \$150 \text{ million}/(1.04125)^{12}$$
$$- \$150 \text{ million} - \$14.25 \text{ million} * 0.66 - \$7.5 \text{ million} * 0.66$$
$$= \$15.624 \text{ million}$$

According to our calculations, the firm will save $15.624 million by retiring the debt. However, we are making a very strong assumption

---

[3]The tax deductibility of the transaction costs are more complicated. The issue costs, (i.e., the fees that the investment banker charges) is usually amortized. The legal expenses filing the issue with the SEC are tax deductible. For this chapter, we are making simplified assumptions for pedagogical reasons.

regarding how much debt we are issuing to refund the bond. In particular, we are assuming that the amount of debt we raise equals $14.25 million (0.66) $A_{12,6.25\%*0.66}$ + $150 million/$(1.04125)^{12}$ = $179.979 million. This is the amount of debt that has the identical after-tax payment as the original debt outstanding of $150 million with a 9.5% coupon. The above approach is the equivalent loan approach.

But your boss does not want to float more than $150 million of debt. It can be shown[4] that if the plan to retire debt is not to float an amount of debt different from the face value of the retired debt, then the profit of refunding is given by:

$$\left\{ \sum [(CR_{old} - CR_{new}) * \text{Face Value} * (1 - T)]/(1 + R)^t \right\}$$

$$- \text{Call Premium}(1 - T)$$

$$- \text{Transaction Costs of New Debt}(1 - T).$$

Note that we no longer use the after-tax cost of debt but rather we use the before tax cost of debt. CR_{new} is the coupon rate of the new debt, which should equal R, the discount rate, which in our example is 6.25%. CR_{old} is the coupon rate of the old debt, which in our example is 9.5%. Thus, the profit of the refunding is given by: $(0.095 - 0.0625)$ ($150 million)*$0.66 A_{12,6.25\%}$ − $14.25 million*0.66 − $7.5 million*0.66 = $12.25 million. Note that this answer is less than the $15.624 million we had before, but remember in the previous approach, you were issuing almost $180 million in new debt to retire existing debt, while this last approach you were issuing $150 million. Now recall, that according to Modigliani and Miller, assuming no change in the risk of default, the greater the level of debt you issue, the greater the value of the firm. Thus, the first approach will always yield a greater profit. Which approach should you use? Easy! Whatever your boss tells you.

Multiple Choice Questions

The correct answer is in **bold font**.

---

[4]Your instructor will have to show you the derivation of this formula. Note that the formula assumes identical maturities of the old and new issues.

For questions 1–10, assume the following information. The ATWACOC is 12%, the cost of debt is 8% and the corporate tax rate is 34%. The firm is considering acquiring a $10 million machinery to expand production. The life of the asset is 10 years and you should assume straight line depreciation. Further assume that the NPV of the expansion plan is −$120,000. The NPV is based upon the assumption of acquiring the equipment through normal financing channels, without consideration of leasing or other special financial arrangements.

1. The bank is willing to lease the asset to you for 6 years. The annual lease payment is $1.88 million. Normally, your firm would hold onto the purchased asset for 6 years and then sell it in the secondary market. You estimate you could sell the asset for $4 million. The incremental value of the lease is:

   a. **$21,171**
   b. $135,449
   c. $665,627
   d. None of the above

2. Given your answer in question 1, you recommend:

   a. **Reject the project**
   b. Accept the project but lease the asset
   c. Accept the project but purchase the asset
   d. Not enough information

3. The bank is willing to lease the asset to you for 6 years. The annual lease payment is $2.0 million. Normally, your firm would hold onto the purchased asset for 6 years and then sell it in the secondary market. You estimate you could sell the asset for $6 million. The incremental value of the lease is:

   a. $21,171
   b. $135,449
   c. $665,627
   d. **None of the above (The correct answer is −$1,046,002)**

4. Given your answer is question 2, you recommend:
   a. Reject the project
   b. Accept the project but lease the asset
   c. Accept the project but purchase the asset
   d. Not enough information

5. The bank is willing to lease the asset to you for 6 years. The annual lease payment is $2.3 million. Normally, your firm would hold onto the purchased asset for 6 years and then sell it in the secondary market. You estimate you could sell the asset for $2 million. The incremental value of the lease is:
   a. −$704,546
   b. −$40,513
   c. $135,449
   d. None of the above

6. Given your answer in question 5, you recommend:
   a. Reject the project
   b. Accept the project but lease the asset
   c. Accept the project but purchase the asset
   d. Not enough information

7. The bank is willing to lease the asset to you for 6 years. The annual lease payment is $1.7 million. Normally, your firm would hold onto the purchased asset for 10 years, which at that time would have zero salvage value. You estimate that if you choose to lease you could repurchase the asset at the end of the lease for $4 million. The incremental value of the lease is:
   a. $262,334
   b. $618,801
   c. $1,098,461
   d. None of the above

8. Given your answer in question 7, you recommend:
   a. Reject the project
   b. Accept the project but lease the asset
   c. Accept the project but purchase the asset
   d. Not enough information

9. The lease financing company is willing to lease the asset to you for 10 years. The annual lease payment is $1.25 million. The incremental value of the lease is:

    a. $262,334

    b. $618,801

    c. $1,444,124

    d. None of the above

10. Given your answer in question 9, you recommend:

    a. Reject the project

    b. Accept the project but lease the asset

    c. Accept the project but purchase the asset

    d. Not enough information

11. The firm has $250 million debt outstanding. The coupon rate of the debt is 9%. The debt matures in 15 years and the principal is fully paid at the end of the 15th year. The CFO of the firm is told by the firm's investment banker that similar debt can be issued at par with a coupon rate of 8%. However, to prematurely retire the existing debt, the firm will have to call the debt at $275 million. Let the tax rate equal 40%. Assume that the investment banker charges no fee to affect the refunding. Then the firm should:

    a. Call the bond since the new debt will save the firm $2.5 million in interest per year.

    b. Call the bond since the profit of refunding the bond is $782,120 using the equivalent loan approach

    c. Not enough information

    d. None of the above

12. The manufacturer salesman finds out that you plan not to buy his equipment for the list price of $15 million. The salesman tells you that if you buy the equipment, you will be able to borrow $10 million from the manufacturer at 7%. Your normal borrowing rate is 10% and your tax rate is 40%. The term of the manufacturer loan is 12 years and the $10 million principal will be repaid at the end of the 12th year. The value of the subsidy is:

    a. $1,509,092

    b. $1,890,359

c. $2,316,655

d. None of the above

Advanced Problems

(1) You plan to export 1 million hand-held calculators per year for 5 years. The suggested retail price is $30 per unit. The government wishing to expand exports will lend you $50 million at 8% with the principal being repaid at the end of the fifth year. You will use this newfound lending capacity to retire existing debt with a coupon rate of 14% that is selling at par in the market. Assume a tax-rate of 40%. Assume further that you plan to use the full value of this loan subsidy to reduce your unit export price for calculators. How much can you cut your unit price?

(2) The Kiddushin company has the following balance sheet information:

Security Class	Book-Value	Coupon Rate (%)	Maturity (years)
Senior Debt	$175 million	9	12
Junior Debt	125 million	7	10
Common Stock	750 million	—	—
Retained Earnings	175 million	—	—

The senior debt is priced at par in the market. Junior debt is privately placed. However, other firms with a similar debt structure as Kiddushin is currently priced to yield at 10%. The beta of the common stock is 1.5. The current risk-free rate is 8% and the market premium is 10%. There are 20 million shares outstanding of Kiddushin. The current price per common stock share is $40. The corporate tax rate is 40%. Determine the ATWACOC.

(3) Kiddushin Company of problem 2 is considering a new investment. It is planning to buy new die-cutting machinery to replace

existing die-cutting machinery that was bought 5 years ago. The new machinery will cost $25 million and has an expected life of 10 years. The annual depreciation rate for this machinery is $2.5 million. The old machinery had an original cost of $15 million and was depreciated on a straight-line basis. The original expected life of the old equipment was 15 years. The new machinery will result in annual cost savings of $7 million. The old machinery can now be sold at $5 million. Would you replace the machinery?

(4) Assume now that the new machine can be leased at $3.3 million per year for 10 years. What do you recommend now?

(5) Consider an alternative lease option for the die cutting equipment of Problem 3. Assume that you may lease the equipment for only 5 years at $2.8 million per year payable at the end of each year. Assume that you can purchase the leased die cutting machine at expected market price of $15 million. What would you recommend now?

Solution to the Advanced Problems

(1) This is a subsidized loan problem. Essentially, the amount of savings is the amount that you can cut the price. First, we will find the PV of the subsidized loan savings using the following formula:

Incremental Benefit of a Subsidized Loan

= Amount Borrowed

$- \sum[$Interest portion of the loan$(1 - T)$

$+$ principal portion of the loan$]/(1 + R(1 - T))^t$.

The firm is borrowing $50 million at 8%. Since the principal is repaid at the end of 5 years, the annual interest payment is $4 million per annum. Consequently, using the above formula, we find

$$\$50 \text{ million} - \$4 \text{ mm}(0.6)A_{5,8.4\%} - \$50 \text{ mm}/(1.084)^5$$
$$= 7,111,743.$$

To find the price discount, we want to equate the PV of the revenue loss to that of the PV of the subsidized loan. Let X be the revenue lost per year. Note we need to take the after-tax revenue loss, so we multiply X by 0.6 which is the one minus the tax rate.

$$0.6X A_{5,8.4\%} = \$7,111,743.$$

Since $X = \$3$ mm and we are exporting 1 million calculators per year, the price reduction is $\Delta P = -3$.

(2) To do this problem, recall that the value of the private bond should be based upon the going market rate of 10%. Hence, the value of the Junior Debt is given by $0.07(125 \text{ mm})A_{10,10\%} + 125$ mm$/(1.1)^{10} = 102$ mm. The rest of the table is filled out like we did in the capital budgeting chapter.

Security Class	Market Value (mm)	Proportion	CoC (%)	Contributing Cost (%)
Sr. Debt	175	0.162	5.4	0.87
Jr. Debt	102	0.095	6.0	0.57
Common Stock	800	0.743	23	17.08
	1,077	1.0		18.52

(3) For this problem, remember to use incremental cash flows based upon the assumption that you replace the machine. Hence, at $t = 0$, there is a \$25 mm outlay but you sell the old machine for \$5 million, resulting in a book loss of \$5 mm. The cash flow at time zero is therefore -25 mm $+ 5$ mm -0.4 (5 mm) or $-\$18$ mm. At $t = 1 - 10$, the "Sales $-$ Costs" component increases by \$7 mm. Notice also that the depreciation expense increases from \$1 mm to \$2.5 mm resulting in an incremental tax savings of

0.4 (1.5 mm). The cash flow implications of this problem are summarized in the table below.

	$t = 0$	$t = 1-10$
Sales − Cost		7 mm
− LTI	−25 mm + 5 mm	
−ΔWC		
− T(Sales − Costs − Dep)	−0.4 (−5 mm)	−0.4 (7 mm − 1.5 mm)
Total	−18 mm	4.8 mm

The NPV $= -18$ mm $+ 4.8$ mm $A_{10,18.52\%} = \$3,179,580$. Replace the machine.

(4) In this case, the lease is considered to be an installment sale and only the interest portion of the lease payment is considered to be a lease. Since the contract does not specify which part of the total "lease" payment is lease and which is principal, we first calculate the implicit interest rate on the "loan" and develop an amortization schedule to calculate the after-tax payment. The table below derives the implicit interest rate of the loan:

N	I	PV	PMT	FV
10	? 5.395%	−25 mm	3.3 mm	0

Next, we amortize the loan as we did in the time value of money chapter.

t	Principal Balance	Interest Pmt	Principal Pmt	$(1-T)^*$ Interest	Total Payment	PV of total Pmt
0	$25,000,000					
1	$23,048,667	$1,348,750	$1,951,250	$809,250	$2,760,500	$2,619,070
2	$20,992,143	$1,243,476	$2,056,524	$746,085	$2,802,610	$2,522,792
3	$18,824,669	$1,132,526	$2,167,474	$679,516	$2,846,990	$2,431,443

(*Continued*)

(*Continued*)

t	Principal Balance	Interest Pmt	Principal Pmt	$(1 - T)^*$ Interest	Total Payment	PV of total Pmt
4	$16,540,260	$1,015,591	$2,284,409	$609,355	$2,893,764	$2,344,772
5	$14,132,607	$892,347	$2,407,653	$535,408	$2,943,061	$2,262,540
6	$11,595,061	$762,454	$2,537,546	$457,472	$2,995,018	$2,184,519
7	$8,920,615	$625,554	$2,674,446	$375,332	$3,049,779	$2,110,494
8	$6,101,882	$481,267	$2,818,733	$288,760	$3,107,493	$2,040,259
9	$3,131,078	$329,197	$2,970,803	$197,518	$3,168,321	$1,973,621
10	$0	$168,922	$3,131,078	$101,353	$3,232,431	$1,910,395
					Sum =	$22,399,904

We then determine the PV (at time 0) of the payments, as computed in the rightmost column. Note that we have multiple debt classes, and we have used the after-tax borrowing rate of our Senior bonds (5.4%), rather than our average after-tax borrowing rate of 5.62%. This is because the lease is *secured* by the asset; if we default, the creditor can seize the asset and take it away. This makes the lease most similar to a secured loan, so the rate of our Senior debt is the appropriate rate to use.

The table says that the Equivalent Loan of the Lease equals $22,399,904.

Hence, V_{lease} = [Amount borrowed] − [Equivalent loan] = $2,600,096. Yes, we should lease.

(5) In this situation, the lease description is consistent with the definition of a true lease according to the IRS. Now:

V_{lease} = Purchase Price − PV of the After-tax Lease Pmt for 5 years − PV of the Tax Benefits of the Depreciation assuming that you bought the asset at $t = 0$ − the PV of the Salvage Value discounted at the ATWACOC + PV of the Depreciation based upon the Salvage Value discounted again by the ATWACOC.

$$V_{\text{lease}} = \$25 \text{ mm} - 0.6 * (\$2.8 \text{ mm})A_{5,5.4\%} - 4(\$2.5 \text{ mm})A_{10,5.4\%}$$
$$-\$15 \text{ mm}/(1.1852)^5 + 0.4(\$3 \text{ mm})A_{5,18.52\%}/(1.1852)^5$$
$$= \$25 \text{ mm} - \$7.194 \text{ mm} - \$7.574 \text{ mm} - \$6.414 \text{ mm}$$
$$+ \$1.586 \text{ mm}$$
$$= \$5.404 \text{ mm. An Even Better Deal, take this one!!}$$

CHAPTER 8

MERGERS AND ACQUISITIONS

The Board Meeting

You left your home in East Brunswick at 6:30 am to catch the 7:05 am NJ Transit Train from New Brunswick to Newark airport. You have to catch an 8:20 am Continental flight to Dallas to attend a board meeting that begins at 3:00 pm at the Dallas headquarters of GEM Inc. This was your first day as the new CFO of the firm and your family is making the move to Dallas at the end of the month. GEM is a $1.2 billion manufacturer of specialized tools. Over the past few years, the earnings per share have been flat and the board of directors are anxious in getting GEM out of its rut. The stock price-earnings multiple of 8 is below the industry average of 23. The members of the board of directors are desperate for a growth strategy that would boost the price of the stock. As you settle in your first-class seat, you begin to rehearse your presentation to the board.

You have performed your financial ratio analysis and have discovered operational problems. The company's trade credit policy is too lax and industrial customers are taking too long to pay their bills. GEM needs to modernize its plants and reduce overhead and fixed costs. However, you recognize that these fixes will increase the profit margin of the firm but it will not produce long-term growth for the firm. You have decided to make a pitch for acquiring other firms.

Types of Mergers

There are three types of mergers. A *horizontal* merger is when two firms in the same market join together. One such example is when two local men's garment stores in Brooklyn decide to merge and locate to a new large retail space. There are hundreds of such establishments in New York City. The benefit of such a merger is that there might be operational synergies whereby economies of scale can be achieved. For example, each firm did not have enough business for two salesmen but they both needed more than one. Neither company hired the second salesman which became problematical around the holiday time. People avoided their stores during the holiday season because the waiting time was unbearable. The owners can share the cost of a third salesman if the retail outlets merged. The downtime for the three salesmen has decreased significantly because of the merger. As a result, the sales per staff increased significantly.

However, traditionally most people think of horizontal mergers as creating a monopoly or extracting monopoly rents from the consumer. In Economics, small firms such as the example denoted above are not expected to affect the equilibrium price of the product. Instead of having 100 garment retailing establishments in Brooklyn, there are now 99 stores competing with each other. If the new garment store increased their prices on men's suits, the other 98 could exploit the price differential and gain the upper hand. However, if two firms join together and have significant market share, it is possible that the new entity could dictate price to the consumer. For example, consider the following description that can be found at http://www.learnmergers.com/.

Staples, Inc., a superstore retailer of office supplies, wanted to acquire Office Depot, another giant retailer of office supplies. This action would have left the newly merged Staples in the position as the only large office supply superstore in most places around the country. This creates an unfair advantage for Staples in the market. Market research showed that Staples would have then been able to increase their prices up to 13% after the merger. The Federal Trade Commission recognized the results this action would have on the market and took steps to block the merger, saving billions of dollars for customers.

However, sometimes the FTC does allow two large establishments to merge. This is particularly true in the financial services industry where economies of scale are important for survival. Chemical Bank acquired Chase Manhattan in 1996. The two companies saved over $100 million per year in rent costs when Chemical moved its headquarters from one side of Park Avenue in NYC and moved into Chase's headquarters, one block further south and on the east side of Park Avenue. It was hoped that by joining the two banks, the cost of financial services will decline enabling the larger bank to compete against global financial institutions. More recently, Chase acquired Washington Mutual when Wamu's toxic mortgage loan would have forced it into bankruptcy.

Not all horizontal mergers work out. For example, Daimler Benz, the German automaker of Mercedes Benz acquired ailing Chrysler to achieve geographic reach in the valuable North American automobile market, but we know that did not work out.

A second type of merger is the *vertical merger*. This is a merger whereby the supplier and customer join together. One example of such a merger is when Time Warner Incorporated, a major cable operating firm merged with the Turner Corporation, which produces CNN, TBS, and other programming. One of the benefits of this type of merger is that the cable distributor does not have to pay market prices for programming since it owns the programming. Moreover, competing cable distributors would be at a cost disadvantage in pricing their services to its customers.

The third type of merger is a *conglomerate merger*. This merger occurs when two firms offering different products or services join as one firm. Note that these two firms prior to the merger were not in direct competition with each other. Conglomerate mergers can serve various purposes, including extending corporate territories and extending a product range. One example of a conglomerate merger was the merger between the Walt Disney Company and the American Broadcasting Company. Note that the merger enabled Walt Disney, a producer of movies and creator of theme parks to extend its products to produce TV shows for ABC. However, most conglomerate mergers are done to diversify the profits streams of the two companies, in order to reduce the volatility of the earnings per share.

Financial economists are dubious about the benefits of such diversification. One reason is that if the stockholders want such diversification, the stockholders can simply hold shares in both companies. So why should any firm pay a premium to acquire another firm simply because of diversification? In fact, one can argue that such diversification can actually harm stockholders' wealth. Diversification may result in reducing the aggregate dividends of the stronger partner in order to bail out the weaker partner of the merger. This is known as the co-insurance effect and it can have a deleterious impact on stockholders wealth.

We can show this effect mathematically. Assume a single period model. Let X_i be the operating cash flow of firm i. Let R_i be the promised debt payment. Note that if the firm is solvent, bondholders receive R_i and stockholders receive $X_i - R_i$. If the debt payment is greater than the operating cash flow, the bondholders receive X_i and the stockholders receive nothing.

Consider the following situation. Two firms, A and B, decide to merge. There are absolutely no operational synergies involved with the merger. This implies that the total operating cash flow of the merged entity is simply $X_A + X_B$. The only thing going for this merger is that when firm A does well, firm B does very poorly. And if firm A does poorly, firm B does very well. Note the inherent diversification. Let us further assume that if either A or B does poorly, we mean that without the merger the relevant firm would be insolvent. Let us further assume that the debt obligation due in one year is R_A for firm A and R_B for firm B. Now consider the following two situations. The first situation is that B does poorly, but there are sufficient profits in A to save B. This implies that $X_A > R_A$ and $X_B < R_B$ but $X_A + X_B > R_A + R_B$. Now let us us look at the stockholder's situation. If A and B merge, the stockholders of the shareholders of the joint entity receive $X_A + X_B - R_A - R_B$. Had the merger not taken place, then firm A's stockholders receive $X_A - R_A$ while the shareholders of firm B receive nothing. Let us compare the cash flows available to firm A's shareholders if the merger takes place to what they receive if it does not. The incremental cash flows are: $[X_A + X_B - R_A - R_B] - [X_A - R_A] = X_B - R_B < 0$. Notice that shareholders of firm A give up $R_B - X_B$ of their dividends to pay off the bondholders of firm B to keep the merged firm from going bankrupt. Of course, you can imagine a second situation when the stockholders of firm A are even worse off if B does so poorly. For example, B does so poorly, there are insufficient profits from A to save the company. In other words, B drags the stockholders of A into bankruptcy.

Now this does not mean that conglomerate mergers offer no benefits. There can be operational synergies when duplicative staffs are eliminated or the weaker partner benefits from stronger management of the bidding firm where wasteful and inefficient managerial practices are eliminated. It is also possible to extract unused tax credits. For example, if the merger is tax-free, the tax attributes of the target are brought over to the merger. Generally, a tax-free merger occurs when the bidder acquires the target via an exchange of voting stock. That is, the bidder firm issues new voting equity to the shareholders of the target firm. The target shareholders surrender their holdings of the target firm to the bidding firm's management. In this case, the target's assets, liabilities and income are carried directly over to the bidder's balance sheet and income statement. If the target firm suffered in the past negative income, the bidder firm could use the negative income to reduce its positive income thereby reducing the income tax liability of the merged entity. Note that without the merger, such a transfer of tax losses cannot take place.

However, the co-insurance effect exists even if the merger is not primarily motivated by diversification. Any merger that reduces the volatility of cash flow or equivalently, reduces the probability of default, yields benefits to debt holders as a class at the expense of the existing stockholders. For example, bidder A currently has a single A credit rating on its debt. As a result, the coupon rate of the debt is 250 basis points above the equivalent treasury security. Now if the firm merges with another for appropriate reasons, we would expect that the expected cash flow of the merged entity would be greater than what was the sum of the cash flow of the bidder and target. This implies that the probability of default has declined. Note that for most debt, the coupon rate is fixed. Even those corporate debt securities that have a variable rate, the current rate is based upon the contractual spread over the reference interest rate. This spread was determined based upon the original credit rating of the security. Since the reduction in default risk does not change the existing fixed coupon rate or the original spread, the value of the debt must increase. This is value that should normally accrue to the shareholders. Hence, there will still be some co-insurance effect that effectively reduces the benefits to the stockholders. How do you avoid the co-insurance effect? One way is to increase the amount of leverage the merged firm uses so that the risk of default of the merged firm is not different that it was from before.

Issues Concerning GEM's Acquisition Policy

Now that you are settled in your new office in Dallas, you begin working on merger possibilities. One possibility immediately comes to mind. There is Garo Die Cutters, Inc., located in Minneapolis. It has annual sales of $300 million and specializes in making metal dies. Its earnings per share have increased at 7% per annum over the last few years and the company is fast becoming the number one die maker in the Midwest. You understand that the board will have some tough questions for you and you are determined to be prepared to answer those questions.

The first question is obviously how much should you pay for the company? You estimate if you take over the company and implement operational efficiencies that would occur as a result of the merger, Garo's unlevered cash flow will be $25 million. Garo's After-tax Weighted Average Cost of Capital (ATWACOC) is 17% and assuming a growth rate of 7%, Garo's assets are worth to your company, GEM, $25 mm/(0.17 − 0.07) or $250 million. Since the value of Garo's debt is $80 million, the value of the equity to GEM is $170 million. Currently, Garo's stock price is $25 per share and there are 4.25 million shares outstanding. This means that currently the value of Garo's common stock is only $106.25 million. This implies that there is much room to maneuver in the negotiations in terms of the final offer price.

The next question that will be asked is whether GEM should buy the assets or the equity of Garo? You understand that if you buy Garo's assets, you do not assume Garo's liabilities and the maximum offer price should not be greater than $250 million. If you buy the common stock, your maximum offer cannot be greater than $170 million. If you buy the assets, your stockholders no longer guarantee the debt of GEM, thereby avoiding any co-insurance effect. But it increases the price tag of the merger!

The last question that the board will want answered is whether or not GEM should acquire Garo using cash or an exchange of stock. If cash is used, then Garo stockholders, including the CEO of Garo, Gary Roberts, who owns 35% of the company, will be out of the picture once the merger is completed. However, it is also true that if cash is used, Gary Roberts will incur a substantial capital gains tax liability and therefore Mr. Roberts might oppose the takeover because of his incremental tax bill. Or, he might demand a larger stock price offer to compensate for his personal tax liability. You know that Mr. Roberts' opposition can sink the merger deal since he controls major portion of the stock and it will be hard for GEM to acquire at least 50% of the common stock to consummate the merger without Mr. Roberts' cooperation. On the other hand, you can use an exchange of voting stock. In this case, GEM will offer an agreed-upon amount of common stock shares of GEM to acquire at least 50% of the common shares outstanding of Garo. In an exchange of stock, the IRS does not recognize the acquisition as a taxable event. Mr. Roberts will not have to report any capital gains implied by the exchange of stock until he sells off the shares of GEM that he receives as a result of the merger. This could reduce the offer price that GEM has to offer. On the other hand, Mr. Roberts will own a significant amount of GEM stock. He will likely demand a seat on the Board and he has a reputation of being quite ornery!

Evaluation of Mergers

The way to evaluate a merger is no different from how we evaluated Carob Inc. in the Capital Budgeting chapter. However, there are some interesting twists and curves we must traverse. Let us begin with some definitions. This part of the notes is primarily taken from framework used by Brealey, Myers, and Allen in their Principles of Corporate Finance textbook. These definitions are taken from the viewpoint of the bidding firm. The *Cost of the Merger* is the premium that the bidder pays the target to acquire it. The *Gain of the Merger* is the NPV of the merger to the bidder firm. The total gain of the merger is the sum of the *Cost of the Merger* and the *Gain of the Merger*.

The Cost of the merger depends upon whether you are acquiring the firm by cash or by exchange of stock. Before proceeding, note that there is a significant difference between the use of cash and of stock to acquire a target. When you use cash, the target shareholders go away because they have been bought out, but if you use exchange of stock, they become junior partners of the merged entity. Consider the cost of cash mergers:

Cost of Cash Mergers:

$$\text{Cost} = (\text{Aggregate Price Paid for Target}$$
$$- \text{Market Value of the Target})$$
$$+ (\text{Market Value of the Target}$$
$$- \text{Intrinsic Value of the Target}).$$

Note that the market value of the target in the first bracket is cancelled out by the market value of the target in the second bracket. I am sure you have two questions. First, why even introduce the term market value of the target? Second, why should the market value of the target be different from the intrinsic value of the target? To answer these questions let us define the intrinsic value of the target, which is the value of the target assuming no change of firm ownership or management. In other words, the value of that firm assuming no pending merger. The market value of the target might already include a merger premium! For example, assume that Exxon acquires an energy firm that specializes in producing energy via windmills. You might expect that if Exxon is willing to buy such a firm, all of the windmill firms will be in play. In which case, the price of all windmill firms might actually increase at the announcement of the Exxon's decision to buy a windmill firm because the market expects other mergers will follow. Hence, the value of the remaining windmill firms will take into account the probability that a merger offer will be forthcoming. This is important to note that should your oil company be the second company to acquire a windmill, it should understand that the price of the windmill firm has already reflected this possibility. For the remaining part of this chapter, we will assume that the market value and the intrinsic value are the same.

Consider now the cost of exchange stock mergers

Cost of Exchange of Stock

Cost = The product of the (% of Merged Entity Owned by Target)
    and (Value of the Merged Entity)
    − The Intrinsic Value of the Target

Note that the equation for the cost of exchange stock is much more complicated than that of cash. The reason for this is that after the merger is completed the target shareholders will own a piece of the merged entity. Let us do a simple example: A wishes to buy firm B. Firm B's after-tax weighted average cost of capital is 25%. B's cash flow is expected to remain in perpetuity $10 million per year assuming no merger. With the merger, B's cash flow will increase to $13 million per year. Assume that the total gain is split evenly between the bidder and the target. Further assume that there are 10 million shares of the target outstanding and 20 million shares of the bidder outstanding. The current stock price of the bidder is $25. Assume that the target has no debt. What should be the exchange offer assuming A is acquiring the equity of firm B?

Note that the synergized value of the target is $13 million/.25. or $52 million. The current value of B's equity is $40 million. Hence, the total gain is $12 million. Thus if the total gain is to be split, cost = $6 million. Let x be the number of shares that firm A will issue to acquire firm B. Note also that the number of shares after the merger will be 20 million $+x$. Hence the percentage of merged entity owned by the target will be $x/(20 + x)$. The value of the merged entity is the sum of the value of the bidder, which is $500 million and the synergized value of the target, which is $52 million. Thus, we are solving for x in the following equation.

$6 million = $[x/(x + 20)][$500 mm + $52 million] - $40 million

$x = 1,818,182$ shares of the bidder to the target.

GEM's Acquisition Policy Revisited

You arrive at the board meeting to persuade the board to consider acquiring Garo. Once you suggested the possibility, the Lead Director, Sharon Gold nods her head in agreement. She knows Garo and thinks that suggestion is at least interesting. The CEO and Chair, Anjav Patel, bellows out, "A very fine suggestion," and you begin to relax. That is always a mistake. Dr. Jonathan Phizer, a board member with 10% stock ownership in GEM, interrupts. "Tell me what you know about Garo and at what price do you think we will need to finalize the deal."

You explain the synergies you expect from the deal and what the potential resulting cash flows are. You begin your power point presentation and you state that you are assuming that you can split the total gains of the merger with Mr. Roberts and his stockholders. "First, the board must make a decision as to whether we should acquire Garo's assets or its stock. I recommend that we buy Garo's stock since it would reduce the total price we pay for the merger." The board unanimously assents to this point of view. You continue: "Note that the total gain of the merger is the difference between what we believe to be the value of Garo's stock under our management and what it is worth today. According to my calculations, Garo's equity should be valued at $170 million if we take it over. It is currently priced at $106.25 million. This is a net gain of $63.75 million. If the total gain is split, our Net Present Value (NPV) should be $31.875 million and the premium we pay Garo is also $31.875 million. If we pay cash, our stock offer should be the total cash paid divided by the number of Garo shares outstanding. That is our aggregate cash payment is equal to the sum of $106.25 million, the current equity value of Garo and the $31.875 million premium. Divide that by the 4.25 million shares outstanding, we get our offer of $32.50 per share or a 30% premium. Usually cash premiums are around 25% so our offer will be considered to be serious. However, Mr. Roberts will not be happy. First, if we give him cash, he is totally out of the picture and Mr. Roberts is not interested in retiring any time soon. Second, he will have a substantial capital gains tax bill to pay and I do not think he will agree to our offer unless he is compensated for the extra tax liability."

I am about to talk about the exchange of stock offer when Dr. Phizer raises his hand and asks: "This is a very thorough analysis, but what if your assumptions concerning the value of merger are biased upwards?" Always the skeptic, you think of Dr. Phizer, but you do not show your annoyance. Instead you reply, "That is a very good point and that is also the beauty of the exchange of stock. Assume that we are suffering from hubris and we are over-estimating the benefit. In this case, the value of our stock will not increase as much as we want and Mr. Roberts' and his stockholders will also not receive the anticipated amount. Of course, if we are underestimating the benefits of the merger, then GEM's stock price really soars and we all benefit. Dr. Phizer smiles knowingly and turns to the CEO and Chair. "She has a head on her shoulders, Anjav. Continue, please!"

You feel a lot better about your presentation and you continue. To find the number of shares we will need to offer, we use the following equation:

Cost of Exchange of Stock

Cost = The product of the (% of Merged Entity Owned by Target) and (Value of the Merged Entity)
    − The Intrinsic Value of the Target

The premium we plan to pay, which is the Cost of Exchange of Stock is $31.875 million. The intrinsic value of the Garo's stock is $106.25 million. GEM has 60 million shares outstanding and it current stock price is $20 per share. Hence the value of the merged entity is the $1,200 million of GEM and $175 million synergized value of Garo.

Thus we are solving for x in the following equation:

$$\$31.875 \text{ million} = [x/(x+60)][\$1,200 \text{ mm} + \$175 \text{ million}]$$
$$-\$106.25 \text{ million}$$

$x = 6,700,354$ shares. "Before you make any final decisions," I blurt out, "Mr. Roberts will own 35% of these shares or 2,345,124 shares. Our total outstanding shares after the merger will be 67,000,354 shares, so he will own 3.5% of the shares. The beauty of using exchange of shares in this case is that Mr. Roberts will not own enough shares to demand representation on the board."

Anjav Patel says, "I like this analysis but I have one worry. Mr. Roberts' total compensation as CEO and Chair of Garo is roughly $1.8 million. He may not want to retire and therefore he might oppose the merger?" You have your answer ready because you foresaw that question. "I would suggest to Mr. Roberts that we will retain him as the President of the Garo division at a pay of $1.8 million and we will give him a golden parachute of $2.5 million should he be terminated within the next two years."

Sharon Gold, the lead director then speaks. Mr. Chair, I recommend that the Board accept this proposal and we form a team to meet with Mr. Roberts about the possibility of a merger. The board unanimously accepts the recommendation and you go to your office smiling like a Cheshire cat.

Merger Problem

In the leasing chapter, we had the following problem:

The Kiddushin company has the following balance sheet information:

Security Class	Book-Value ($)	Coupon Rate (%)	Maturity (years)
Senior Debt	175 million	9	12
Junior Debt	125 million	7	10
Common Stock	750 million	—	—
Retained Earnings	175 million	—	—

The senior debt is priced at par in the market. Junior debt is privately placed. However, other firms with a similar debt structure as Kiddushin is currently priced to yield at 10%. The beta of the common stock is 1.5. The current risk-free rate is 8% and the market premium is 10%. There are 20 million shares outstanding of Kiddushin. The current price per common stock share is $40. The corporate tax rate is 40%. Determine the ATWACOC.

The table below summarizes the solution to this problem

Security Class	Market Value ($ mm)	Proportion	CoC (%)	Contributing Cost (%)
Sr. Debt	175	0.162	5.4	0.87
Jr. Debt	102	0.095	6.0	0.57
Common Stock	800	0.743	23	17.08
	1,077	1.0		18.52

Now consider the following problem. The Elimelech Company has decided to buy up the common stock of the Kiddushin Company. Assume that the growth rate of the unlevered cash flows of the Kiddushin is 6% per annum. The Elimelech Company has $5 billion of equity and 50 million shares of common stock outstanding. Elimelech's management feels that they can increase cash flow base at time zero by 20% while maintaining the 6% growth rate. The Elimelech Company would also increase the leverage ratio to 0.5. Assume that changing the leverage would not increase the cost of debt. If the total gain is to be split between the two companies, what should be the exchange ratio?

Solution to the Problem

First, let us find CF_u, the unlevered cash flow. Note that the value of the firm is $1,077 million and the ATWACOC is 18.52%. Given a growth rate of 6%, then we have the following relationship:

$$V = CF_u/(0.1852 - 0.06) = \$1,077 \text{ million}$$

implying that CF_u of Kiddushin is $134.8 mm. Moreover, given the 20% increase, under Elimelech management, the expected CF_u is now $161.81 million.

Next, let us find the new ATWACOC. Note that the relationship between the ATWACOC and R_{eu} is given by Equation (6.8) of the financing decision. In our case, L is the sum of the proportion of Senior Debt and Junior Debt, which equals 0.257. Accordingly, $18.52\% = R_{eu}(1 - 0.4(0.257))$. Hence, $R_{eu} = 20.64\%$. The new ATWACOC is given by $R_{eu}(1 - TL_{new})$ or $20.64\%(1 - 0.4*0.5)$ which equals 16.51%. With this information, we can determine the new value of the firm using $V_{new} = CF_{u,new}/(ATWACOC_{new} - \text{growth rate})$. That is,

$$V = \$161.81/(0.1651 - 0.06) = \$1,539.58 \text{ mm.}$$

However, that includes the value of debt. The value of equity is found by subtracting out the value of current debt of $277 million, implying the value of equity once taken into account all synergies will be $1,262.58 mm.

To find the exchange offer, note that the intrinsic value of Kiddushin's equity is $800 million. The synergized value of its equity is $1,262.58 mm. The total gain of the merger is $462.58 and therefore if the gain is to be split, then the cost is $231.29 mm. Our formula to calculate the number of shares given to the target is:

Cost = % owned by Target (Equity Value of the acquirer

+ The synergized equity value of the target)

− the intrinsic value of the target.

Or

$$\$231.29 \text{ mm} = (X/[X + 50])[\$5,000 \text{ mm} + \$1,262.58 \text{ mm}] - \$800 \text{ mm.}$$

Solving for X, the number of shares exchanged is $= 9,856,937$.

EPILOGUE

Concluding Remarks and Appreciation

The chapters included in this book represent the notes I provide to my Corporate Finance students. It is meant to provide a unifying framework to make financial decisions based upon time value of money. The time value of money requires two inputs: cash flows and the appropriate interest rate to discount cash flows. As can be seen in the Present Value of Money notes, present value can be used to evaluate stocks, bonds, real estate, determine amortization schedule of loans and determine a retirement plan for individuals. Time value of money can also be used to determine the yields of investment, including the yields of bonds and stock.

The discount rate depends upon the risk of the cash flows. Hence, riskier investments require a higher interest or discount rate. Generally, investors and corporate financial officers take their cue from the markets in order to determine the appropriate interest rate. For example, if I expect a guaranteed set of cash flows, like the money promised to me by the State for winning its lottery, I might use the yield of a long-term treasury bond to discount the cash flows and compare that present value to what I am being offered as an immediate payment of my winnings. A more risky cash flow would require a higher discount rate and one might want to find the yield of an investment traded in the market that best reflects that risk. This is the reason why the third chapter of the notes, Risk and Return, is included so you have an idea how to measure return and risk of market securities.

However, it may not always be possible to find the comparable investment in the market place to determine the appropriate discount rate. It would be nice if we had a model that will tell us the exact risk–return relationship in the market place. One such model is the Capital Asset Pricing Model, which states that the risk of any investment is measured by its beta. You can look up the beta of any stock using Finance.Yahoo.com. The fact that this measure is easily attainable as well as other information on that site (such as earnings per share, the name of the CEO, etc.) indicates that *Wall Street* believes that beta has some merit.

The culmination of the first few chapters of this book is the Capital Budgeting chapter. In this chapter you learn how to evaluate corporate investment projects. We use time value of money concepts to calculate the After-Tax Weighted Average Cost of Capital (ATWACOC). The ATWACOC is a proxy for the return demanded by the owners of the firm, the debt holders and stockholders. A project is acceptable only if the return on the project is greater than the ATWACOC. The basic principles of capital budgeting can be used to evaluate the value of common stock as illustrated in the Carob Inc. case that is found in the Capital Budgeting chapter.

Since the ATWACOC is blended rate of the yields of outstanding bonds and equity of the firm, it makes sense to understand how the financing decision impacts upon the value of the firm. In essence, the optimal financing decision is based upon finding combination of debt and equity financing mix that minimizes the ATWACOC. We learn from that chapter, that taxes and bankruptcy costs help determine that optimal mix. It would be nice if one can develop a simple mathematical model that takes into account the tradeoff between the tax benefit of debt and bankruptcy costs. In fact, I know several academicians that have developed such models and as a result have earned tenure at their academic institution. But these models are overly simplistic and rely on too many assumptions that ignore other important psychological factors that determine the financing decision of the firm at any given moment. For example, the more confident management is about the market's undervaluation of the firm's equity, the more likely that management would want to borrow instead of issuing new common stock. That is why the chapter includes several techniques to help make the decision. For example, the break-even earnings per share analysis allows the manager to find the sales level that would equate the earnings per share if debt financing is used or if new equity is issued. If management is confident that sales would exceed that break-even point, then the manager would use debt financing. We also include a section that provides the simple relationship between the level of debt outstanding and the ATWACOC. Clearly if the firm increases its financial leverage such that the ATWACOC can begin to increase, the firm is less likely to increase its leverage unless such increase fulfills a strategic initiative of the management.

The last two chapters provide examples on the use of the time value of money in making the lease versus buy decision, to determine the dollar benefit of receiving a loan at below market interest rates, to determine the profit of refunding a bond, and or to determine the stock exchange ratio to acquire another company.

Like all books, although the authorship is mine, I did receive help from colleagues and friends. I received many significant comments from John Longo, Ben Sopranzetti, Peter Murphy and Vadim Reynus. I also must acknowledge the emotional support and encouragement of my wife, Joyce, who has been by my side for over 40 years. I doubt that I could have accomplished anything in my career without her strong support. Finally, I must thank God for giving me many advantages that enable me to enjoy a very rewarding career at Rutgers University. I hope you enjoy the book. I know I enjoyed writing this book, which is based upon my class notes.

INDEX

Printed in the United States
By Bookmasters